The Hidden Seasons

Tristan Gooley is an award-winning and internationally bestselling author. Through his journeys, teaching and writing, he has pioneered a renaissance in the rare art of natural navigation. Tristan is the only living person to have both flown solo and sailed singlehanded across the Atlantic. He has explored close to home and walked with and studied the methods of indigenous peoples in some of the remotest regions on Earth. Further details of Tristan's most recent work, events and courses are available at naturalnavigator.com.

Also by Tristan Gooley

How to Read a Tree
How to Read Water
The Secret World of Weather
Wild Signs and Star Paths
The Walker's Guide to Outdoor Clues and Signs
The Natural Explorer
The Natural Navigator
How to Connect with Nature

The Hidden Seasons

A Calendar of Nature's Clues and Signs

Tristan Gooley

Illustrated by Neil Gower

hodder
press

First published in Great Britain in 2025 by Hodder Press
An imprint of Hodder & Stoughton Limited
An Hachette UK company

The authorised representative in the EEA is Hachette Ireland, 8 Castlecourt
Centre, Dublin 15, D15 XTP3, Ireland (email: info@hbgi.ie)

1

A CIP catalogue record for this title is available from the British Library

Hardback ISBN 9781399733540
ebook ISBN 9781399733564

Typeset in Baskerville by Hewer Text UK Ltd, Edinburgh
Printed and bound in Great Britain by Clays Ltd, Elcograf S.p.A.

Hodder & Stoughton policy is to use papers that are natural, renewable
and recyclable products and made from wood grown in sustainable
forests. The logging and manufacturing processes are expected to
conform to the environmental regulations of the country of origin.

Hodder & Stoughton Limited
Carmelite House
50 Victoria Embankment
London EC4Y 0DZ

www.hodderpress.co.uk

For Shoo
X

Contents

1

Opening the Back of the Clock

On a cool, blustery March morning I arrived at St Mary the Virgin Church in the coastal town of Rye, a once notorious smuggler's haven in East Sussex. I paid a small fee to gain access to the tower, which promised the best view in the town and thanked the old lady who took my money for her warnings: 'There are eighty-five steps. And mind your head!'

My pulse throbbed below my jaw as I paused next to the turret clock that had been installed in 1561, making it the oldest of its kind in the country. I scanned the open workings of the antique timepiece, looking from the pendulum to the escapement and then from one dark metal cog to another, trying to make sense of the elaborate mechanism. But I am no horologist and much of it remained puzzling.

The Rye turret clock has a claim to fame beyond its great age: it once struck an Orwellian thirteen. After many years of wear, the notch for the number six failed, the holding arm bounced out and the clock struck seven more times instead of six.

At the top of the tower, a plastic owl was meant to scare the pigeons, but it failed to fool them and they shat where they pleased, coating the wooden beams with their mess. I squeezed past stone walls and guiding rails, around the church's mighty bells, before lifting a narrow wooden trapdoor and emerging into bright grey light and cold air. A narrow walkway wrapped around the church's spire and offered a view worth double the climb. I could see for miles in all directions and the land offered up its history. The river Rother cut bright curves on its way past two castles, many churches and a smuggler's watchtower.

The rooftops below were bright green on one side and bright orange on the other. Two seagulls perched on the apex, the line dividing green from orange, and a third swept in and joined its colleagues. The birds faced towards the orange and had their backs to the green side of the roof. They confirmed there was a southerly breeze. Unlike the old clock in the tower, I could decipher the workings of this instrument without effort.

The orange colour on the roof was a lichen called *Xanthoria*, which turns a more determined golden colour in direct sunlight; it is much more common and much brighter on south-facing roofs. The green was a mix of algae and mosses, more common on the shaded, damper north side of roofs. Perching birds face into the wind – it stops their feathers ruffling and allows them to take off quickly. They acted as a weathervane and, paired with the colours on the roof, gave me information as easy to read as a clock face.

An hour later, I was walking out of Rye towards the sea under clearing skies. The yellow daffodils were in bloom, and there was a sprinkling of green dots in some trees but most were still bare. I could hear a single songbird, a chaffinch, and the pale wings of a butterfly passed at the edge of my vision. I sensed early spring in the land, but had no real understanding of what was going on in the clock. Why did I see a flower, a butterfly, and hear a bird when I did? What unseen forces regulated these individuals? I had spent decades walking through landscapes, growing more confident in my reading of Nature's signs for navigation, but all the time I was half blind to the timekeeper behind them. I decided I wanted to change that, to open the back of the seasonal timepiece.

How do the plants and animals know what time of year it is? What part is played by the sun, moon, stars and weather? By investigating the inner workings of the seasons, we learn when, how and why things change. Next, we discover the key moments to look for, which lift our focus from science to experience. Soon we find we can anticipate and celebrate predictable changes, which few notice, and decipher any surprises. When Nature strikes thirteen, it's good to know why.

Some of the most rewarding observations are seasonal but not confined to a single month. In this book I want to share the best times to seek out some of my favourite clues and signs in nature, but also to reveal why they appear when they do and why that sometimes varies. January comes towards the end of the book for a reason: the unorthodox calendar I have chosen will give you the best chance of success early on, then lead you towards a less explored place. By the end of the book, you will no longer see seasons in terms of months but, instead, identify more than one season in each day and know how to unwrap and decipher each moment.

My first tip: see nothing in isolation. If you notice one thing, notice two and try to leap over an imaginary boundary. There is nothing wrong with noticing that two plants come into flower at the same time – it is an observation that will pass most by – but try to take an extra step and make a pair with another part of the nature spectrum: a blossoming flower with a bird's song; a falling leaf with a cloud shape; a constellation with a scent. Soon we will meet the science that explains the pairings but, as our ancestors knew long before we uncovered the science, there is satisfaction in the pairing alone. It sharpens our powers of observation, deduction and prediction. And it's joyous. When we know what to look for and what it means, seasonal moments that were once hidden suddenly shine brightly.

2

Late February

Mast Flowers

—

Bulbs and Perennial Punctuality

—

Catkins

—

Small Leaves

—

Long Memories

Mast Flowers

The natural year has no formal start date but, if we know what to look for, the second half of February is when we see the wheels turning. Some plants get a head start, showing leaves or flowers weeks before others. But how and why?

The overnight rains had cleared and cars pushed puddles in arcs over the pavement. I was early for my meeting with Professor Rosemary Fricker at the Cambridge University Botanic Garden. Professor Fricker is a neuroscientist who has researched the neurobiology of diseases including Parkinson's and Huntington's. She also leads a team of phenology researchers at Cambridge University Botanic Garden where they call her Rose. Phenology is the formal study of seasonal phenomena.

Rose had kindly invited me to join the researchers on their routine patrol of the gardens to record seasonal events in a carefully chosen selection of the eight thousand plants that grow there. This is part of a plan to improve our understanding of the plants' seasonal responses to external influences, including changes in climate. At Cambridge they are introducing nuance. In the past almost all records were binary – a plant was either in flower or not; there were no shades between. But at Cambridge they are refining the process and using increments, marking some plants as 30 per cent in flower and others at 90 per cent.

Questions started flowing to Rose. A tall postgraduate called Edward stopped us as we passed an alder. His finger flicked over the iPad in the crook of his arm. 'Do I mark this alder as a hundred per cent in flower, 50 per cent in flower or zero per cent in flower?'

I was intrigued. How can a tree be fully in flower, half in flower and totally not, all at the same time? It turned out that the database software didn't differentiate between male and female flowers. The male flowers were out, but the females weren't. Edward felt this qualified as 50 per cent in flower, but Rose told him to mark it as 100 per cent, but to add a note that they were males only. The small dilemma was testament to the fresh detail the team were recording.

We passed a Persian ironwood tree with dark bark that had peeled away in great swatches to reveal a golden honey colour beneath. I learned that this ironwood blossomed strongly on alternate years, putting on a magnificent display of flowers one year and underwhelming the next. Many trees have 'mast years' in seeds – when an oak or beech, for example, puts out a bumper crop every few years to inundate greedy grazing animals and improve the chance of a seed to take root – but I had not expected to find this habit in tree flowers.

At the edge of the path, the sunlight caught a sprinkling of white snowdrops and then the bright yellow of daffodils.

Bulbs and Perennial Punctuality

Daffodils are one of the landmark flowers that herald the loosening of winter in many parts of the world. They have much in common with snowdrops, although they look quite different, much taller, with bright yellow trumpet flowers. Both are geophytes, plants that store resources like carbohydrates below ground in unfavourable seasons, which gives them a huge advantage in the cold pre-vernal months.

Annual plants complete their life cycle in a single year, germinating, flowering and spreading their seed over a few months. It is a strategy that clearly works, as any horticulturalist will tell you: leave a patch of fertile earth bare for a few warm months and some enterprising annual plant will call it home. Gardeners call these opportunists weeds, but the shaming does little to deter them.

There is a major drawback to the annual strategy – it means a standing start in spring. Annuals have a tiny reserve of energy in the seed, just enough to fuel some root growth and a green shoot to poke its head above the soil, but that is all. From that moment onwards, the annuals are on a tight budget, and they can use only energy they have harvested from the sun, which makes them shy as winter weakens. They simply can't hope to reap enough sunlight to sustain the growth they need to survive in February, let alone January. That means we don't find annuals winning early-spring races.

Geophytes are perennials, growing for many seasons, and this allows them to prepare more thoroughly for the following year. They draw energy down and store it below ground in organs like bulbs, tubers or rhizomes. This gives them a head-start the following year and they can start growing, sometimes even flowering, before the sun is high and strong enough to provide energy. To the annuals, this arrangement is grossly unfair, but Nature is never one-sided: at the end of the growing season, many annuals throw thousands, sometimes millions, of minuscule seeds into the air. The geophytes can't copy this strategy as their plan revolves around big, heavy bundles of energy.

Wherever you are, the first flowers you see as winter surrenders slowly to spring are very likely to be geophytes.* I see snowdrops, crocuses, lesser celandines, anemones, daffodils and

---

* There are also geophytes in harsher climates that wait out a too-hot or too-dry season, then leap up as the heat breaks and cool air or rain moves in.

bluebells passing on the baton to each other as spring matures, beating most annuals into flower by some margin. The early purple orchid has root tubers that help it earn the 'early' in its name. If we see plants poking above the soil very early in the year, we can think of icebergs – a fuller story lies below the surface.

There is a second deduction we can make too. If a plant surprises us by getting going earlier than most others in that habitat, it is much more likely to be a perennial than an annual. The stinging nettle is a good example of this: its flimsy form pops up in so many places near humans each year that it has earned a reputation as one of the most opportunistic weeds. That ubiquity might make us suspect an annual, but each year it gets going early. Its shoots and leaves poke up before most of the neighbouring plants, the clue that it's a perennial and, barring intervention, will be back in that spot next year. Punctuality means perennial.

Catkins

Rose had a challenge for me and led me to a hazel, a tree species I thought I knew well.

'Can you spot the female flowers?'

Hazel trees are monoecious, with male and female flowers growing on the same tree. But, as is normally the case with flowers, males and females are not equal in size, shape or colour.

As I searched, I played with the male flower, a catkin, in my left hand. It was one of the hundreds of thin pale green cylinders that hung down and pointed at the ground. Each catkin is a bundle of about 240 smaller flowers. It took a little scouring of a branch, but I did finally spot the diminutive female flower. Protruding from the branch there was a small green bud, barely bigger than a Tic Tac, with what at first appeared to be a magenta-red spider at its tip. The bright red 'legs' were the 'styles' of the female flower.

I won't be the first to have found the practical implications of monoecious trees confusing. Why have male and female sexual organs on the same plant? Won't they just fertilise each other? In which case, what's the point? The main biological advantage of clumsy, depleting, risky, unpredictable sex is to introduce new genetic material to the offspring. If you are going to put male and female flowers on the same branch, why not cut out all that effort and be asexual?

The hazel, like other monoecious species, blocks its own flowers from fertilising each other. A single gene in the plant's DNA is responsible for stopping sexual reproduction within the same plant or others with the same genetic fingerprint. This is why commercial growers of hazelnuts and other monoecious species have to make sure they keep at least two varieties within the same plot. A hazel's ability to stop its flowers fertilising each other has a catchy scientific name: 'sporophytic self-incompatibility system'. Try saying that after eating a dry biscuit.

The hazel's female flowers are worth seeking out and as cute as kittens, but let us turn back to the larger, plainer, male flowers, the catkins, because they hold a phenological clue. We will see many catkins on trees in the pre-vernal weeks, when winter has weakened and spring has yawned and stretched for the first time. If we follow a series of simple logical steps, the catkins will whisper a seasonal sign in our ear.

Trees can't move so they always need assistance to pass their pollen (plant sperm) from male to female flowers. They do this by enlisting the help of pollinating animals or the wind. There are some interesting global patterns within these habits, because almost all tropical trees rely on animals for pollination and almost all high-latitude trees rely on the wind. As we move from the equator towards the poles, animal populations decline and wind-pollination becomes more important. As we climb higher up mountains, the same trend applies, which is logical: animals find life easy at sea level in the tropics and difficult high up on a boreal mountain. The wind is undeterred by ice and snow.

The same trends work on a smaller scale within woodlands. Many of the tallest plants – the canopy trees – are wind-pollinated, but it is rarer among the smaller plants in wood-land, the under-storey, as the wind is unreliable near ground level. (Short plants that rely on the wind live in open terrain, including many of the most important crops – wheat, maize, barley, rye, oats and rice.)

We will return to the animals, but catkins are a sign that a tree is wind-pollinated. Many trees rely on wind-pollination or 'anemophily' (literally 'wind-loving', from the Greek), includ-ing hazels, oaks, ashes, aspens, elms, birches and most of the conifers. On the broadleaf trees, catkins hang down or project out from the branches to catch a lift for their pollen on a breeze.

Now for the final pieces of the jigsaw. The wind slows close to the ground. Try reaching to the ground on a blowy day and you'll find the wind appears to stop altogether near your feet. This isn't a problem for tall trees, like spruces, firs, pines and most of the other conifers, because they reach far enough above the ground to catch a breeze, even in a valley, but it's a chal-lenge for the smaller wind-pollinated trees. Now add one more layer of difficulty for the small trees by covering them with leaves that snuff out the weak low forest winds. Small broadleaf trees have to beat the leaves and they do this by hanging out their catkins before leaf budburst. Catkins are a sign that we sit in the delicate season between winter and leaves, when breezes can still flow over low, bare branches.

Catkins can be eye-catching, but they are rarely as attractive as animal-pollinated flowers and tend not to have strong or interesting scents – the wind is unmoved by either beauty or aroma. A bunch of catkins would make a poor bouquet on Valentine's Day, unless the recipient was an open-minded botanist. But they have their admirers and Rose told me her favourite plant in the whole Cambridge garden was a variety of the goat willow tree, in the *Salix* genus, which had a glorious display of showy catkins, fluffy white with strong tints of pink. Pretty catkins: a sign of an unusual plant, one that relies on wind and animals, in this case bumblebees.

Small Leaves

The group moved on, past a sign that announced proudly, 'Winter Garden: a masterclass in using foliage, flower, stem, structure and scent for winter interest'. I felt like a child being pulled out of a toy shop just as I'd found *the toys*. I begged for a detour into the Winter Garden.

The first thing that struck me was not the plants in the beds, but the wonderful golden colour covering one side of an otherwise dark conifer. Horticulturalists breed golden varieties of many plants, including some conifers and other evergreens. This tree was a golden cultivar of the Lawson cypress – *Chamaecyparis lawsoniana* 'Winston Churchill' – and I couldn't resist showing the group how the golden colour formed a compass. It was a much brighter, more vibrant yellow on the southern side, thanks to more direct sunlight reaching it.

Our focus moved to the main attraction, the planted beds. There were snowdrops, periwinkles, hellebores, winter aconites, winter honeysuckle, viburnum and many others, all perennials, of course. Then I spied an extraordinary bare bush, a scene of organised chaos. Picture an image that shows the neural pathways in the brain but made of tiny twigs. The bush had hundreds of thin ruddy-brown wiry stems that branched off each other constantly, as if they couldn't stand to be part of the same plant.

I had never come across such determined anarchy in a single plant before and knew there had to be good cause. Nature never does crazy, wonderful things for a gardener's benefit. There was also bound to be a reason this curious plant had found a home in the Winter Garden so I set about quizzing my tour guides as to what it might be.

I learned it was a species of shrub with a long formal name, *Muehlenbeckia astonii*, with highly descriptive common names: the zigzag plant and the wiggy-wig bush. A native of New Zealand, it's one of a handful of plants with the Maori label *mingimingi*, meaning 'twisted'. It's a favourite in exotic gardens around the world, but is struggling in the wild.

The reason for its haphazard appearance is that the branches are 'dichotomous': the growing buds split and fork into two branches instead of continuing growth in a straight line. This weakens the plant's structure and means it can never grow mighty – tall plants have a single stem and the tallest trees a single trunk. But it offers one important evolutionary advantage. It makes such a mess that grazing animals struggle to penetrate and nibble the foliage. It is a cunning defensive strategy, an 'anti-herbivory' tactic, and a sign that the plant has evolved to live alongside grazing animals. Crazy branches on wild shrubs mean hungry animals nearby.

The seasonal answer lay in a different part of the plant. Plants need to gather a certain amount of solar energy over the course of the year and have to choose the size of their leaf. Some plants are in a hurry and throw out massive leaves, which harvest the light quickly, but why don't all plants do that? It isn't a strategy that works well in exposed or extreme places: the bigger and floppier a leaf, the more vulnerable it is to injury from wind, cold, dehydration, heat or even sunlight. That is why big leaves are more common in shady places. We don't see large evergreen leaves in temperate zones – but there are plenty in the tropics, with little risk of frost or drought. The hazel tree puts out catkins very early but its large leaves come much later.

Small leaves can cope with testing conditions, but they take longer to get the job done. Plants with small leaves need lots of them and longer seasons than plants with big leaves, but that's fine – they're hardier and much better suited to dealing with the weather outside summer. The small leaves of the zigzag bush are out for much longer than most deciduous shrubs, so long, in fact, that the plant is termed 'semi-evergreen'. Conifers take this tactic to extremes with their tiny needles and year-long green seasons.

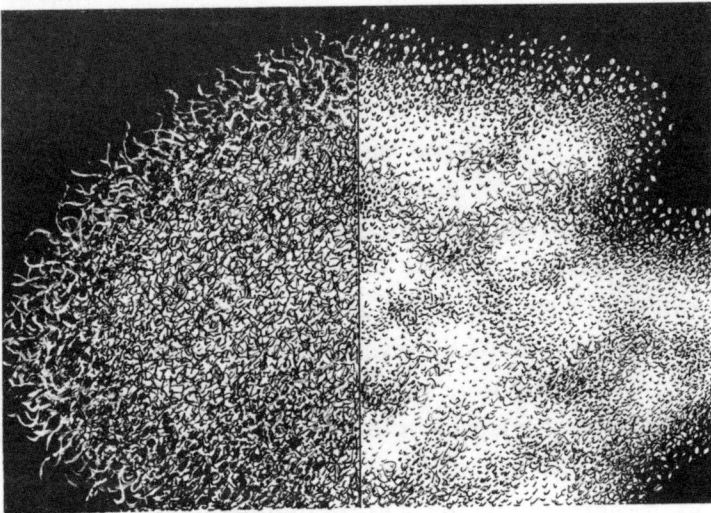

Muehlenbeckia astonii, *the 'wiggy-wig bush'*

Long Memories

Margeaux Apple, the collections coordinator, explained that they keep paper and digital records of each species in the Cambridge garden.

'We work in curation ... we consider ourselves a type of museum. You know if you see a Picasso in a gallery, you can back that up with information about its provenance. With our plants we can tell people when we got it, where and who from. Our records should do that for each of our plants. I should be able to give you their provenance.'

The team logged the full background of every new plant, not just the exact species, but where it came from in the world precisely. We're not talking about another botanic garden, but the plant's heritage and its journey to its new home: its neighbours, its coordinates, how it was received. Was it wild? How exposed was it? Was it on the south-facing slope of a mountain?

'When we collected plants in Kyrgyzstan, we noted all of this information and passed it on to the horticulturalists to help them plan where to plant it. It can then be used for future conservation, because we can tell other organisations that we have plants from very specific genetic populations that perhaps nobody else has. But we also do audits to see how a plant is doing each year, which includes when it blooms and when it fruits.'

Gathering so much detail about the provenance of plants may seem extravagant. Surely if we know the exact species of a plant and understand its environment, we also know its nature and nurture so we have all the information we need to predict and understand its behaviour. Not quite. On our walk, we passed a *Ginkgo biloba* tree, a fascinating specimen, which sits in a lonely part of the genetic family tree. Ginkgos are extraordinary trees, living fossils, like crocodiles, that once survived only in the valleys of China; it is still treasured there for its role in traditional medicine. It is a tough tree and has now spread, with help from humans, across the world and we understand it well. We know that it can thrive in a range of soil types, and can cope with root compaction and heat much better than most other trees – hence it is one of the most popular trees in New York City. We know the *Ginkgo* species; we understand how it responds to its environment. That completes the picture and allows us to predict the full story of the plant. Surely that's all there is to it. That was the prevailing view for about a century, but there is an intriguing twist to the story. Each year we learn more about the memory of plants.

Plants carry over experiences to future generations. We know this to be true, observations prove it, but the science is still young. For many years it was believed that two plants with the same genes could be expected to behave in near-identical ways if planted in the same habitat. Now we know there will be variation thanks to epigenetics, the way certain genes may be 'switched on' or not. The environment influences this for living plants and animals, which we would expect, but scientists were surprised to discover that the switch leaves 'marks' on the DNA that can be passed on to the next generation. This has profound implications for all organisms, including humans: our lifestyle before we became parents may change the development of our children, even though we pass on the same genes. For example, men who smoke before becoming fathers may make asthma and obesity more likely in their children – even if they never smoke a single cigarette after the child is born. It is possible in theory, but too early to know, that smoking a single cigarette in adolescence could affect the life of a grandchild. There are hopefully as many positive implications in epigenetics: could reading Shakespeare in adolescence improve the prospects of the children we have?

Back to the plants. Before moving to Cambridge, Margeaux worked at Holden Forests and Gardens in Ohio. Even though it was February, I couldn't resist asking her about the colours of maples in autumn, whether she had noticed any patterns that might help us predict the timing of the display.

'We had a bunch of red maples – *Acer rubrum*. It's an incredible tree. Its range goes from Nova Scotia all the way down to

Florida. But the ones from Minnesota, every year they were first to turn red and the first to drop their leaves. They were prepping, right? They said, "We're in Minnesota still. It's gonna get cold real quick. We gotta finish up what we're doing." Every year they were the first.'

How did those trees know they were from Minnesota when they had spent so many years in Ohio? They had the same genes as their slower neighbours, so the answer was deeper than that. Something was going on, very possibly epigenetics, that meant they had a long memory. And we know from the habits of other trees that it is highly likely their offspring will be early to turn red too, even though they've never spent a minute in Minnesota.

Whichever month we are in, the season we see will be shaped by current and recent conditions, as well as events long ago.

3

Seeing the Light

At high latitudes, as we draw closer to the North or South Pole, there is not enough solar energy to sustain large organisms year-round, and in some weeks of the year life may be restricted to a few lichens having a difficult time. Closer to the equator, in the tropics, there is always enough energy, and patterns are dictated by water levels. There are wet and dry seasons, but no summers or winters as we know them.

In this book we focus on the northern temperate zone, a part of the world that swings between fat and lean energy times. Nature has worked out that for most organisms in this zone it makes sense to start again each year. They are trying to complete the major functions of life – taking on water and food, growing and reproducing – in the window when millions of years of experience have proved their chance of success is best.

The lurch between extremes of energy and action puts on a show in all seasons, especially spring and autumn. But this is not gentle theatre for the performers, it is the most barbaric circus – one small mistake and death follows swiftly. Give birth or unfurl leaves before a major cold snap and it might be your last mistake. Each year the plants and animals must step into the Coliseum of spring. Evolution has honed their sense of timing, giving them the best chance of survival, but how? We also know that timings vary from year to year, but why? Let's unscrew the back and peer inside the seasons' clock.

It contains many pieces, some big, others tiny, and we'll go through them until we understand how Nature keeps time. At first, we'll focus on spring and lean a little more towards plants than animals, because it will be easier to see how the mechanisms work. Plants underpin animals. All animals rely on plants, directly or indirectly – herbivores eat the plants and carnivores eat the herbivores. Many birds feed their young on insects, but the insects follow the drumbeat of their food plants. The great tit needs plenty of caterpillars for its chicks and the caterpillars feed on oak leaves. If we understand how the oak keeps time, we'll understand more about the caterpillars and birds, but also the moths that follow the caterpillars that don't become bird food.

An Early Mystery Solved

Robert Marsham, a Norfolk naturalist, started recording signs of spring in 1736 and continued until his death in 1797, making him the father of phenology in the UK and possibly globally. Family members continued his tradition and notes on 'Indications of Spring' ran until 1958 when, sadly, they stopped. Marsham noted many signs that remain popular to this day – snowdrops, swallows, cuckoos and butterflies – as well as less savoury examples: he informs us that his chamber pot froze solid overnight in the unusually harsh winter of 1739.

Marsham, like everyone else, knew that days become longer and warmer in spring, which coincides with increased activity, growth and arrivals from abroad. He must have known, too, that Nature was responding to the changes, but he couldn't have known how to tease apart the two influences.

In 1914 a young Frenchman, Julien Tournois, published research showing that hops and cannabis plants flowered most rapidly when the daylight hours were short. Unfortunately, soon after, he was killed in action during the First World War, which meant, as one commentator remarked, he was 'unable to develop his ideas further'.

In 1920, a pair of scientists in America, Garner and Allard, performed an experiment that was beautiful in its simplicity. They sowed Biloxi soy beans over successive weeks, waited and watched. The early-sown plants had a head-start and grew to be bigger than the late-sown ones. Soon the scientists found themselves with lots of beans of different ages and sizes. So far, so predictable, but what the pair noticed next was enlightening: all of the plants, young and old, little and large, began flowering at the same time. This proved that the soy beans were not counting time from sowing to flowering, but were tuned to an external reference. Having ruled out other causes, the pair settled on the length of day, and the science of photoperiodism was born. It would be another twenty years before scientists proved that plants responded to the length of night, not day. We now know that changes in proteins called phytochromes are responsible for time measurement in plants, and that melatonin is secreted from the pineal gland in animals at night, which gives their brains a calendar.

How Plants Read Their Calendar

Photoperiodism is ubiquitous and powerful, but it is a gradual chemical process, very different from the fast 'photonastic' movements we see when daisies and dandelions open their flowers at the start of the day. Once an organism senses that the length of night has reached a certain number of hours, it sets in motion key seasonal processes.

Many plants flower when the day grows longer than a critical period, such as fourteen hours. They are known as long-day plants and include peas, potatoes, carnations, wildflowers and crops we see on the way to midsummer. (We live mostly by day, so the convention remains that we focus on its length, even though we know that plants and animals gauge night.)

[25]

Short-day plants flower when daytime shrinks below a certain critical period, such as eleven hours. They include some onions and spinach, as well as most of the plants that are known for cheering winter along, like poinsettias and chrysanthemums. More energy is available during long days – the sun is up for longer, and is stronger – which is one reason why short-day plants tend to be shorter than long-day plants. Think of peas climbing up supports in summer while spinach spreads low in cooler months.

Some other plants, known as day-neutrals, do not take their primary cue from the length of day or night and respond to other internal and external cues. They include many cucumbers and tomatoes.

The photoperiod clock governs many other aspects of a plant's calendar, such as the germination of seeds, the formation of tree buds, budburst, leaf growth, branching habit, the colour of leaves, bulb development, dormancy, and readiness for frost. Tubers, as we have seen, form as part of a plant's plan for the following year and are triggered by days shortening.

There are a few intricacies within this framework. Some plants need a certain sequence of long then short days or vice versa; others are rigid in their requirements and will not flower if the hours aren't right, while yet others are more flexible. Oats are sticklers for long days and won't flower without them; barley likes long days, which make it more likely to flower, but it sometimes blossoms regardless of day length.

Tinkering and Discoveries

Agricultural scientists have used photoperiodism to bend the plants to producers' needs. During the 'green revolution', they developed wheat varieties that were less sensitive to the length of night, making it possible to grow them in countries nearer the tropics. 'Night-break lighting' – turning the lights on in the middle of the night – allows growers to tell the plants what time of year it is: by turning lights on and off, they can produce crops in line with supermarket demand, not sunset times. The horti-culturalist and journalist Alys Fowler lamented the state of her indoor plants in winter and used similar tactics on a much smaller scale: 'I can torture them no longer so I've changed a few light bulbs, added a few timers and now, even in my darkest corners, life grows.'

Horticulture is big business and the research has followed the money, leading to intriguing discoveries. Studies found that dormancy could be delayed in catalpa trees by extending daylight using either tungsten-filament or fluorescent bulbs, but the gap between leaves – the 'internode' – grew longer for the plants under tungsten. Plants are sensitive to colour and respond in different ways to light from each end of the spec-trum. Light from the blue and ultraviolet end influences *the way* plants grow, the direction in which stems head, for example. Light from the red end shapes their concept of time. It is a bit of a stretch, but I like the idea that our choice of blue or red shirt in the morning might tweak either the plant's compass or its clock.

Most plants have leaves that grow larger when the day is longer than the night. When plants in winter conditions are exposed to an hour of light in the middle of the night, their leaves start expanding. Potato leaves are more upright when days are long, and droop more when nights are longer. Tomato leaves turn yellow (chlorosis) if exposed to more than eighteen hours of continuous light. Grasses grow fewer but larger leaves in summer and produce more offshoots – 'tillering' – during short days. As summer turns to autumn, we expect leaves to change colour, but before that happens the leaves shrink: chlorophyll content reduces dramatically as the days shorten.

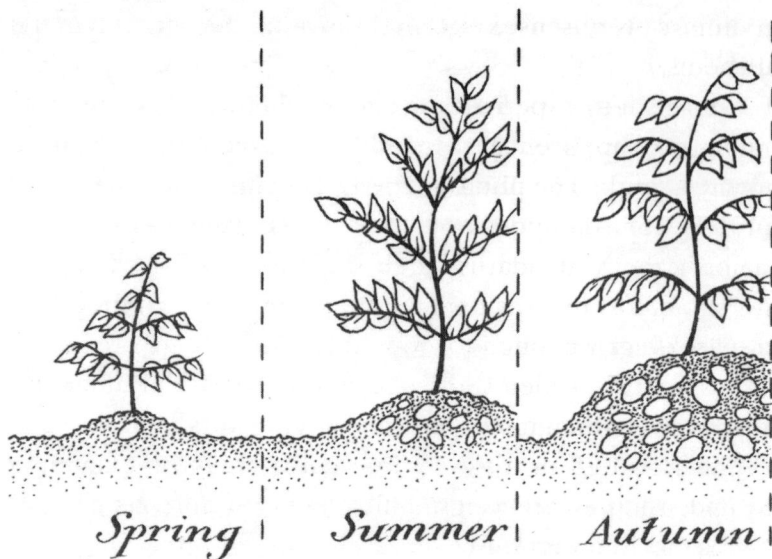

Spring | Summer | Autumn

Leaf angles change with seasons

Some plants, including members of the *Ranunculus* family, grow leaves with different colours or shapes when they sense night contracting. Black locust trees have leaves that are darker and more rounded when night is longer than day, but the same leaves turn lighter, more yellow-green, and change shape to be more elliptical, when the days grow longer. Some succulent plants, including the *Kalanchoe* genus, have thin leaves when the days are long; they grow thicker, fleshier, more succulent as they shorten.

Seeds are sensitive to the length of day. Only a third of birch seeds will germinate if the day isn't at least as long as the night, but 90 per cent will germinate when the day lasts twenty hours.

So, if we notice plants thriving during the long days of summer we should expect them to be taller with bigger leaves, and bigger gaps between the leaves, than plants that do well much earlier or later in the year. Short-day plants are smaller in almost every sense, often denser and bushier, with more offshoots.

Humans may experience jetlag when travelling west or east but, as we have seen, plants suffer a seasonal jetlag if moved north or south. The photoperiod calendar for each plant is set for their home latitude. When they are transported from south to north, their calendar is off: further north they are not sensitive enough to the way nights grow longer faster so they don't prepare quickly enough for winter. Black locust trees in Russia and aspens in Sweden showed signs of delayed dormancy and frost damage when moved north.

Plants evolved in a world different from the one we have created, so they are thrown out by streetlights, which they confuse with daylight, but not by moonlight, which they have evolved alongside.

How Animals Read Their Calendar

In animals, photoperiodism governs the timing of reptile growth, insects sprouting wings, new fur or feathers, hibernation and many other rhythms. However, most animal seasonal changes link back to the reproductive cycle – the need to be in the right place at the right time for mating and to give the young their best chance. As the days lengthen, fish, mammals and birds migrate north; gonads and antlers grow. Male birds sing more frequently as the days lengthen, as their testes grow, and then, as days and gonads contract in autumn, the songs reduce. Short days act as a brake on sexual development, but can't hold back the tide for ever.

In a series of slightly surreal experiments, scientists learned that hamsters' testes shrink when nights are kept long and stop working altogether for a while; after a month they are growing again. Similarly, sheep remain asexual for a long period if the days stay short, but eventually mature sexually. White-crowned sparrows can be kept asexual for years if nights stay long, but spring back to fertility when long days return.

Each animal has its own schedule and there are big differences. Birds may lay an egg a day or two after fertilisation, which hatches a couple of weeks later; a horse waits almost a year before giving birth. Horses have ovaries that develop when the days grow long, but many other mammals with shorter gestations respond to shortening days. Sheep have a gestation period of about 152 days, for deer it is closer to two hundred, but both need to give birth in spring. Deer and sheep respond to shortening days, but deer start earlier. We hear the noise of stags rutting from late September and see rams at work in early November: their internal clocks have been marking off sunrise and sunset times.

Things are more complex with insects, not least because of multivoltinism, or having multiple broods per year, and diapauses, or pausing development at certain stages. Some insects, like aphids, produce asexual female offspring if the days are too long, and fertile young during long nights.

Plants sense the photoperiod through their leaves, mammals through their retinas. Birds sense the light of day through their pineal gland, and migration dates are more dependable than we might imagine, thanks to the regularity of the sun. Insects, as always, are complex. 'Photoreception has been located extraretinally in the dorso-frontal neuro-secretory region cells in aphids and silk moths', or somewhere on their back, near their head.

Curiosity prompted me to look into the most popular month for human births. It is September in the USA, which is nine months after the long hours indoors of midwinter. But here's the weird thing, it's September in Australia too, nine months after midsummer. I haven't managed to discover why that is, but my best guess is that the festivities near Christmas lead to lovemaking regardless of when the sun rises. Did our ancestors, raising their offspring before central heating, know to get romantic in summer so as to have more babies in spring? I'm not convinced that's how romance works in our species.

A Major Weakness

The genius of photoperiodism is that it sidesteps the current weather. No matter how many heatwaves or storms blow through in spring and autumn, the length of days and nights is dependable. We don't know how many frosty mornings there will be next April, but we know when the sun will rise and set, even if it is behind clouds, and organisms keep time by counting dark hours, not intensity of light. (Thick clouds can nudge the clock out by thirty minutes for some species, but it won't last for enough days to cause an issue.)

Photoperiodism works especially well in spring and autumn in the temperate zone, because this is when we experience the fastest changes in sunrise and sunset times and therefore the most dramatic changes in the length of day and night. The length of day changes more in a single week in late March and September than in the entire months of June and December.

Farmers know when to sow crops and how to manage the courtship diaries of sheep, cattle and horses, but plants and animals in the wild, as far as we know, have zero concept of future seasons. There is a temptation to anthropomorphise when it comes to the seasons,* to imagine that animals are, at some level, thinking, Better get going if we want to be ready in

---

* As you may have spotted, I do it deliberately sometimes to help convey some ideas. It is easier to teach and learn when we imagine ourselves in the game.

time for spring. But, of course, they don't think months ahead or make plans for the future: they react to the present. Animals respond to current night lengths, which allow them to behave as though they are predicting and preparing for seasons and weather changes many months away. This is the wizardry of photoperiodism – internally clocking the time between sunset and sunrise allows their bodies to gaze into a crystal ball.

Photoperiodism has one major weakness: it is ambiguous. The day is the same length in late March and late September, but the following six months could not be more different. This is why, however clever and critical photoperiodism is, it would be risky to rely solely on it. The consequences of thinking September is March would look a lot like death. Plants and animals need to pair photoperiodism with at least one other gauge of annual time and the most popular option is temperature, which we will meet soon.

4

March

The Spring Equinox

—

Rising Sap and Stone Fruits

It was one of those March days when the sun shines hot and the wind blows cold: when it is summer in the light, and winter in the shade.

Charles Dickens, *Great Expectations*

Seesaw Moments

You are doubtless familiar with the expression 'four seasons in a day' and we do get days when the weather is not only changeable but volatile with sudden shifts in mood. They mark a moment.

One day in early March, I set out on a walk into cold air, my face freshened further by blustery breezes but warmed by fulsome sunshine. I chopped my planned walk short when I saw clouds to the north that made the hills look feeble. Beating a retreat, I glanced over my shoulder at the menacing white pillars and a brisk pace kept me ahead of trouble. Respect is recommended for any cloud taller than it is wide.

Closing the door of my cabin behind me, I heard a light drumming on the roof. The percussion picked up and soon a cacophonous hammering of ice pellets bounced off the roof, the gravel track and everything else I could see out of the window. I opened the door again and stood under the parapet of the cabin roof, safe from lightning, sheltered from the icy onslaught, yet able to savour the sights, sounds and even the feel of the hail that bounced off some tree roots and on to me. The intensity was glorious, although not wholly unexpected. Hail means that a storm cloud – cumulonimbus – towers overhead. If you meet hail, it's a warning that lightning and thunder may be brewing.

Hail never lasts long continuously. It can't. It falls from towering isolated clouds and as soon as they pass or dissipate the hail stops. Hail can arrive in bursts, to stop and start, but that means a series of tall clouds is passing over the same spot; there will be breaks between the hail showers.

By the time the hail stopped, barely five minutes after it started, the ground was carpeted in ice baubles and I picked up a handful to study them more closely. The small ice pellets were just large enough to divine two shades. There was a pure white and a translucent grey. The white is the ice from the freezing top of the cloud; the grey is water that froze nearer the bottom. As I studied the hailstones, I felt the sun on my face again and it lit the hail, highlighting the small differences in the ice.

My walk took me to the edge of Madehurst village where my boots landed on tarmac for the first time that day. Then a March genie appeared before me. The sun cut between two trees at the edge of the road and lit the wet tarmac. Above it, twirling in bright light, a pillar of steam rose into the cold air. The steam and hail may appear to have little in common, but they whisper the same message.

The genie granted Aladdin three wishes after he rubbed a magical oil lamp, but the March steam genie has its own rules and offers different gifts. For steam to rise off the land, we need cold air, water on the ground and strong enough sun. Black tarmac absorbs the sun's energy very well and gives some of the best and earliest displays, but the steam can be seen over foliage and other surfaces too. Colour is critical and you won't see this effect on bright surfaces, I never see it rising over a white chalk path. If you stay sensitive to this phenomenon at this time of year, you may sometimes notice small wisps of steam rising off dark evergreen leaves, like ivy, but not from lighter leaves nearby. A curl of steam rising above frosty leaves offers one of the most sublime displays.

We may occasionally spot it at other times, but it is a classic early-spring sign. Until March the sun isn't strong enough; later the air is too warm. The steam tells us that the seesaw is starting to tip: the sun has risen high enough to warm the land, but the air is still cold. The hail sends the same seasonal message on a different scale. Both are examples of thermals, warm air rising through cold, and emblems of an unstable atmosphere.

March thermals make tall clouds, hail showers and storms more likely and they have another knock-on effect – they change the winds we feel. Winds grow gustier when the sun is strong enough to stir up the air because the wind can no longer travel in a straight line and instead is jostled and obstructed by the pillars of rising air. If the sun is out on a cool spring day and you spot clouds towering up, notice that there is no such thing as a steady breeze.

At these times, we may feel a deep stirring as our brain tries to reconcile gathering warmth and light with turbulent skies. Artists exploit our sensitivity to these moments, none more so than Constable, who described the sky as 'the chief organ of sentiment' in a landscape painting. We can revel in these emotions if we enjoy the ride, but if they prove unsettling, we can overrule them with optimism. We haven't met four seasons in a day but we have witnessed one of the seesaw moments of spring. The sun is moving us, over bumps, to warmer times. However volatile and discombobulating a March day may be, we know the direction of travel and can salute the towering clouds with traditional lore: 'March comes in like a lion and goes out like a lamb.'

The Tadpole and the Supertanker

In March 1975 a successful eighteen-year-old student slipped and fell into a large icy Michigan pond, where he lay submerged for thirty-eight minutes. The first responders did not rush the young man to the hospital. They were heading for the mortuary with a lifeless body when they heard gasping. Two weeks later he was back at his college and continued to get excellent grades. Almost fifty years later I saw a tadpole in a pond.

After a March night of violent storms, I rose early to check the house and garden for damage and paused at the edge of our pond. For a couple of minutes, little appeared to be going on. But there is a simple trick to making things happen at the surface of calm water: move until your view across it mixes light and dark reflections. I stepped around the edge until I could see the dark treeline cut the pond in two and focused on the tops of the reflected trees, the line that divided light from dark. When we look across a mix of light and dark reflections the slightest disturbance jumbles them and we spot the patterns easily. Suddenly the surface was a sea of action. The activity had always been there but I had been blind to it until I changed my perspective.

I saw countless breeze-whipped ripples and then a couple of whirligig beetles scuttling over the surface, leaving their signature patterns – a thousand tiny circles emanating from a frenetic skittish spot. The motion of the beetle reminds me of a drop of water on a hot stove, zipping fast, never stopping and without apparent destination.

Whirligigs are small black beetles that have paddle-like back legs that propel them over the surface of the water. Many pond insects are small and light enough to treat calm water like a table-top and rest on the surface tension. Sitting on water appears to break the laws of physics, but anything will float if its surface area is vast compared to its weight and volume. A sweet demonstration proves this in the kitchen: icing sugar floats on water, caster sugar sinks; the first is powdery and has a much higher surface-area-to-volume ratio than the second.

I peered down through the surface of the water near the rock I stood on. A solitary tadpole wriggled among the rush stubble at the edge of the pond. Tadpoles tell us that the water is warming, but there is water and water. Everyone knows that water warms as winter turns to spring and then summer, but few appreciate the different speeds at which this happens and the impact it has on the nature we see.

In boats we learn that we can stop a rowing dinghy dead in about two seconds by jamming the oars into the water. The International Maritime Organization stipulates that, in an emergency, all ships in the world must be able to put the engines into full astern and bring the ship to a stop within twenty times of its own length, ideally within fifteen. Consider for a moment that ships have been built that are almost half a kilometre long – the *Seawise Giant* was 458 metres long and weighed 657,000 tonnes. The rules state that a ship weighing more than a street of houses must be able to stop within about seven kilometres. Big ships have inertia, it takes a lot of energy to change their speed or direction; it takes time. Small boats can change direction in a beat. There are some interesting parallels between size and temperature in bodies of water. If you are planning to fall into a pond in spring, make it a small one: it will be safer and much more interesting.

Small Changes Feel Big to Small Creatures

The days lengthen in spring, the sun's arc nudges higher in the sky, solar energy pours in and everything the sun touches gets warmer, but it happens at very different speeds, depending on the surface the sun hits. As we saw earlier, tarmac responds dynamically: a road may be thirty degrees warmer at dusk than at dawn, but the sea may not noticeably change temperature from one week to the next. A pond may be six degrees warmer in the afternoon than it is at daybreak. A small pond changes noticeably more than a large one, and a narrow deep stream is totally different from a wide shallow one. The temperature fluctuations at the surface of fresh water are much greater than they are a few feet below. And we haven't even begun to consider how some parts of the water may be shaded or more exposed to the wind. There are a thousand seasons in every stretch of water, but how does that change what we see?

Two keys unlock this world of wild change. First, look for the biggest differences over the shortest distances. Second, enlist the help of the smallest animals. In practical terms this means we get to know a patch of water well enough to appreciate its temperature habits, then marry them to the changes we see in the insects.

For decades scientists have used insects as 'bio-indicators' to monitor the wellbeing of water systems, because nothing gets past them. Aquatic insects are sensitive to every variable in their watery world: pollutants, nutrients, pH, flow speed, turbulence, oxygen, light, plant life, predators . . . If anything alters in the environment, the insect populations change rapidly.

We may see the same river flowing from high ground to low, but the insects reflect different worlds at each stage. Sediments flow downhill, oxygen levels change and microscopic plants, like phytoplanktons, do better downstream. This leads to differences in the water that may be imperceptible to us, but are seismic enough to divide the insects into groups that thrive in each zone. Temperature fluctuates, which changes almost everything else in the water also. As water warms, microbes stir into action and plants photosynthesise more; it also alters the solubility of oxygen and pollutants. It even changes how electricity conducts, which affects species that shock their prey, like eels and catfish (as well as those that sense fluctuations in electric fields caused by the movements of prey at sea, like sharks).

A few degrees will change an insect's universe. As cold water warms, the insects grow faster, eat and excrete more quickly, have more offspring that hatch earlier. Some insects even change colour. The parental effect explains the explosion in numbers we so often see. In a cold environment, a species may tend towards a single brood in a year, known as univoltinism; the same insect in a warmer environment may have as many as three broods – multivoltinism. Thanks to the compounding effect, a hundred insects quickly become a hundred thousand. The next time you find yourself walking through warm moist air near still water and beating a thousand flying insects away from your nostrils, say, 'Multivoltinism,' and it will magically take your mind off them.

Big fluctuations in air temperature over the course of a day lead to more species and variety, as long as the thermometer stays within limits. Cool mornings and warm afternoons lead to lots of different species, but freezing or sizzling temperatures will kill off many. Prey welcome warm days – it is harder for insects to hunt in hot air.

By early summer, there will be grand differences and fascinating displays in every patch of water, but late March is the time to start honing observational skills. This is when small worlds morph before our eyes. A walk from a large lake in the morning to a small pond in the afternoon offers two contrasting worlds: the pond will be many degrees warmer than the lake. But we can explore without moving far, by getting to know one stretch of water well. Compare deep shady areas at dawn with sunlit shallows in mid-afternoon and you'll travel to another country as far as the insects are concerned. Aspect plays a vital role. Water flowing from east to west will have one bank open to the southern sun, a different habitat from the opposite north-facing bank. A stream that runs from north to south will have an east-facing bank that soaks up the morning rays while the opposite bank will heat more after lunch.

A breeze leads to stirring, mixing shallow and deep water and changing the picture we see. This effect is important in spring because, as the sun warms the water, many lakes get stuck in a stagnant arrangement called 'stratification': a warm layer of water lies over a colder layer and the two do not mix. You may have experienced this when wild swimming – in a dive about a metre beneath the surface you meet a shocking drop, up to 10 degrees, in temperature. It's enough to shock most unsuspecting swimmers back to the surface with a gasp. Stratification can help explain big differences in late spring. Perhaps there are two lakes near to each other, one exposed to constant breezes, the other sheltered by dense woodland: the water in the first is well mixed; in the other it is stratified.

According to the Smithsonian Institution there are about 10 quintillion insects alive at any one time in the world – 10,000,000,000,000,000,000 – and hundreds of thousands of species. There are about seventy-six aquatic insect species in freshwater habitats, so getting to know them all by name is a game for another lifetime. Our aims are more modest and much easier: we spot the different worlds on, in and around fresh water and understand some of the factors at play. Then we pair our observations of insect life and behaviour to those microworlds. We see through the cloud of midges to the shallow water at the lake edge, the sunbeams landing there and the shelter from the wind offered by the pair of alder trees and appreciate that all five pieces, midges, sun, trees, wind and water are part of the same seasonal jigsaw.

At the start and end of the day, the height of each flying insect above water maps the extreme fluctuations in microclimate there. As the temperatures warm through spring and into summer, we find the species changing but also their comfort near water at the warmest and coolest times of day. It is common to see clouds of insects very close to the surface of water in the afternoon, but much rarer near cool daybreak.

March is not the month of greatest activity, but it is the time to familiarise ourselves with the character of the water we see. The tadpoles fire the starting gun – they prompt us to focus on factors like depth, aspect, gradient, shade and flow before the insects do their best to overwhelm us.

Our reward for an early start is that we are ready to spot the most fun displays through spring and into summer. As the sun dips in the west, the east side of water receives the last of its rays. Many insects migrate there as dusk approaches. Roosting insects, including dragonflies, will be active until the sun drops near the horizon when they alight on vegetation to find their spot for the evening. A west-facing stem is a fine place to spend a summer dusk, but not at dawn. The commute near sunrise flows the other way. Sometimes this journey is a proper flight, but often it is a small hop. If you rise early, you may spot a dragonfly relocate. Many adults, including the common green darner, roost on the west side of a shrub and make a small flight to the east at daybreak to absorb the sun's warming rays.

Early Elder

I followed a path up the domed back of a hill on my way to meet a hedge-layer in Wiltshire. A pair of kites patrolled above the woodland to my east and the cacophony of a rookery.

A kestrel hovered by a distant road. Whenever a bird of prey hovers over the same piece of ground, it has to face into wind or be blown off that spot. They flap their wings just enough to counter the wind, keeping them pinned over some unsuspecting rodent and making a fine weathervane. A kestrel hovering by the road reveals the wind direction and improves any long road journey.

When I met Tom Fortune, he was doing kind battle with some young ash trees and sap poured from the wounds. 'Ash is brittle when it comes to laying. Hazel and blackthorn bend beautifully, but ash just shatters.' He pointed to the places where the ash had refused to bend and ruptured.

I was just in time: the hedge-laying season runs from September to March, when tools are downed to protect the birds and other wildlife. Tom works in woodland management in the off-season and was keen to point out that it was low impact, not the intense logging of commercial timber operations: the heavy machines destroy the intricate root networks under their tracks.

This led to a chat about the public's perception of working on trees. There is a widespread belief that cutting down any must be a negative action, but biodiversity is improved by good management. The manner of the work and the age of the witness elicit different reactions.

'Use a chainsaw and people come running to question what's happening. Use an axe and they leave you alone. The young say, "Why are you cutting down trees?" Wiser heads say, "So nice to see this work."'

We walked alongside a hedge Tom had been laying on a windswept chalky hill. A great tit sang loudly from the woodland edge. Ash was not Tom's only enemy: 'Elder is a hedge-layer's nightmare. Normally we cut it out because it can't be laid, but this farm's organic and it's great for the pollinators.'

The elder is one of the first broadleaf trees into leaf each year. I had seen buds bursting weeks before I met Tom, and the sap was well into the leaves by the time we were walking his patch. It has branches in the sweet spot for early leaves, a few feet above the cold ground.

Elder trees make poor hedges but they have so many other uses and are treasured by many who practise traditional skills. Elder stems contain white pith that is easily removed, leaving a hollow tube, once commonly fashioned into a flute or blowpipe for fanning the flames of a fire. Its name comes from the Anglo Saxon word '*æld*' meaning 'fire'. Tom used the French word for this fire blowpipe, *bouffadou*, as he had been taught how to fashion one by a French shepherd. (I have since heard the name comes from the legend of a witch called Bouffanelle, who could summon the Devil by blowing into a fire with a hollow magic wand.)

Foragers will know the flavour of the elder flowers and berries of warmer months and the plant features strongly in traditional medicine, the inner bark as a cathartic and the flowers used to make a healing ointment. The berries have also been used as a fabric dye. The leaves were once a popular insect repellent, but they do not deter all insects and some moths favour it. Uncooked, many parts of the plant are toxic.

Elder is helpful in natural navigation. It does well in disturbed places and signals a nutrient-spike, telling us we will find humans nearby. The further from a building you find it, the stronger the likelihood that you will find an animal's home within touching distance – it is common around rabbits' burrows. Elder likes lots of light and is more common on south-facing slopes. A bumper crop of blossom or berries is a strong sign that the plant receives plentiful sunlight.

The elder is a seasonal nexus plant. It signals a line between winter and spring, the edge of homes and the gate to a wilder wisdom.

Water, Place and Time

'There's been so much water this year,' Tom said, referring to the relentless February rain, 'that the willows are going hell for leather and I've seen that already in a couple of hedges that have willow in. Amazing.'

Willows mean water. A long line of willows in the distance nearly always marks a river or stream. But it was interesting to hear Tom point to water-loving trees getting an early start in wet years. I asked if he had seen this in any other plants that favour moist habitats. He had noted the wild garlic being especially early that year too. Heavy rain had brought spring forward for the thirstiest plants.

On the far side of the hill, the path ran steeply down to the shelter of a wooded valley. The sun, freed from the cooling gusts of higher ground, warmed the land and a butterfly dipped and soared by the edge of the path. My eyes had not adjusted to the brightness and it took me a few seconds to spot the corners of the wings of the well-named orange-tip. This was a seasonal moment. I had not expected to see that butterfly for a few weeks yet, but it was ahead of schedule, as most things had been that spring so far.

The colour marked it as a male and sent me in pursuit. All butterflies give us clues to season, weather, direction and habitat. They make maps of moments as well as places. And this one was hinting that there was water nearby – they favour moist habitats.

The simpler the relationship between any animal and plant, the clearer the map they make. We expect to see sheep grazing on open land, not in the heart of dense woodland. Butterflies favour certain plants for food and for important stages in their reproductive cycle. The orange-tip teaches us how to follow a stepping stone approach to map-making with animals.

If we watch any butterfly as it visits flowers, a pattern will emerge, a signature behaviour. The orange-tip favours four-petalled flowers within the brassica family and I often see it flitting between garlic mustard or cuckoo flowers. Those plants share a habitat preference – they thrive in moist environments. Any plant that prefers such places is trying to tell us it is very shady or we are near water, perhaps both. Garlic mustard is also known as hedge garlic or Jack-by-the-hedge, and is found on the shaded side of hedges or on north-facing ground. The cuckoo flower does well with more light, but tells us we will find water nearby. The orange-tip, after a couple of steps, leads us to a compass and a map. But where is the calendar? The clue is in the flower's name.

The naturalist parson Gilbert White recorded how the cuckoo flower would open its flowers from 6 to 20 April, and the cuckoo could be heard from 7 to 26 April. Although I hear cuckoos less frequently than anyone did in White's day, when I do, I know to look for pretty pink four-petals as a sign that I'm nearing a river. I met this happy triangle of signs on a walk towards the river Clyde in Scotland last spring: birdsong, wildflowers and water made a calendar and a map.

The Spring Equinox

Some dates are artificial, like 1 January, and others are rooted in astronomy, like the solstices and equinoxes. The former wouldn't exist if humans hadn't invented them; the latter are astronomical moments that exist independent of human culture.

The March equinox would, if it could speak, make a good case for being called the beginning of the year. A campaign speechwriter could do worse than enlist the Roman poet, Ovid:

Come, tell me, why does the New Year start in the cold,
When it would surely be better in the spring?
Then it is that all things flower and a new age begins,
And from the bursting vine the new bud swells . . .

Then the sun's rays soothe and the visiting swallow comes
And fixes his mud nest under the lofty beam.
Then the field yields to the farmer's plough and is renewed.
This is the time we should rightly call New Year.

Ovid, *Fasti*, 1 149–60, from Jeremy Mynott*

Earth rotates about its axis and orbits the sun. We call each rotation a day and each orbit a year. When the North Pole points as far as it can towards the sun this is the June Solstice. The sun is well over the northern hemisphere at this time, which gives us the longest days. When the South Pole points as far as it can towards the sun, this is the December solstice. Halfway between these two points the sun is over the equator and we have the equinoxes in late March and September.

On the vernal equinox, close to 20 March each year, the sun rises due east and sets due west. For the next six months, until the September equinox, it will rise and set north of east and west.

You will hear it said that day and night are of equal length on the equinox – the word 'equinox' means 'equal night' – but there is a nuance to this that goes beyond pedantry: we get more light hours than dark on those dates. The times of sunrise and sunset on the equinox split the day and night into equal halves, but we experience some light for about half an hour before sunrise and after sunset, which stretches the days. This is 'twilight', and it's a good time of year to delve into it, because it has a significant bearing on outdoor experience at this time of year.

---

* From Mynott, Jeremy, *Birds in the Ancient World*, OUP, 2019.

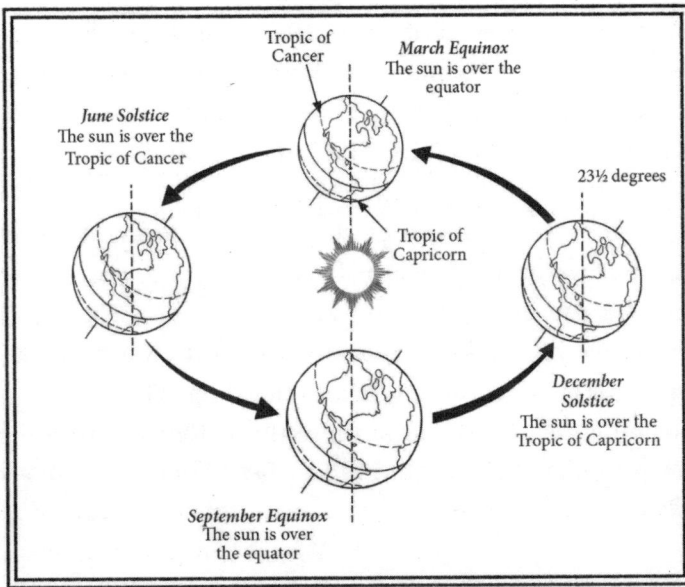

Twilight stretches with latitude: the further from the equator you are, the longer it lasts. Twilight is shorter in England and the USA than it is in Scotland and Canada because the angle of sunrise and sunset grows steeper as we move towards the equator, where it is at its steepest, 90 degrees. The sun falls and rises vertically at the equator and moves horizontally at the Poles. Ironically the idyllic low-sun time – cocktail hour – lasts just twenty minutes in the tropics, but hours in the Arctic.

If you're spending time near the coast, the March and September equinoxes are times to watch for big tides. The sun and moon form a line that passes through Earth twice a month, during a full or new moon, causing 'spring tides' about two days later. (The word 'spring' here has nothing to do with the season; it is used in the sense of rising or springing forth. Spring tides occur in all seasons.) During a full or new moon near the equinox, the sun is over the equator and lined up with Earth and the moon, meaning that the effects combine. 'Equinoctial tides' take place a couple of days after the full or new moon nearest the equinox.

While tide-watching, give some thought to the wind and air pressure. If storms are on their way, there will be low and falling pressure – good sailors check their barometers. Air is heavy, but when air pressure falls precipitously, this takes a weight off the ocean and the water rises as much as a foot. When there has also been an onshore gale, we have all the ingredients for tidal onslaught and flooding. The worst coastal floods include at least two of these three: storms, spring tides and equinoxes. In late March and September, all three can combine.

Rising Sap and Stone Fruits

Miles Irving placed a cup on his kitchen table and I sniffed the steam rising above the homemade rosebay willowherb tea. He told me it was traditional in Japan. I waited for it to cool and we discussed Miles's professional path since we'd last met.

For many years Miles had been a successful professional forager supplying restaurants, but he had stepped away from the business, frustrated at the superficiality of his customers' approach. 'I've never felt the foraging business was about selling something to make money. It's about putting something in someone's hands . . .' His face lit up as he explained his aim of fostering engagement and understanding, but fell again. 'It's not happening with the restaurants.'

He'd spent time teaching, but wasn't convinced he was having the impact he desired there either: 'I'm a scout going back to where we used to be,' he said, with new zeal in his voice. He talked about a time that summed up his philosophy. 'There were acorns lying on the ground everywhere. It was embarrassing, a high level of rudeness to leave them there! It was my responsibility to take care of that. To teach people. You can do this with the acorns, this with the hawthorn . . . Then I leave them to their biscuits made from acorn flour.'

I took a sip of willowherb tea, it was pleasant, slightly musty and less fragrant than I had imagined. Later we headed out for a walk in Kent's North Downs. Our conversation bounced off our observations and, nibbling sheep sorrel leaves, I learned that dandelion contains five thousand bioactive compounds. We reached the edge of the woods, reliably mapped by the birch trees that thrive there. Miles pulled a knife from his pocket and I could tell from his energetic movements that he was about to share something interesting. He cut a small hole in the bark and the sap began to trickle and drip. He had been making birch syrup and asked if I knew which side of the tree was most dependable for tapping.

I thought about it for a few seconds. In spring, birch and maple are unusual. Unlike most other trees, which pull their sap upwards to their leaves, birch and maple create positive pressure and push sap up from below. Pumping sap helps them to clear any frozen pipes in early spring and allows them to grow much further north than other broadleaf trees. It explains how they can survive alongside conifers in the brutal north of Russia. But that didn't answer Miles's question.

I guessed the south-west side of the tree, as this is where the biggest roots were – they grow larger there to anchor trees against the prevailing south-westerly winds.

'Nope. The north side.' Miles grinned. Why? I couldn't understand it. 'Don't know, but there's twice as much on that side. Works for me every time.'

Some old hands recommend tapping the north side as it's cooler and the sap is less likely to dry or congeal in the shade, but I've never heard of it being the best side for flow rates. Sap flow is stronger with taller, thicker, older trees, which is logical, and flow is meant to be better on the downhill side, but I'd never heard that aspect has a big impact.

In the weeks after our walk, I tried to shed more light on this, but have so far failed. I learned, though, that prospectors have tried using birch sap to work out if there are valuable mineral seams in the ground below. They sampled birches over a decade and found spikes in levels of metals such as cadmium, lead, silver and zinc in the sap of trees near deposits.

Soon we were admiring the blossom on a pair of blackthorns. There were no leaves on the trees, just a frothy white blossom, doing best on the southern side. There is a jubilant rebellious-ness in a tree bearing flowers so early, before its first leaves – it's one of my favourite early-spring signs.

Blackthorn is a spreading, colonising plant, and I often find it closing over little-used paths. If you can't find a path you were expecting to lead you out of a field in March, look for a patch of white blossom. You will find your overgrown path, but if there is no clear route, I don't recommend trying to beat your way through blackthorn. It's a painful battle. The long, strong thorns can puncture tyres and make light work of clothing or skin.

The blackthorn blossom is part of an early-spring pattern that stretches around the world and percolates through many cultures. The blossom of stone-fruit trees signals spring widely. I once walked among the almond blossom in the foothills of the dry mountains of southern Spain. It signals early spring in many Mediterranean climates. The almond tree inspired the iconic multi-branched candelabrum, the menorah, of Jewish ceremony:

There shall be six branches going out of the sides thereof: three branches of the candlestick out of the one side thereof, and three branches of the candlestick out of the other side thereof; three cups made like almond-blossoms in one branch, a knop [the cuplike sepals, which protect the petals] and a flower . . .

Exodus (25:32–33)

The Hebrew word for almond is *shaked,* and the tree is used as a metaphor for swiftness and courageousness in the Bible: it isn't easy for a plant to blossom during the cold early weeks of spring. The almond symbolises 'waking' for the same reason.

The Japanese have recorded cherry blossom dates for more than a millennium. In 2021, the *Washington Post* reported that the blossom in Kyoto, Japan, was the earliest in twelve hundred years of records, coming out on 26 March that year. I imagined these records tumble regularly, but Nature likes to surprise us: the previous record was set on 27 March 1409.

The blackthorn, almond and cherry trees are part of the *Prunus* genus, which also includes peach and plum trees. They are the 'stone fruits' (also known as 'drupes') – a large hard seed encased in a soft flesh that we often consume. These glorious rebel trees are seasonal vanguards and dare to throw out sprays of bright blossom before most others have shown signs of leafing.

Trees are the ultimate perennials and store lots of energy from the previous year so they don't need the sun's to start putting out leaves or flowers in spring. Trees have another advantage over smaller plants. They hold their flowers off the ground, well above the hardest frosts. The *Prunus* genus has evolved to flower very early: they specialise in meeting the earliest flying insects. There are always risks in early flowering, but the rewards can be seen in the beautiful displays and, later, the abundance of the fruits across the world.

We were nearly back at Miles's home when we stopped to pick some nettles for lunch. They had their usual tough, hairy texture, but the acid droplets hanging from the hairs couldn't penetrate our gloves. Nearby we saw a small patch of lamb's lettuce, which looks delicate but is surprisingly hardy, coping with freezing temperatures and even snow. 'It's got its own anti-freeze,' Miles explained.

Indoors, we took off our boots and continued our chat as Miles prepared soup. He combined the nettles with wild garlic, seaweed and mushrooms to make a heavenly broth, inspired by a Japanese recipe. Out of the window I could see the white blossom of the blackthorn trees running in a line over the hill.

5

Cold and Warm

A Failsafe

Photoperiodism works beautifully if you can rule out confusing autumn with spring, and evolution devised a cunning way to do this. Many plants will only respond to lengthening days if they have been through a cold period, when the temperature drops below a certain threshold. It is a logical safety switch – 'If there hasn't been cold weather in recent months, it can't be spring.' Most native deciduous trees require a chilling period before they will begin to grow again. There are exceptions, but the vast majority that we see leafing in spring have worked out it is safe to do so, thanks to 'vernalisation'. Some seeds require the cold period to germinate and many plants will not flower without it. We can think of it as a gate that is open or closed: once there has been a cold spell, the gate remains wide open. Invasive plants have a less strict need for chilling than natives, an advantage in a warming world.

Now we have length of day and a failsafe system for checking it really is spring, but if that was all, we might expect plants to germinate, leaf and flower on exactly the same day, at pretty much the same hour, each year. We know they don't and that there is significant variation from year to year, but why?

Counting Warmth

René Antoine Ferchault de Réaumur was a pioneering French entomologist, in the first half of the eighteenth century, who took a keen interest in the effect temperature has on organisms.

(He has been credited as the founder of ethology, the study of animal behaviour, and might have done more in that field had he not died from injuries sustained by falling from his horse.) He joins us here, briefly, because he noticed that Nature reacted to warmth in spring in a way that was quantifiable. By combining measures of temperature *and* time into 'degree-days', de Réaumur devised a way to keep a score of cumulative change and paint a better picture of spring as Nature senses it.

Humans using supercomputers struggle to predict the weather more than ten days in advance with any accuracy, and Nature doesn't bother trying. Instead, it gauges the past and present as best it can. Plants have specialised proteins and enzymes that respond to changes in temperature and help them keep tally of warming weather – they count the warm hours. This 'thermal sum' gives them one of the final major pieces of information they need to decide when it is time to break dormancy and grow, grow, grow. Yellow star thistle, for example, needs five hundred degree-days to flower. Two months of mild weather that is nine degrees above the base temperature needed will trigger flowering, but one very warm month that averages seventeen degrees above that level would have the same effect (60 x 9 = 540 or 30 x 18 = 540).

Perhaps there is an easy way to overcome the problem of frosts. Why not wait until the risk has passed by late spring? There is a different danger in delay: organisms need to beat the competition to resources, including food or light, and to prepare for the next generation. If they wait until the last minute to avoid the risk of cold snaps, their competitors could get a head-start of weeks, robbing them of food or light. There is risk in going too late or too early. As gardeners know, there is no perfect way to guarantee that the last frost of spring has passed, but counting warm hours and doing thermal sums is the most popular method in nature.

Some species have hard and fast rules: if the thermometer doesn't stay high enough for long enough, nothing happens. For others there is a balance between photoperiodism and temperature: if the days grow long enough, they will compromise and lower their need for warmth – 'Oh, go on, then, if you insist. Let's call it spring.' Some plants are casual chefs, throwing ingredients together until it tastes about right. Others are sticklers for accuracy and formality. The budburst of the sessile oak, for example, can be predicted precisely if the temperatures over the previous ten days and length of day are measured.

Many Smaller Worlds

Warm days mean earlier spring, but there is a fascinating world within this basic rule for a simple reason. The temperature that matters is not the one in the forecast, but the one the plants sense, and the more we zoom in, the more intriguing things become. But let's start by taking a step back.

The further from the equator we are, the cooler spring temperatures will be on average for any given date. We expect spring to start at the equator end of any region and progress towards the Pole and that is what we find. (The same rule applies in the southern hemisphere, where plants on North Island, New Zealand, nearer the equator, flower before those on South Island, nearer the Pole.) Latitude has a secondary knock-on effect. Plants at higher latitudes start later and finish earlier because the season of kind temperatures is shorter.

Warm temperatures wash away from the equator in spring, then back again in autumn. We can think of latitude as a beach: the tide rises and falls. The bottom of a beach is underwater for a long time, the top for a short time. Plants grow for a long time near the equator end and a short time near the polar end.

[59]

Flowers start and peak earlier at lower latitudes. In one study, the lower-latitude plants flowered over a six-month period and peaked earlier; the plants further from the equator flowered for only four months and peaked later.

Plants halfway up a mountain experience a colder world than their relatives in the valley and will germinate, leaf and flower later in spring. Researchers in the Niuheliang Reserve in China found that spring phases were delayed by 1.84 days for every gain of 100 metres in altitude. There were similar but slightly weaker effects at the end of the growing season too, with autumn phases advancing 1.66 days per 100 metres. The combined effect was the season shortening by three and a half days for every 100-metre gain in altitude. But we don't need the academics' data to make this true: the moment you see the first flowers or butterflies of the year, walk uphill for twenty minutes, catch your breath and watch them disappear. (Or, make them reappear by walking downhill in autumn.)

We may expect seasons to change as we walk higher up a hill, but it's easy to overlook the micro-seasons we pass on the way. If you spot a bowl or hollow in the land on the lower slopes of a hill, it is worth investigating for seasonal anomalies. It may be out of the wind, making it warmer, but it will also act as a pool and collect the cold dense air that rolls down the hill after a clear night leading to a 'frost hollow'. The cold air will retard developments in spring and accelerate them in autumn. If this is a place we pass only once, it will be enough for us to notice a slight difference in size, flowering or leafing times or insect activity. But if it is part of a regular route, we should befriend it over weeks and years. One spot confused me because the plants were both behind and ahead of others on that route. Eventually I appreciated that those at the bottom of the dip were slowed in spring by frost and those just above it were profiting from the shelter – there was a seasonal brake and accelerator within the same modest landscape feature. (The mystery was greatest in spring, but it was solved, as is often the case, at a different time of year. One October I spotted a line of hard frost that reached only halfway up the bowl.)

The season changes as we climb a hill, but also if we stay at the same level and walk around it. Aspect has a powerful impact on the biology of a region and will change the plants and animals we see. Where a species is found on all sides of a hill, spring starts earlier on the warmer south-facing slope than it does on the northern aspect. By monitoring nine wildflower species over sixteen different microclimates in Indiana, scientists established that the plants came into flower six days earlier on the south-facing slopes. This doesn't sound dramatic, but the flowers in this case were only 115 feet apart. To put this in context of latitude, we'd have to travel 110 miles north to see the same six-day delay. Another study, this time in the Lake Michigan area, found an even greater gap between the peak flowering dates – a full fourteen days later on the north-facing slopes, equivalent to a journey north of 242 miles or heading 1400 feet up a mountain.

Of course, nature isn't sensing aspect, it cares neither for north nor south, but reacts to every change in its environment. We find huge differences over tiny distances because direct sunlight has a major effect and there is always more of it on the side of any hill facing the equator. Step over a ridge from north to south and you enter a much brighter zone. The wildflowers and insects experience different micro-seasons on each side of a tall tree. A dozen different wildflowers grow on the cleared land outside my cabin; those to the north of the tall spruce tree blossom and go to seed later than those at either side of the tree, open to direct sunlight from the southern sun. In late summer I'll tweak a few petals from the wild marjoram and compare the scent of the fresh pink flowers in the shadier zone with the drier, stiffer ones in the sunlight.

Gradient also plays a part. Spring starts earlier and autumn comes later on gentle slopes – steep gradients delay spring and accelerate autumn. But every landscape will also shape the flow of the wind, making some areas colder and others warmer:

Gruinard House, standing beside the tumultuous Gruinard River, must surely be in one of the most sheltered and one of the most delightful situations in the West Highlands. Larch woods keep off most winds, yet the sun is not hidden by them; it is not surprising that the trees come early into leaf here.*

Seton Gordon noticed that the trees were coming into leaf early because they were benefiting from the magical combination of being open to the sun and sheltered from the wind.

At the start and end of the growing season, there is a 'stretching effect': the earlier in spring or later in autumn that seasonal events occur, the greater the impact of temperature fluctuations. A couple of degrees early in spring may have a bigger, much more noticeable impact than a more substantial rise in temperature later in the growing season. The stretching effect comes about because early plants are more sensitive – the earlier a plant flowers, the more strongly it reacts to temperature changes. For the same rise in temperature, spring flowers advance by 6.2 days on average, while summer species advance only by 3.8. And the quickening stops altogether later in the season; species that flower in September don't bloom earlier in warm weather.

You can see the same stretching effect when looking at aspect too. The differences in flowering timing between the north and south sides of any hill are greatest early in spring and almost disappear by the end of May.

---

* Gordon, Seton, *Highways & Byways in the West Highlands,* 1949.

There is a similar stretching effect in trees, where early trees, like birches, accelerate more determinedly in warm springs than the more laid-back species, like oaks. The early-leafing trees win the race in all years, but the margin they win by is greater in warm springs. Warm stretches; cold compresses.

Plants show some niche temperature responses that we might never guess. As the weather warms in spring, those pollinated by insects accelerate more than those that are wind-pollinated. Plants in their comfort zone, near the centre of their habitat range, accelerate more than those near the fringes.

It's time to zoom in. Plants are sensing the temperature at their extremities, at their apical bud (the top) and in their root tips. This could, in theory, mean that the sunbeam that regularly catches the top of one plant will trigger petals to open earlier in that single flower than the one a few feet away that catches the sun only on its lower leaves.

Animals Clear the Bar

We find comparable patterns in the animal world, especially the insects, in which temperatures govern birth, development and mortality rates. There is a minimum for each species, a bar the temperature must climb over before anything happens. Once the thermometer rises above this minimum threshold, degree-days become important and, again, a short, warm period may have the same effect as a longer, just warm-enough one. Insects are very sensitive to high temperatures so it has to stay within a certain window; too high and the numbers start falling, a little higher and they all die.

The lower the latitude, the earlier insect life cycles start and the longer they last. Then there is the added dimension of voltinism: the lower the latitude, the more life cycles an insect may get through in each warm season, which can change the total numbers exponentially. Drive south for an hour and the season may be just long enough for an insect to go through its life cycle several times more, which can make the difference between a few and a swarm. At higher latitudes, the insect season will be very short and we find a spike of activity in a narrow window. You may have experienced this in northern regions, it's as if there are no insects one day and a blizzard the next.

Weather plays a big part in determining the arrival dates of spring immigrants and the temperature in March affects the schedules of birds. The weather conditions at their origin, destination and en route are all important. The dates that ten common birds arrive in the UK are influenced by the temperatures in March here, but also those in Spain. And birds must contend with rain and wind too, both of which can delay arrivals if unfavourable. In fact, the single biggest factor affecting arrival dates for some bird species, like song thrushes, can be tailwinds, which may help them and reduce the energy they need for the long journey.

Migratory schedules are affected by issues as diverse as the quality of feathers grown during the season before, the availability of food en route and the vagaries of the weather. Rain makes flying harder and slower, but can improve the food options through arid regions. This makes precise prediction tough, but we can say that a warm spring is likely to bring things forward and rainy weather will probably slow them down.

The Clocks Are Changing

In 1831, an English clergyman, the Reverend Leonard Jenyns, received an unusual invitation, as he recounted in his diary:

This year I had the offer of accompanying Capt. Fitzroy, as Naturalist, in the Beagle, on his voyage to survey the coasts of S. America, afterwards going round the globe:- declined the appointment w<u>h</u> was afterwards given to Charles_ Darwin Esq. of Xts' College Cambridge.

Mr Jenyns turned down the invitation citing the demands of his parish work, although secretly he knew that his health was not robust enough to withstand such a journey. This was a small fork in history for which we can be grateful. The *Beagle* voyage helped Darwin formulate his theory of natural selection, once referred to as 'the best idea anyone has ever had'. But it was the right decision for Jenyns, too, and this 'methodical, studious and quiet' man applied his naturalist talents elsewhere. He developed into a zealous recorder of seasonal events.

In his introduction to Jenyns's book, *A Naturalist's Calendar*, Francis Darwin (third son of Charles) wrote:

The Calendar may be respectfully applied to test the accuracy of the poets. Thus Shakespeare is quite right in making the daffodil come before the swallow dares, since the latest daffodil flowers on 4 April, and the swallow does not appear till 9 April at the earliest.

Jenyns's *Calendar* is a list of events and dates, but has a power of its own. By pinning dates to specific events, Jenyns shines a light on major differences between his time and our own: the climate has changed and the dates have shifted, mostly coming forward. This is a book about the seasons as we experience them each day, not climate change over decades, but we should try to understand the surprises we see each year. If you have ever asked, 'Where are all the X this year?' the answer may lie in mismatches.

We understand so much more than we did a few decades ago about how temperature affects the seasons because climate change has shot to the top of the environmental research agenda.* It remains a challenge to tease out the relevance of broad changes to the seasons in our backyard, because global average temperature changes over a year have little impact compared to regional fluctuations at key times. The plants and animals don't read the latest data from the IPCC, but they react to a hard frost in our local park.

Many of us sense spring creeping forwards and the data support this. A study in Massachusetts found that spring flowers bloomed twelve days earlier on average in 2013 than they did in 1929 and this was true for native and non-native species. That simple figure hides a more variable and nuanced picture. Of the 292 species included in the study, 220 flowered earlier and 72 were later. And there were wild swings in individual species: pineappleweed (one of my favourites for reasons we will return to) accelerated by 55 days, while yellow star grass flowered 33 days later.

The fussier the butterfly and the fewer plants it chooses as host, the more sensitive it is to temperature changes and the earlier we are likely to see it in warm years. And butterflies that overwinter as adults appear earlier than those that are larvae in winter.

Unlike plants, animals are mobile and will not suffer a habitat if they can relocate to a better one; warming temperatures have had a northwards-nudging effect on many over the decades. The life stages of forty-four butterfly species in the UK have advanced, but most of them have also moved north.

---

* Funding for research into the way climate change affects nature has skyrocketed from a few papers per year in the 1980s to more than 200 recently, and has included work better to understand how climate influences phenology.

Parenthood forces animals to compromise. They want the best conditions for their offspring, but this often means enduring sub-optimal conditions themselves. Birds that wish to feed their young on caterpillars that are abundant during a narrow window suddenly find their whole life cycle flows back from the calendars of these wriggling insects, which in turn march in step with the leaves of their food tree. But this introduces a serious potential pitfall: what if these three clocks – bird, insect and leaf – don't have the same timekeeping mechanisms?

In 1773 the French scientist and watchmaker Ferdinand Berthoud measured the effect of temperature changes on his marine watch. He noted that an increase from 32 degrees Fahrenheit to 92 degrees Fahrenheit slowed the watch, which lost six and a half minutes over twenty-four hours, a serious problem. He investigated the cause and found that the spring lost elastic strength when warm, which caused it to run five minutes slow, but that this was exacerbated by expansion and elongation in the balance. In the eighteenth century, if you bought a dozen clocks from different clockmakers and subjected them to fluctuations of temperature through the seasons, you would find that they all gained or lost time in slightly different ways – they would no longer be in synch. And this is what we find in nature when the climate changes. North American songbirds are reaching their breeding grounds earlier because temperatures are warmer along their routes, but the plants they need at these grounds are not responding to temperature rises at the same rate – they are coming forward by only a third as much.

Across the world, birds are laying eggs earlier, thanks to rising temperatures, but insects, their food staple, aren't keeping up. At first, the effect is to shorten the window of overlap and species will adapt where possible. Caterpillars in the Netherlands are advancing faster than the arrival dates of the pied flycatchers that prey on them and the birds have responded by shortening the time between touchdown and breeding. However, if the mismatch worsens there comes a snapping point when the birds and insects no longer overlap at all, which leads to a crisis in that species.

At Wytham Woods in Oxfordshire, the great tits have been laying eggs earlier over recent decades, but the caterpillars have not kept up. And the same challenges face migrant species: the red admiral butterfly is arriving earlier but its host plant, the stinging nettle, hasn't followed. Newts are arriving at ponds earlier than they used to, but frogs, their food, are still on old time. Mismatches like this are now common because each species keeps time in its own way. Each has a unique relationship to photoperiod, temperature and other factors. If a plant or insect is more sensitive to temperature than the animal that feeds on it, it will advance more rapidly in warm conditions, leaving the animal behind. Sometimes the animal's response is greater and it overshoots. Oak buds are bursting earlier in the Netherlands, but the winter moth eggs are hatching even earlier, leading to weaker populations of moths. On a much smaller scale, microscopic plants and animals in water are reacting differently, which impacts the appearance of water, as we will see in June.

Weather and temperature fluctuations have many indirect but powerful effects on seasonal timings, not least in the way they change the availability of water and food. Rainfall in arid regions triggers flowering in plants and a spike in insect and other animal activity. Perennial herbs need a good wet season for a healthy, timely bloom, but annuals are much fussier: they are sensitive to water levels in a narrow window, sometimes only days long. Trees in cold regions, like the Norway spruce, only start photosynthesising once the ground thaws and liquid water becomes available.

Flow rates are important for fish in running water where spawning peaks after fast flows. The height rises at these times also, bursting banks and filling floodplains, which opens up food opportunities. As water slows it warms, which may prompt some insects to leave the water and embark on the land stage of their lives. Invisible water also has an effect – high air humidity accelerates the budburst of oak, birch and spruce.

Food beats a different drum. Research has shown that bird migration dates are influenced by the seasonal replacement of feathers – moulting – and the timing of this is swayed by the availability of food at the departure region. We may see a bird on a perch for the first time in the year because, two months ago, warm weather thousands of miles away brought some berries to ripeness early. The following year a different bird is earlier than we expect, but this time wet weather in another region has led to a spike in insect numbers, plentiful food and an earlier moult.

6

April

Canopy Beaters

—

Bumblebees and Flower Signs

—

Rabbit Habits

—

Eye-catching Colours

—

Lamb and Lunar Wisdom

—

The Leo Method

—

The Lyrids and Eta Aquariids

Canopy Beaters

Some people see a rabbit or a frog when they look at the moon, but does the moon leave its mark on animals in spring?

The fastest route to the lambing sheds would have been a road walk of only fifteen minutes, but the hills were begging and I set off deliberately in the wrong direction. Near the edge of the woods there was a sprinkling of flowers, common violets, primroses and bluebells – my first bluebells of the year. It was now the season of spring ephemerals, the woodland flowers that blossom before the canopy trees are in leaf. They have raced into bloom earlier than most wildflowers, before the forest darkness seals over them.

The canopy-beating flowers like a mixture of sunlight and shade each day. The species will vary depending on where in the world we are, but this group shares the trait. The bluebells stretch in thick carpets for hundreds of yards near the edge of the trees. This is their happy place, the zone where some sun can break in, but where it will soon pass behind a tree trunk or branch. Early flowers are a sign that you are standing where you will see sun and many shadows.

There is always a trade-off when trying to win races in nature and these early-flowering plants don't have it easy. Frost-scorched leaves are common in April. Spring ephemerals have a lower chance of survival, but high rates of reproductive success if they make it.

I followed a deer trail through the flowers to the edge of the woods, where the violets and bluebells gave up in bright light. I saw primroses still flourishing in a clear area between the trees and a forestry track. After I'd walked among the flowers for a minute, a pattern leaped to my eyes. A pair of spruce trees stood outside the main wood and their dark bullet shapes stole much of the light from the sky. The primroses were doing very well near the tall conifers, but only in a pair of thick stripes. The two lines of pale yellow flowers were directly north of the spruces and mirrored their width. The flowers mapped the midday shade. Outside the protection of the woods, the primroses struggled to cope with the sun near the middle of the day when it was high in the southern sky and at its most powerful. The micro-habitat just north of the trees was perfect for those wood-land flowers: they enjoyed some weaker sunlight near the start and end of the day, but rested in full shade for a few hours near the middle. There was a compass in the flowers, formed by tree shadows.

Bumblebees and Flower Signs

A bumblebee was hovering a couple of inches over the ground, joined soon by another that emerged from a hole at the base of a fence post. Australian Aboriginal tribespeople developed techniques for tracking bees. They got down on their hands and knees to search out the tiny specks the bees drop to the ground, revealing their habits and hives. At this time of year, we don't need indigenous-level skills because the bees have few options. The spring ephemeral flowers offer them a rare source of nectar and pollen, which means the sight of one will likely lead to spotting the other. I listened carefully to the first bee's buzz and gauged its size – the bigger the bumblebee the slower the vibrations of the wings and the lower the pitch of its buzz.

Bumblebees can fly in air temperatures as low as 10 degrees centigrade, which allows them to get an early start in spring, but they need a body temperature of 30 degrees to fly. That is a wide gap to close and they achieve it by disconnecting their wings from their muscles and working their flying muscles until they reach the required temperature. It's a bit like when we jog on the spot to keep warm, but it looks less ridiculous.

There are no accidents when it comes to the shape, colours and scents of the wildflowers. They are all part of the pollination plan and give us a strong clue to any insects the flowers are hoping to attract. Lips or bell shapes are a sign that bees are welcome – 'Where there's bells there's bees.' Umbellifers have broad horizontal platforms – umbels – made of dozens of small flowers that make good landing pads for flies and hoverflies. Wide open flowers attract a wide variety of pollinating insects, including butterflies and beetles.

Bees also like broad tubular shapes with a landing platform, but thin tubes with no platform are a sign that moths aren't far away. The flowers they favour often have strong scents as they are more likely to be nocturnal pollinators. And the earlier in the season a moth-pollinated flower blooms, the stronger its scent is likely to be – it takes a lot of perfume to create a good scent in cool air.

Wildflowers that reflect sunlight stand out better than those that don't, which is why insect-pollinated flowers orient to catch the light. This leads to one of the simplest, most logical but most beautiful natural navigation compasses of all. We get most of our light from the south and that is the direction in which most wildflowers face. There is an art to reading flower compasses.

The flowers don't care about natural navigation. They respond to the light they receive, regardless of where it comes from. If something is blocking the sun's light, the flowers will not face that way. You will see the perfect demonstration of this around the base of solitary trees. One early spring morning, I was walking past the edge of Wiltshire's Tollard Royal, when I saw the most magnificent display of daffodils. Perhaps a dozen were clumped around the base of a mature tree trunk. The flowers on each side showed a preference for facing outwards – no light was coming from the direction of the tree. Looking more closely, I could see that those on the south side faced perfectly south, while those on the north side faced north. Those on the east and west sides of the tree had compromised, facing south-east and south-west respectively. The flowers aren't fools: they will make the best of every situation and face towards the greatest light. In the open this gives fair compasses that are easy to read; in crowded situations it leads to puzzles that tickle the mind.

Flowers face the greatest light

The second nuance to the flower compass is no less beautiful, but even subtler. The flowers and insects are in partnership and need to work together, which means being sensitive to their partner. In open ground the flowers are likely to face south, but if you see a slight consistent variation in a species, this is a clue to the flower knowing its partner insects' habits well. All animals are habitual, and pollinators don't spread their patrols evenly throughout the day. Some favour the morning and others start later. If a flower is trying to attract an insect that is busiest in the morning, which is very common, it will do better facing slightly closer to south-east than south, to catch the mid-morning light as the sun arcs from east to south.

April is a month of flowers, showers and fast-changing weather. This makes it the perfect month to look for how flowers herald weather changes. There are different examples to look for across the seasons, but get started early with the chickweeds that are open in fine weather, half closed in passing showers and fully closed as rain starts. Dandelions and daisies close at night or when rain is approaching. Red clover has leaves that respond to bad weather, rising and pointing upwards, revealing their pale undersides.

Small plants are at risk from grazing animals. Deer would make short work of the flowers if they hadn't developed some resistance. Early-spring flowers tend to be unpalatable to the grazing animals, or they would struggle against the ravenous appetites of mammals in spring. They use an array of tactics to put the animals off, including poisonous sap and hairy stems and leaves. If you are watching the same area carefully as spring progresses, you may spot this difference between early and later spring flowers: the first flowers show little damage from grazing, but the next wave suffers badly.

April is the best month to start looking for the 'species spike' by paths. If lots of people or animals follow the same route repeatedly, the footfall kills off all plant life and leads to a line of bare earth in the ground – an obvious path. It stands out as the logical route for the next group to follow. Once a popular path is formed it tends to be self-clearing because no new plants can get going with so many feet crossing the same ground repeatedly. This is a well-known trend, but it leads to a common misconception: many people assume that trampling is bad for biodiversity. The opposite is often true – a little footfall changes the habitat and makes it harder for one or two species to dominate. A few feet landing on the ground actually improves species diversity, which leads to a spike in species numbers near to paths. Trampling also changes the plants, making them shorter and leading to more flowers.

We can think of there being three zones around the paths in open country. There is the path and, as we've seen, it's too brutal for plants to thrive there. Then there are the wilder, untrodden areas a few metres away on each side that we can see from the path but that remain undisturbed because nobody walks over them. In this untrodden zone, we find one or two species thriving. These are the plants that are ideally suited to the conditions – the soil, moisture, light levels and climate are perfect for them – and they dominate and displace most other species. If the soil is kind it leads to lots of green, but little variety.

Then there is the third and most interesting area: the two strips at the edge of the path, where the footfall isn't heavy enough to kill off the plants, but just frequent enough to make it hard for any species to dominate. This is where we find a spike in diversity and the greatest number of different wildflowers. This zone is perfect for flowers and grasses, because they aren't bullied by the tall or woody species, which struggle because they are less tolerant of trampling. Many of those plants are perennial and can be seen in some form through the winter, but April is a good time to tune into this effect because then we can enjoy the waves of blossoming times through spring and into late summer.

Dandelions, plantains, daisies, clover and pineappleweed thrive in these zones.

Once you've spotted this effect a few times, you will soon notice that it is rarely symmetrical. There is a dependable spike on either side of the path, but one side normally does better than the other. There are lots of reasons for this, but common causes are asymmetries in footfall, light levels, moisture and nutrients – if owners encourage their dogs to walk and mess on the side of the path away from the houses, we find more nutrient-hungry stinging nettles thriving on that side. It is very satisfying for natural navigators when light levels cause this effect, because then we have another compass. This effect is strongest when the ground rises gently on either side, with slopes facing towards the path; the north-facing side is a steady green, the south-facing a blaze of wildflower colours.

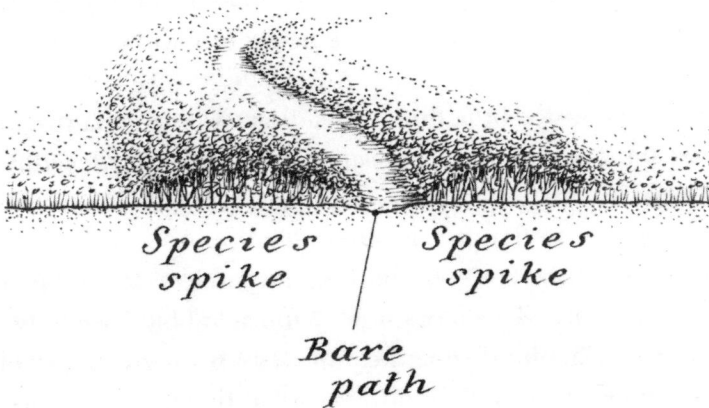

Species spike *Species spike*

Bare path

Practise looking for these effects and soon you will find your perspective shifts from 'Oh, look, a line of flowers' to 'A line of clover running away from the main path ... Clovers are a sign of footfall ... This must be a secret path, known by locals ... Where does it lead?' Or a sudden eruption of marsh marigolds in sunshine warns us that we soon pass through a cloud of midges, and we stumble on a pond.

Rabbit Habits

There was motion, dark specks against the rounded green whaleback of a hill. A herd of about twenty fallow deer broke out of the distant woods and began snaking their way over the pasture. The herd compressed and swelled, concertinaing as they ran across my view and then towards me, appearing to spread widely as they moved from left to right, then bunching into a tight knot as they turned towards me. They paid no attention to the sheep at the other end of the large field. Few animals worry about sheep and equally few enjoy spending time on their exposed, close-cropped, urine-and-dung-strewn fields. A pair of crows dropped from a bough. Crows are the shepherds' enemy in spring, their merciless habit of pecking out the eyes of vulnerable lambs being one of Nature's most detested habits.

The deer wasted little time in heading away from pasture and towards the crops lower down: better cover, better dining options. I watched them pass out of sight as breaks in the clouds sent shoals of sunlight across the valley.

The brambles have established themselves alongside the fence and, tucked in alongside them, a rabbit warren faced south-west. Shepherd lore dictates that the warrens will only ever face between south and west, and although I have noticed a bias towards that, it is not a trend cast in iron. The badger setts are more strongly aligned, facing into the prevailing south-westerly winds. All sensible land animals will give some thought to the wind when making a home. It is critical for comfort – no one wants to sleep in the teeth of a gale. It's also vital for safety, and an exit that faces into the wind offers a scent and sense of what lies ahead. Each animal must weigh up their priority, comfort or safety?

Near the warren, I found the telltale dark spots in the grass. Rabbits leave the warren along trusted routes and bound with a practised rhythm, landing on the same blades of grass repeatedly until it is beaten down and darkened. Poachers use the animals' predictability against them, and it has always been easy to snare a rabbit. A gloved hand, to guard against scent, places the snare halfway between the dark landing zones and the rabbit obligingly leaps into the tightening noose.

Eye-catching Colours

I passed through a scruffy wood where carpets of moss stretched between shade-loving plants, like dog's mercury. A single bright white down feather lay on the moss and then another. Soon I saw a dozen or more of these perfectly white fluffy decorations, all lying as single feathers, tiny islands of white on the dark mossy bed. If there had been a dozen in one spot, I would have suspected a fox or raptor kill and scanned the nearby stumps for a 'plucking post'. I regularly see a wood pigeon eviscerated at the centre of a grey-feather explosion, mounted like some macabre tribute on top of a decaying tree stump. Many predators will move their kill to a raised area to pluck, tear or feed: it improves their view and helps them remain vigilant at a vulnerable time. Even predators are vulnerable soon after a kill, because an easy meal is on offer and animals struggle to feed and scan their environment at the same time.

There was no plucking post and no signs of a kill, and now I suspected the feathers were signs of a calmer chapter, a spring moult, when a bird changes its feather outfit to suit the warming season. Birds, cats, dogs and foxes shed their coats in preparation for the heat of summer, so we will find fur and feathers dotted around the wild and our home at this time. Our old friend photoperiodism lies behind it, triggering hormonal changes in the animals. I contemplated this as I peeled off my outer layer and stuffed it into the backpack. We must congratulate ourselves if we dress appropriately for the whole length of an April walk. It's almost impossible. Layers off when the crest lies ahead, back on again as we start downhill.

The light levels dropped beneath the oppressive canopy of the yew trees. The shade was deep enough to kill off most plants beneath the trees – the yew has few friends in the plant or animal kingdom. Outside its deathly parasol, life sprang up again in a mixture of low-lying plants, and a little further away I saw a pair of elders in leaf.

Most trees' leaves start pale and grow darker through spring and into summer, reaching their darkest hue late in summer. The earliest leaves are anaemic in appearance because the tree is holding back some chlorophyll until later in the season when the leaves are less vulnerable to animals. Sensibly, trees don't like to feed the thieving grazers with any more nutrients than absolutely necessary. When the sun cuts through the bare canopy to light the early low leaves the effect is sublime, a fluorescent display of fluttering pale lime.

I walked on and soon met a joyous effect I call 'the celebration'. When sunlight fights its way through a gap in the canopy to light one area of the woodland floor, it creates a rare bright patch in the forest, an oasis. The plants change dramatically in these zones and it lifts the psyche to see a celebration of flowers flourishing in the heart of dark woodland. Notice how they aren't putting on their show directly below the break in the trees: they thrive to the north of the canopy opening, as the light pours in from the south.

'The celebration'

The tips on the spruces were sprouting, painting the ends of the branches with a vibrant, near-neon green. I plucked one of the spiky tips and chewed it, releasing the sharp, sour, then slightly bitter flavour; spruce tips are an excellent source of vitamin C. They also contain antioxidants and minerals, including magnesium, potassium and phosphorus, and are treasured within traditional medicine. They make a decent herbal tea and other beverages too. One Alaskan brewing company claims use of spruce tips goes back at least ten thousand years in their region, the ancestral land of the Huna Tlingit people.

The bright green sprouts are soft to the touch and young spruces are among the gentlest of conifers. After years of crossing coniferous forests away from tracks, I've grown grateful for any branches that don't scratch my face until blood trickles. Young spruce branches are kind, which is probably why they've been harvested for use as bedding and flooring in many northern cultures.

I turned my attention to the bramble bush that hugged a gate and saw a dark red in some of its leaves. It was arranged in a messy horseshoe shape and the colours changed as I walked around it. Many plants contain anthocyanins, which have a number of important roles, especially in early spring and late autumn. Anthocyanins show up as a range of colours from red through purple to blue and even sometimes black, depending on acidity levels within the plant. They lie behind the colours we see in fruits, including blueberries, bilberries and raspberries.

Anthocyanins protect plants against unseasonably cold temperatures in spring and late autumn. They also shield them from the harmful effects of excessive solar radiation, working as a form of botanical sunscreen. The most intense sunlight comes in the middle of the day, when the sun is due south, and we find more colour on the southern sides of plants that use anthocyanins. If you spot a red or purple tint in leaves, study the plant from all angles. You are likely to find richer reds or purples on the side that gets most sunlight, the southern side for most plants. One more colour compass for the bag.

This is the month of many shades of mud. In winter, the soil soaks up abundant water and takes on a heavy dark hue. In late summer, the water disappears into plants, animals and the air, leaving pale, dusty ground. But in April the earth swings between the two, wet at times, cracking dry at others, sodden in places, parched in others, and none of this is random.

The ground is a great narrator, but it speaks in whispers and we need to bend down to hear its stories. Every change in colour or shade is trying to tell us something about the rain, the wind, the frost, the arc of the sun. Start by noticing the bold differences, the way the soil changes colour under the umbrella of a tree perhaps. Each tree holds its own kind of umbrella and they morph through the year. Spruces make great umbrellas year-round, birches poor ones for half of the year. The trees that keep off the rain, also keep out the sun. The soil under each tree reflects this.

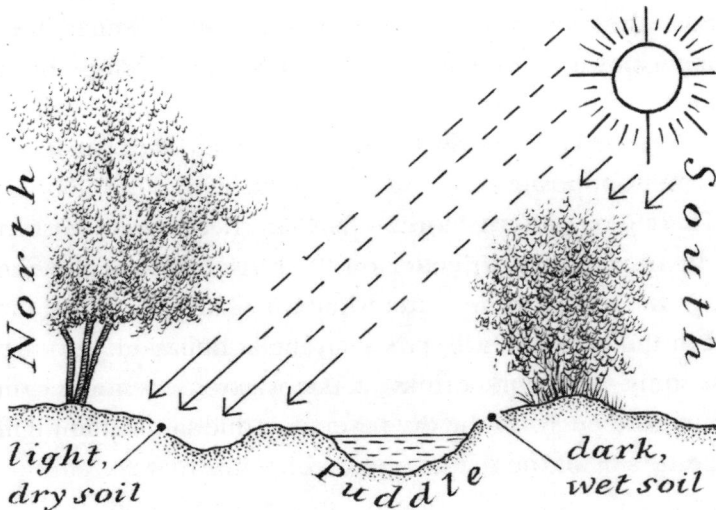

North

South

light, dry soil

Puddle

dark, wet soil

We find darker mud and more puddles on the southern sides of tracks as this is where the sun struggles to reach. But this is only a basic demonstration of a simple, powerful principle. Whenever we see moisture and dryness next to each other in the land, there is a cause, a story, and within that many clues to place and direction. The next time you squint as the sun bounces off glistening wet ground you are watching compasses forming. Within minutes there will be drying bright zones and a hundred wet shadows. Only the other morning I enjoyed noticing the moist disc to the north-west of a flowerpot on the garden terrace, in the shadow from the south-easterly sun. Before April is out, I expect to see one on the north-east side when the sun follows a shower in the afternoon.

The sun works hard in towns and cities too. By April, many have had enough cold and find the sun a welcome visitor. This leads to interesting urban patterns as people cross the road to enjoy the warm rays on the south-facing side of the street. It is a fun month for noticing more activity, more life, more bars, restaurants and cafés on the sunny side of the street. When the sun comes out after rain, it dries only the parts of the roads and pavements it can reach. I'll never forget walking down a Soho street to see a hundred happy people enjoying their drinks at tables on a dry pavement in the sunshine, talking loudly and laughing maniacally at the wet pavement opposite.

There are patterns within patterns. On streets that run north–south, cafés do better on the side that faces the rising sun in the east. Bars do better when they catch the falling sun's rays in the west; you will have seen the bubbling energy of the first sunlit after-work drinks of the season, laughter swirling around the posse on the dry pavement, puddles still lining the opposite side of the road.

When clouds appear like rocks and towers,
The earth's refreshed by frequent showers.

Old weather lore

April is famous for showers and it's the best month of the year for studying them. Shower clouds form quickly, drop their rain, then move on or dissipate. This leads to a popular misconception that they pop up randomly and are impossible to predict. The opposite is nearer the truth: they are disciplined clouds that follow clear rules and form regularly in the same places. More showers fall over hills, woods, towns and islands than over the neighbouring areas. Showers are seen as random for cultural reasons – we have grown used to getting our forecasts on a regional level, not thinking locally. A national or regional forecast has no choice but to say, 'A chance of showers later in the day.' On a local level, we can come to know the places the showers fall and when, and say, 'It will be wet in the woods/in the east end of town/on the far side of the hill after lunch.'

In any sky that mixes clouds, rain and blue, the sun will break through to meet the rain. These are all the ingredients we need for daytime fireworks; April is a grand month for rainbow-hunters.

Large rainbows form when a low sun is directly behind us and shines on raindrops directly ahead. The light enters the raindrop, bends, bounces and returns to our eyes. Each colour bends a slightly different amount in the water, but they do it in predictable, repeatable ways, which is why we always see the same pattern in the colours from inside to out: red, orange, yellow, green, blue, indigo and violet – Richard Of York Gave Battle In Vain.

Rainbow arcs are part of a circle and its centre is opposite the sun, the 'antisolar point'. The lower the sun, the more of the circle we see, the bigger the rainbow. April is a great month for rainbows for two reasons: first, we have the weather that provides both rain and sun and, second, the sun is not yet too high in the sky. We may have showers in June, but the sun is too high for much of the day for a good-sized rainbow. If our shadow is shorter than our height, the sun is too high for rainbows.

The strength of the colours in the rainbow reveals clues about the nature of the rain. A strong red is a sign of large rain-drops or, as I like to remember it, 'Lots of red means a wet head.'

The rotation of the earth sets up global wind patterns that explain why most of our weather arrives from the west. Bringing the pieces together, we can see that rainbows may help us to navigate, as they are always opposite the sun, but they also offer a neat short-term forecast. A rainbow early in the morning means you are looking west with fair weather behind you and a shower is on its way. A rainbow near the end of the day is normally a cheerier sign: the rain has passed and sunny weather has returned. There may be just enough warmth left in the day for the sun to paint some compasses into the wet ground. To find stories in a rainbow and the patterns in the puddles in the same half-hour is truly an April treat.

Lamb and Lunar Wisdom

I descended, following a long straight path past friends' houses in the village, past the pub, the church and out to the fields beyond. Ewes walked with a slow, steady gait, the exhausted new mothers pursued by their bouncing lambs. A ewe stops and two lambs nuzzle in towards her, prodding her with their noses, then suckling. The lambs' tails start a mad dance, shaking and twirling. It's a signal – it tells the mother that they have latched on to a teat and are nursing. A wagging lamb's tail looks like happiness to us but it means something else to the ewe: 'Don't go anywhere just yet!'

Feeding signs are so important at this time of year in animal husbandry. Where we might see only the cow, the farmer will spot the glistening shininess of the teat and, in it, a story of a full and healthy calf. Lambs are born with no functional immune system, they must pick up antibodies from the colostrum in the ewe's milk within twenty-four hours of birth. The early feeds are vital to a lamb's survival in its first weeks.

Lucie called to me from the edge of the large lambing shed and I moved towards the bleating. The sounds rose in waves and subsided long enough for the chirps of sparrows in the rafters to cut through, before another wave of young and old sheep noises filled the air. It was all hands on deck: Lucie was working alongside her husband Richard and older son, Ted, to stay on top of the climactic point in every sheep farmer's calendar. With hundreds of lambs born in a twenty-one-day window and a quarter of the ewes needing help of some kind, it was always frenetic. (Ted, the loyal sheep farmers' son, was fitting in late shifts as a break from working on a dissertation about military morale in Sicily as part of his history degree.) I promised not to get in the way, but couldn't resist trying to make sense of the choreography of new life in the barn.

'The traditional way is the fifth of November to the first of April,' Lucie said, as a ewe started giving birth a few feet away. Then she patiently deciphered the many insiders' codes for me. There were two different types of dye mark on the ewes and several colours. The faded blue above the tail was from five months earlier, 'tupping time'.

'That's the ram jumping the ewe,' Richard explained. Success is confirmed by scans in January, then painted in coloured splotches on the ewes' backs, revealing whether one, two or three lambs are on their way, come spring.

'Two hundred per cent average is ideal, two per ewe,' Lucie explained.

'A green dot is a single. Nothing for two, orange for triplets. If it's a quad, it's a double orange dot.' Richard added, 'We've had a few quads.'

But, as always, some of the most intriguing codes are invisible until you know what to look for. Richard and Lucie told me that one of the ewes walking casually past us in the pen was about to give birth, but I couldn't see the clue that gave this away.

'How do you know?' I said, feeling the excitement I get when I sense I'm about to glean some small gem of an insider's code.

'Her hormones are revved up,' Lucie said.

'She's come along to try to mother it,' Richard added, pointing to a still form on the straw.

They had noticed the way the pregnant ewe had walked towards the newborn lamb and licked it. When birth is imminent, the maternal instinct is so strong that she will try to mother any newborn lamb she finds, regardless that they have just watched it drop from a different mother. It's an irresistible instinct so they separate the new mothers and lambs from the expectant ewes to stop them trying to adopt lambs before their own are born.

After the birth, Richard climbed over the barrier and gave the new lamb some space. He rearranged its legs and put it into a more comfortable position. The lamb moved its head and made its first feeble efforts at standing.

We were walking over to another barn when Lucie mentioned something that made me stop, turn and ask her to repeat it. She took me back a couple of decades to when she was in hospital with Edward, who was premature, a much more vulnerable bundle than Ted, the strapping, rugby-playing sheep-farming historian who flanked us now.

'I was in there for a week. It was all very quiet, until suddenly, one night, the whole place went bananas. You could hear these women screaming and having babies. I asked a midwife what was going on. "It's a full moon," she said. "We always have lots of babies born on the full moon."'

My eyes were wide. Richard nodded. Lucie continued, 'Ever since then, at lambing time, I've picked up on it, the full moon.'

It is not a new idea, but it's not universally accepted. I felt I needed to press a little, not because I doubted the truth of what I was hearing, quite the opposite. I wanted to enjoy their certainty.

'Over the decades you've been doing this, you've seen a connection between the full moon and lambing time?'

'Definitely,' Lucie said.

'Definitely,' Richard said.

I don't think I'm alone in siding with Richard and Lucie and feeling that there is truth in this, but it is only a gut feeling. I want it to be true, as many do. I hear snippets from nature-watchers in other areas: toads seem to be most active during a full moon. There are other views, of course, and head and heart don't always agree. An academic journal called, with laudable precision, *Biological Rhythm Research*, published a paper titled, with equal acuity, 'Lunar cycle and the frequency of births in sheep'. The researchers will win no prizes for romantic views.

The distribution of lambing dates was similar and non-significantly different among the four moon phases: full moon (24%), decrescent moon (23%), new moon (28%), crescent moon (25%); thus, there was no evidence to support the persistent popular belief that the lunar cycle affects the timing of lamb births.

But what if the moon has an impact we don't see in its shape? The phase of the moon tells us one story. It reveals where the moon is in its cycle relative to the sun and Earth – a full moon means the sun is opposite and the moon is acting as a mirror, reflecting light directly back to us. We see a full bright circle. A new moon means the moon is in the same sector of the sky as the sun so we don't see it at all. In both cases sun, moon and Earth are all aligned.

However, lunar phases aren't the only story. The distance of the moon from Earth fluctuates, and one study in Kyoto, Japan, found that the frequency of human births rose when the moon was far away and its gravitational pull was weaker: 'There was a significant increase in the cases of births, when the gravitation of the moon to the Earth was less than 31.5 N. Results of this study suggest that the gravitation of the moon has an influence on the frequency of births.'[*]

The clouds thickened and lowered towards the end of the day. Before they closed over, the sun broke through low and lit the hills on the far side of the valley. The lush greens of spring were now luminous. I was witnessing a wondrous effect that we can see at any time of year but is very common in spring. At the start and end of the day, when the sun is low, its light will bounce back at us from any land or objects that rise in the opposite direction. When the sky in that direction happens to be dark or moody, it acts as a sombre backdrop and the combined effect is a powerful contrast. The land seems to sing with colour. Knowing this simple pairing allows all of us to take striking landscape pictures with very little photographic skill or practice: we simply put a low sun on our back and face towards dark skies.

I arrived home to find that the eggs a duck had been sitting on by our pond for a fortnight had all hatched, but the ducklings and their mother were nowhere to be seen. I stooped to

---

[*] Wake, R., Misugi, T., Shimada, K. and Yoshiyama, M., 'The Effect of the Gravitation of the Moon on Frequency of Births', *Environmental Health Insights*, Vol. 23, No. 4, 2010, pp. 65–69.

look at the broken eggs. I was searching for stories in the shells. We see more patterns at the blunt end, as this is the leading part during laying and where the greatest pressure is exerted. Lines mean a pause in proceedings and swirls point to a rotation in delivery. I don't doubt that a life could be filled by deciphering the stories in egg shells.

The Leo Method

The constellation of Leo the Lion is a good one to know and he's a friendly and practical character. He's easy to spot and recognise with nine bright stars that form a shape that tallies with his name and make up the twelfth largest constellation.

The best constellations contain at least one very bright star that helps us pick them out and Leo obliges: Regulus is the twenty-first brightest star in the night sky, which sounds unimpressive until we consider that's twenty-first out of the six thousand that are visible to the naked eye, in theory. Regulus rises near east north-east and sets west north-east. There is a fairly bright star above Regulus and at Leo's leading shoulder. It is called Algieba, which means 'lion's mane'. (There is another way of seeing these leading stars – a backwards question mark, where Regulus is the dot at the bottom. If you see a backwards question mark in the sky, you're looking at Leo. Nothing else fits that description so neatly.)

Everything about Leo is user-friendly. The stars that form his head are at the western end and his tail is at the eastern, which means he moves 'forward', that is, head first. His head rises over the eastern horizon before his rump, and his head leads the way across the southern sky and sets before his tail in the west.

Leo can be seen roaming across the southern sky throughout the spring evenings and April is a fine time for a lion hunt.

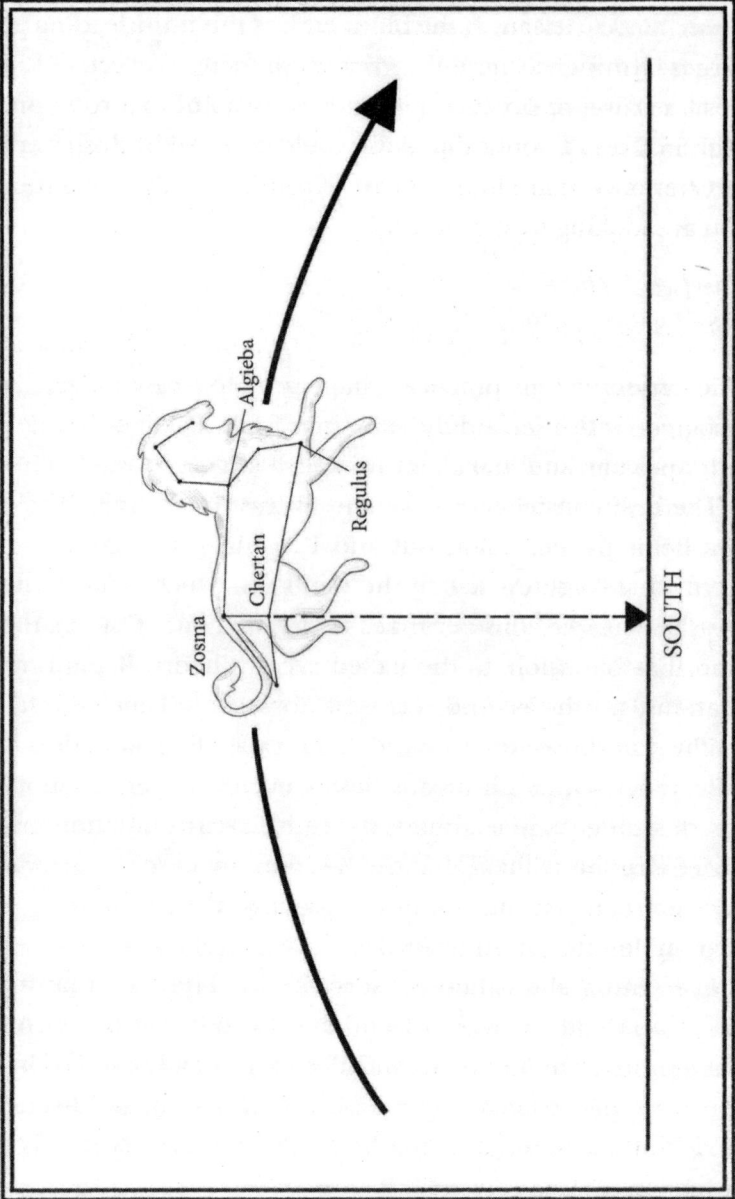

The Leo Method

Having found him, identify the two stars that form his rump, Zosma and Chertan. Now imagine a line that runs down from Zosma, through Chertan and on down to the ground. When this line is vertical, you are looking south. (Whenever Zosma is high in the sky, you are looking close to south. If Zosma is left of Chertan you are looking east of south, and if it is right of it, you are looking west of south.)

The Lyrids and Eta Aquariids

The Lyrids are a major meteor shower and put on a good display throughout the second half of April, when the weather allows. They peak around the twenty-third.

Look above the north-eastern horizon after nightfall, where you'll find the constellation Lyra rising – this is the best place to start the search. As the night progresses, Lyra rises through east, then higher through south-east, and most of the shooting stars will follow too. If you are up very early, before dawn, look high in the southern sky.

The Lyrid meteors form as Earth passes through the debris of a comet. The intensity fluctuates each year – there are never any guarantees when it comes to shooting stars – but this shower is definitely worth taking a chance on. Some years are spectacular for frequency and intensity. There are records going back over millennia – it is the earliest documented meteor shower – and in 687 BC a Chinese chronicle recorded that they were bright enough to make the other stars difficult to see. They were probably referring to instances of the larger meteors that burn up spectacularly as fireballs across the sky. There can be no greater compliment for a shooting star than that it was bright enough to cast a shadow and this has been reported for some Lyrid fireballs. Seeing something like that would surely be worth many less spectacular vigils.

We might expect meteor showers to confer with each other to avoid diary clashes, but they don't. This can work to our advantage in late April because there is an overlap, and the Eta Aquariids range from mid-April to the end of May.

The Eta Aquariid shower radiates from the constellation Aquarius (from the Eta Aquarii star in that constellation, to be precise, hence the odd name of this shower). That means it keeps more social hours for southern-hemisphere stargazers, but we can see it if we look low down in the south-east before dawn.

The Eta Aquariids peak on 6 May, and many think of them as a May shower, but I prefer to consider them in April first, because of their overlap with the more illustrious Lyrids. If we settle into thinking about meteor showers for a month from mid-April, we won't miss much and might catch something fantastic.

For four weeks from Mid-April,
We can seek a skyful
Of shooting stars (yes, meteors)
And possibly a fireball.

7

Strategies

Familiar Patterns

—

The Age and Stage of Plants

—

Grand Plans

—

Fungi Tribes

Familiar Patterns

We now understand the major mechanisms in the great seasonal clock, how they respond to their environment and the interplay. We are ready to look at this scene from a different, more intriguing perspective. Let us imagine a scenario involving the French watchmaker, Ferdinand Berthoud.

One fine Paris autumn morning, Berthoud is invited to inspect a new timepiece that has been fashioned by one of his rivals. With permission, he opens the back of the watch and peers through an eyepiece at the minute wheels, spindles and ratchets. He murmurs with satisfaction, then turns and compliments the watchmaker on their fine craftsmanship. But his thoughts don't match his kind words, because he is secretly thinking, Very beautiful, but the mechanism you have chosen will run slow this spring. Berthoud has spied a component that he knows will lag when temperatures rise again. He thinks he wouldn't place such a piece in a south-facing window. And we can do much the same when we look at landscapes. We can spot the clues that something will respond in a particular way to specific changes in the environment.

Berthoud was allowed to open the back of the watch, and if we put nature under a microscope we will uncover interesting components. There is, for example, a strong correlation between the diameter of tree tissues and the timing of leaf events – trees with narrow water-bearing vessels, xylem, come into leaf earlier than those with wider xylem. The early trees have skinny water pipes, but they don't start early because the plumbing is bad, quite the opposite: the thinner vessels cope better with cold, as blockages from freezing are less likely. The bigger pipes of the later trees mean they have to wait until freezing is less of a threat. Interesting though the microscopic differences may be, they remain invisible to most so this is not where the true satisfaction lies when observing the seasons. For that we turn to the observable clues in trees, smaller plants, animals and fungi.

Our first major clue lies in familiarity. Strong correlations in the seasonal timings of related family members allow us to travel the world and its seasons with confidence. There are about six hundred species in the *Quercus* or oak family and many struggle to name or differentiate the oaks in their local area. That isn't a problem. Once we recognise *Quercus* as a late-leafing type, we can travel between Europe, America and Asia, recognise a member of the oak family and sense a late-spring individual. The same is true of the ash (*Fraxinus*) and walnut (*Juglans*) families.

We know to expect the stone fruits (*Prunus*) to go early, including cherries, nectarines, peaches, apricots and almonds, and other early starters include the birches (*Betula*), whitebeams and rowans (*Sorbus*). Poplars and aspens (*Populus*) are mostly early-leafers. The lime group (*Tilia*) are intermediates, rarely noticeably early or late into leaf.

The Age and Stage of Plants

Genetic trends are fundamental, but perhaps obvious. What patterns yield good clues to timing that we might miss if we didn't know to look for them? With trees, height and life stage play a big role: leaves burst out earlier in trees that are younger and shorter than older trees of the same species in the same forest conditions. One study found the leaves to be eight days ahead in the smaller trees. The juniors start early to harvest as much light as possible before the canopy closes over them. The timing is not reflected at the end of the season: small and tall trees fall more in synch in autumn. This gives the younger trees a slightly longer season and a better chance of coping with the long months of shade after their parents have closed the canopy.

Spring moves upwards

The season's margins are more important than we might guess. One study focused on some trees that beat the canopy by about three weeks, which is a small head-start from our perspective but the trees' experience was very different. They harvested 97 per cent of their annual light energy in that short window.

There are two ways to view this phenomenon. Tall trees leaf later than short, or older trees leaf later than young. Studies that looked at trees by life stage, rather than strictly by height, showed that juveniles were eight days earlier than older trees of the same species and this held true across ten different ones.

There were no examples of older trees coming into leaf earlier than their juniors.

A tree's life stage is always relevant, but height is significant relative to other trees, as this determines whether the leaves will be in light or shade. Height is less important for standalone trees, and isolated mature trees of the same species may share similar timings, even if they are of quite different heights.

If you have lived in the same place for many years, you will have noticed 'ranking' patterns: the trees we come to know follow the same progression from year to year. If we pick ten trees and order them one to ten for the dates when they come into leaf each year, the order is likely to remain constant, even as the dates change with each year's weather. Of course they aren't waiting for their turn to come into leaf, but it can seem like that because they experience similar fluctuations in weather and microclimate year on year. The tree in the warm sheltered spot will still be there the following year, as will the one on the windward edge of the forest.

The order is only likely to change if the landscape and therefore microclimate change. A new housing development may raise temperatures, block gales and bring forward the seasons for the trees on the sheltered side. Or it may block the breeze that was clearing out the cold air in the frosty valley and cause delay. It will definitely have an impact, but not always the one we're expecting. The ranking order holds true in autumn, too.

Canopy trees are more variable in their timings than under-storey trees, showing wilder swings in their dates from year to year. In other words, we are more likely accurately to guess the date of the leaves bursting on an under-storey tree than its tall neighbour. This is also true at the end of the season, when teen-age trees are stricter with their timings than the more mature. It's one more way in which trees differ from us.

Forests are not homogenous blankets. There are always mature areas, young areas and gaps. Storms, fires, animals, diseases and chainsaws lead to gaps in woodland, which change the seasonal timings within them. We find that many young trees in gaps are slower into leaf than same age, same species trees below the taller ones. At first, I thought the reason for this must be light-related: the sun reaches into forest gaps and boosts the light levels – there is no need for small trees in a gap to beat the canopy. But this poses questions. Do they know they're in a gap and, if so, how? Can they sense the difference between the bright light of open sky and the mottled shade of leafless trees? Are they taking their trigger from beneath the ground, sensing nearby roots? The answer lies in temperature: gaps are cooler than woodland as the heat escapes easily.

All organisms are sensitive to vertical as well as horizontal microclimates and there are big temperature differences between the ground and the canopy. As we look high and low, we can expect to see timing differences in individual branches, leaves or flowers and that is before we think about the vertical worlds of mosses, lichens, ferns or insects.

Now we are looking closely, we might start to notice some other micro-trends. The leaves that start slowly catch up. The leaves of under-storey trees burst earlier, but by the time the leaves are fully grown, the canopy leaves have made up a lot of ground. The small trees' leaves grow more slowly than the leaves high above them. Once they reach three-quarters full size, there is little difference between small and tall trees of the same species in the same location.

Smaller plants have a few major disadvantages compared to trees. The struggle for light is vital, but it's easy to overlook their hunger for carbon. Trees start each growing year with reserves to draw upon that the smaller plants, even perennials, can only envy. As the smaller plants grow each spring, they need to take in so much carbon that it forces an early start to the season – they simply have to get their leaves out harvesting carbon dioxide as well as light. There is a longer lead time between leafing and flowering in small plants compared to trees, which leads to one familiar change we see in early spring: the land greens before we see many flowers – the 'greening of the grey', as the Greek poet Hesiod put it.

The gap between leafing and flowering in trees is much shorter – if we see leaves on a tree in spring, it is worth looking for flowers too. As we have seen, some trees, including members of the hazel, birch, ash and stone-fruit families, may flower before their leaves come out, because they were prudent savers in the previous seasons. That strategy is denied to all small plants that don't build up impressive reserves, like bulbs.

Grand Plans

We have focused on trees and then smaller plants for a reason. They are easy to spot, fairly easy to identify, their life stages are transparent and they stay put. There are comparable trends in animals, but they are more complex. Insects, for example, may have different ways of coping with winter, have multiple broods and then migrate. If we get our heads around that, they will still throw curveballs: some beetles and butterflies have a 'diapause' in summer, when they slam the brakes on their development. Their adult phases are split into two, either side of summer. Fortunately, there is a simple, powerful way of looking at animals and plants that helps make sense of seasonal patterns. We turn to any organism, explain that it's tough out there and ask: what's the grand plan?

Nature is brutally competitive and evolution has forced most organisms to pick a strategy that gives them the best chance of surviving long enough in their particular environment to procreate. Once we know it, we gain a helpful insight into seasonal habits.

By some estimates there are 8.7 million different species on planet Earth. If each one followed a totally different plan, it would be mind-bogglingly confusing. Fortunately, there are only two main approaches. Scientists studying organism populations think of each species leaning towards one of two strategies: explosive or slow-and-steady.

Organisms tend to favour either growing rapidly to a small size, reproducing quickly and having large numbers of tiny offspring, or they take their time, grow steadily to a larger size and have fewer offspring. Everything in nature is a game of probability and the likelihood that an individual will make it to parental age shapes the strategy that species will go for. For simplicity, we can think of any plant or animal belonging to either the *Rapid* or the *Slow* group.*

The chosen strategy has lots of knock-on effects for animals: the *Rapid* group live fast and die young, have low intelligence, mature to a sexual age quickly, have a strong sex drive and then care little for their offspring. *Slow* animals are more intelligent and invest more time and resources into raising young.

If an organism is very small it is likely to be *Rapid*. If conditions are right for a few months, we get cholera outbreaks, swarms of flies and clouds of butterflies, because bacteria and

---

* In scientific literature the two approaches were traditionally labelled r-strategy or K-strategy. The *r* stands for the reproductive rate of an organism, the *K* for the carrying capacity of an environment – the maximum number that the local habitat can support. I find the formal definitions confusing and used to think of the labels as *r* for rapid and *K* for killer whale, a slow reproducer. I have not changed the science, but hopefully you can see why I have simplified the language and refer to the *Rapid* group and the *Slow* group instead.

insects are in the *Rapid* group. We don't get sudden swarms of tigers.

Most insects, arachnids, amphibians, reptiles and fish can be considered *Rapid*. Most birds and big mammals (including whales and dolphins) are in the *Slow* group. As a crude rule of thumb, if you can count the offspring easily, it's probably *Slow*. It is, of course, a spectrum and smaller mammals will fall nearer the middle; mice and cats are nearer the middle than mosquitoes or rhinoceroses, but mice are on the *Rapid* side of cats. This is something I'm reminded of seasonally when the temperature drops and mice head in from the cold to our cosy attic. Trapping a single mouse does not affect their population noticeably over the season, but the loss of one of our two cats would make a big difference.

The size of plants gives us a good clue, especially when paired with seed size. Small flowering plants are *Rapid*, while tall canopy trees, like oaks and chestnuts, are *Slow*. Dandelion seeds float in their thousands past our noses, but we hear the thud of a single conker fall from the tree.

We can now make a fast, educated guess at the strategy of any organism we encounter, but how does that help us to read its relationship to seasons? The *Rapid* group are opportunists: they seize any small chance to explode in numbers, however short-lived. The *Slow* group follow a steady, less volatile rhythm. This means that *Rapid* organisms respond more dynamically to fluctuations in temperature, while the *Slow* are more wedded to the annual solar cycle. It's temperature and photoperiod again, of course, but this time seen from the perspective of strategy. A surprise heat wave in early spring leads to dandelions blooming in a field and a cloud of midges engulfing us, but we don't suddenly see a hundred horses or horse chestnuts in the field.

Trees are considered *Slow*, but the size of each species' seeds shines a light on their individual responses to the seasons. We find that many early-season trees, including birches and poplars, scatter millions of tiny seeds on the breeze, putting them well to the *Rapid* side of the big-nut *Slow* trees. The minuscule seeds are a clue to strategy and a hint that these trees will respond more noticeably to a change in temperature. Warm years expand the seasons of the *Rapid* more than the *Slow* and vice versa.

When the temperature changes, small plants and animals respond more dramatically than large ones

Strategy offers us another way of viewing seasons within landscapes. The *Rapid* group are colonisers, springing up in disturbed zones before they're overtaken, slowly, by the climax *Slow* group. If we experience anomalous weather, heat waves or cold snaps, we encounter more dramatic responses in areas of disturbance and upheaval. The edges and gaps of the forest reflect the micro-season in a way that the forest itself does not.

Nature doesn't tolerate rigid rules because any framework leaves gaps and enterprising organisms quickly fill them – the *Rapid* get there first. A tiny insect, a chironomid midge, can survive in the glacial ice of the Himalayas. However, there are patterns and broad trends. Smallness and edginess favour fast fluctuations. If any organism is relatively small, thrives near the edge of the season and in edgy habitats – close to other habitats – we can expect major variability for modest weather changes. A cold, cloudy day changes the dragonflies we will see but barely slows the leaves on the trees.

Fungi Tribes

The approach of fungi to the seasons includes familiar and unusual aspects, which befits organisms that are perhaps more animal than plant but definitely neither.

During my walk with foraging expert Miles Irving, we passed some bracket fungi on a dying tree and I asked Miles if he looks for any seasonal triggers for fungi fruiting. He told me that shii-take mushrooms need cold water to fruit but can't tell the difference between a rain shower and a watering can, which makes cultivation easier. Girolles, on the other hand, mystify and defeat the cultivators. They can get the mycelium to grow without difficulty, but don't know how to trick them into fruit-ing. 'I'm now convinced it's the tree,' Miles said. 'Unless the tree talks to the fungus, it won't fruit. That's my theory.' Soon after our walk I learned how and why he was probably right and it came back to strategy.

Temperature is important for all fungi, especially in autumn. Fungi fruit earlier in spring and later in autumn if the soil is warmer than typical, but their timing can also be influenced by temperatures over the past year and many need a 'cold shock' before they will fruit. A rise of one degree during winter/spring was found to bring fruiting forward by about five days for some species. But temperature is only part of the equation for many fungi and, on its own, doesn't work as a strong predictor across the year.

The need for a cold shock to trigger fruiting explains why we see flushes after the first frosts of autumn. And that is where sensitivity to microclimates adds a layer to our understanding. Anything that accelerates the onset of autumn will bring fungi to fruit more quickly, so they appear earlier as we move north and uphill. Cold weather hits inland locations harder (because the sea has a moderating effect on climate) and fungi fruit earlier there too.

Increasing latitude, altitude and distance from the sea accelerate things in autumn, but delay fruiting in spring fungi.* These factors have a cooling effect in both seasons and fit with our own experience: spring takes its time and autumn arrives early on northern mountains. This holds true for fungi on much smaller scales too – spring is late and autumn comes early to the frost pocket.

Fungi fruit at different times of year, but also follow different strategies within those seasons. Let's look at two common strategies to see how they shape what we see. Some fungi feed on dead organisms, the saprotrophs, and others find nutrition by partnering with living trees, the symbiotic (mycorrhizal) fungi. I think of them as two tribes and they each prioritise different seasonal cues.

We see a lot of symbiotic fungi in spring and summer and lots of saprotrophs in autumn. This comes to life if we think of the way trees burst into leaf, in turn fuelling their partners in those

---

* Spring fungi are really spring/summer fungi. Their fruiting might start in April or May, but can last well into summer.

months, while autumn is a prelude to death and decay, favouring the saprotrophs. The weather affects both groups, but not equally.

Saprotrophs are more responsive to the weather than symbiotic fungi. I find this easy to remember, albeit in a strange way: one group appears cooperative and tuned to its partners. To anthropomorphise the situation further, there are social fungi and sociopaths out there. The symbiotic fungi appear sensitive to other organisms, like trees, and tune their seasonal timing to their habits. The saprotrophic group feed on the dead; they are not swayed by the behaviour of others and tune more to the weather. In summary, we can expect weather fluctuations to have a more dramatic impact on the timing of the saprotrophs on the dead wood than the symbiotic fungi over the living roots.

Rain influences spring's timing more than autumn's but it has a bigger impact on quantity than timing in both. Rain or drought can bring forward some fruiting and hold others back, but the right amount of rain leads to greater numbers for all species.

When it comes to fungi and the seasons, the complexity is either fascinating or frustrating, or both. Whenever we get to grips with one aspect, we find there is another way of looking at things. The symbiotic fungi, for example, can be seen as broadleaf or conifer specialists and they respond differently to temperature changes, broadleaf fungi showing greater variability than those under conifers. And the age of trees influences the timing of fruiting too.

If we try to take in everything we will melt in the face of the extraordinary richness and variety out there. My preferred path is to seek out individual examples actively and quiz surprises reactively. We can hope to build a meaningful relationship with a selection of Nature's signs each month, but this leads to a sensitivity that opens a door to unplanned prizes along the way. When we know a constellation to look for, we actually look and then we see the shooting stars. A focus on the habits of a single fungus or a single place pulls back the veil on the habits of others that would otherwise hide. After interesting weather events, I head to a local hill where broad-leaves and conifers meet. It is home to enough different fungi, that I can be sure to spot any that have boomed as a result of recent change. There are colonies of fly agaric among the birches that grow at the edge of the wood, and a downpour from late summer onwards is a call to those white-flecked red-capped toadstools. Sometimes they heed the call, sometimes they don't. Each year I get a slightly better sense of which one it will be.

8

May

The Dawn Chorus

—

Pookof

—

Water Colours

—

The Naivety of Youth

—

Blossom

—

Ripples and Rises

The Dawn Chorus

The dawn chorus peaks in early May across much of the northern temperate zone and it is, simultaneously, one of the most familiar and least understood seasonal markers. We all know what the dawn chorus is, but scientists are unsure. I have learned to read early birdsong in a slightly unusual way, which I'll share with you, but first we'll try to understand what it actually is.

Many species of birds singing at the start of the day may be the most complex collection of animal signals on the planet. We do know that it fulfils a couple of basic and important roles for the birds: it establishes territory and it helps with mating. Within this simple framework, there are many mysteries. Why sing at dawn? Why do they sing in the order they do? Why earlier on some days than others? Why louder today than yesterday?

It's not immediately obvious why birds would choose to sing at such an antisocial time. Dawn is cooler and darker than daytime, which makes life more difficult for birds, so why do they make such an effort? One theory is that the challenge appeals – it's literally sexy. When animals do difficult or costly things, it proves genetic fitness and makes them more attractive to the opposite sex. The peacock's flamboyant tail is expensive and unnecessary, but its magnificence is irresistible to the peahen. But that can't be the whole story.

Night can be a time of upheaval and predation, and singing re-establishes territories at the start of the day. When a bird sings at first light, it is reminding other local birds that it hasn't died or deserted a territory.

There is some evidence that singing early improves the fertility of females. In some species, male song influences egg numbers and their size, because strong singing changes the physiology of the hen, leading to more investment in her eggs as a direct response to the morning songs. Another hormonal theory proposes that the singing gets the males ready by stimulating their gonads.

Singing is meant to be a beacon, to attract females and deter rival males, and this has some downsides. It is hard to hide when you're belting out your best tunes: singing increases the risk of predators locating you. Maybe dawn is the best time to avoid them. Unfortunately that doesn't stack up. A lot of hunting takes place in the crepuscular hours and there's no evidence that this timing offers any advantage to the birds. A very different theory holds that singing deters predators by signalling that a bird is in great shape and won't be easy prey.

Or maybe dawn is a great time to sing because sound travels well in the cool and calm air at this time. Once the sun has risen, it warms the land leading to thermals, turbulence, gusts and a bumpier soundscape. It's a neat idea, but there's not much evidence to support it.

Foraging is a relentless pursuit at this time of year for many small animals, including birds. Maybe singing early is just good time-management, because it avoids the best foraging hours. Why not sing when it's cold and murky, then crack on with the food search when the sun has risen? The sun's light and warmth make hunting easier for birds and change the foodscape too. It makes sense to wait until the temperature rises to forage for creatures like centipedes, insects, spiders or crustaceans – these animals grow more active when they have warmed up. One scientist suggested we should expect birds that eat insects to sing before grain-eaters: you need better eyes to catch moving food so those birds will sense light earlier. I like this idea, but no clear trends appear to support it.

Like so many aspects of animal behaviour, the truth is probably a blend and scientists will continue to research and debate which mix applies most strongly to each species.

Dawn singing is different from daytime. In many species it is more complex and varied and the differences are distinct enough for us to notice. Early singing is louder too: the blackbirds that light up my local woods with song are definitely boldest near daybreak. Even if the songs were the same throughout the day, they would sound different, because birds pick different singing perches at the start of the day. At dawn, some sing from lower-risk locations and are fussy about things like leaf cover. They prefer early-leafing trees for better concealment at this time of day, which means we hear a different sound from the open branch later.

The sound of a single bird's song increases the likelihood of others starting to sing. This is the domino effect that we have all heard and expect. If we are woken by one bird singing, we know instinctively that the numbers and volume will increase. It's harder for the birds to stand out as individuals, but makes predation less likely for each individual as there is some safety in numbers. The birds compromise: they all sing at the same rough time of day, dawn, but they follow an order within that chorus. For example, larks are followed by robins and thrushes, then warblers and wrens, sparrows, finches and tits. The skylarks I see and hear first thing are always singing from high in the air, well above the trees, the land and most predators. The lark has few avian predators that will trouble it so early, which helps explain why it is happy to lead the chorus, long before the sun has reached the horizon.

Bolder birds that perch in well-lit places, like the tops of trees, sing earlier than those in the darker areas below the canopy.

Birds on high perches sing earlier

Light levels determine the start time of the singing. We know this, it's why we call it the dawn chorus, but it has hidden levels. The timing of sunrise is dependable and predictable so why does the chorus fluctuate?

The weather has a noticeable impact: the thicker and darker the clouds, the less light reaches us and the later the dawn chorus begins. On a cloudy morning, the birds start to sing when the light reaches the same level as it would at their normal singing time on a clear day. A break in the clouds can bring the chorus forward – doubling the impact on our eyes and ears if we sleep outdoors. The clearer the sky, the earlier the land brightens and the birds start to sing.

Temperature also affects their song. It's not the temperature as dawn breaks but the cumulative effect overnight. Birds sing for longer after warm nights: they start earlier and finish later.

The more artificial light we add to the mix, the earlier most birds start singing. Studies have shown that urban conditions affect the hormone levels in birds, including the inner-clock hormone, melatonin. Light pollution brings the dawn chorus forward, but it also stretches it. Street lighting affects the naturally early singers, like robins, more strongly and their song is brought forward disproportionately; the later singers are less affected. Some birds, for reasons that aren't clear, aren't fussed by streetlights – the chaffinch gets up and sings at the same time whether in town or country.

Urban noise also starts the chorus early – the birds are woken early by the bin men, like the rest of us. After growing used to regular loud sounds in their area, some birds anticipate and try to beat them – birds near airports tweak their routine to start singing before the first flights take off each day. Unlike light, human noises affect the later singers more strongly and they rush their songs forward to beat the racket. Town lights pull the songs earlier, towards the light; noise pushes them earlier, away from the cacophony.

Moon phases affect the timing too, but the songbirds aren't sensitive to the phase, only to the amount of light coming from the moon. They aren't looking up at a waning gibbous shape and making plans, but responding to differing light levels (we know this because the effect disappears under thick clouds). The chorus starts earlier during full moons, because they reflect more of the sun's light than new moons or thin crescents. The effect of the moon is significant in spring, but wanes to negligible by midsummer, probably because a bright moon changes light levels dramatically at 5 a.m. in early March, but barely at all in late June when the sun will already be up.

When we see that half the moon is bright, we can guess whether it will affect the timing of the dawn chorus. If the right side is bright, there will be no change. But if the left side is bright the birds will sing earlier. (A first-quarter moon, when the right side is bright, cannot have any impact on the dawn chorus as it rises well after the sun. A third-quarter moon, when the left half is bright, rises six hours before the sun and this must logically influence the chorus, bringing it forward. None of that changes the price of rice, but it's fun to spot hidden cogs in the great birdsong time machine.)

Birds with larger eyes tend to sing earlier. If we pause to wonder why a bird's eye might have evolved to become larger, this odd indicator suddenly makes good sense. Large eyes let in more light so they are an advantage if you need to be active in low light levels. Therefore, large eyes are a clue that a bird (or any other animal) operates at the fringes of light, in the early dawn or late dusk. Owls are extremists. They don't sing in the mornings, like the passerines do, but they have enormous eyes and are busy in the very low light of deep night.

If we are super-sensitive and regular in our habits we may pick up one subtle change through the seasons. Birds tend to sing slightly earlier relative to sunrise at the start of the season. This is the most competitive time in the year, when pairing takes place and females are at their most fertile. As spring progresses, the sun rises earlier and the songs start earlier, but they also slip a bit later relative to the sun.

There is status within the chorus. We kept chickens for many years, including a cockerel that always crowed before the others got started. Sometimes it was a little too early even for country life and the thought occurred to me that we might all feel more rested if we relocated that one eager cockerel. We didn't, and I now know it wouldn't have worked. There is a pecking order in singing, a choral hierarchy: larger or more dominant birds tend to sing earlier than small ones. This has been found to be true across a wide range of species, from tits to kingbirds. A study of common cockerels showed that the dominant bird crows earliest, but if he is removed from the group, one of the others will take over to replace him. The same was found to be true in the wild.

There is also a dusk chorus, shaped by many of the effects we have met, typically in reverse order: if it is brighter later, song starts later. Dusk singing is less strong in real terms, but it also feels less strong, coming after the day's noise instead of the night's quiet.

Pookof

Mya Bambrick led me across her favourite nature reserve, Wood Mills, near Horsham in West Sussex, on an overcast spring morning. Mya was rightly proud of her flourishing naturalist career and her atypical path so far. From an urban background, she was gathering experience as a nature professional. Mya had been an animal keeper, visitor-centre assistant, communities intern, events assistant and volunteer, all by the age of twenty-one and while she was studying for a degree in ecology and wildlife conservation.

I didn't know what we'd discuss during our walk, but I was sure there would be a focus. I have learned over the years that most naturalists profess a love of all nature, but can't help revealing a form of tribalism early on. No one finds rocks, trees, clouds, insects, stars, wildflowers, fish and fowl of equal interest. For reasons as deep as time, we all have affinities, aversions and apathies in life and in nature. Mya is a birder, and during our walk past streams and over boggy fields, she shared her view of the natural world with me through her relationship with the birds. We talked about how a small number of birds seem to prefer cloudy grey days – the mistle-thrush is famous for its rebellion against the weather. It sings from a high perch on the windiest of days, earning itself the nickname 'storm cock'.

Mya talked about how the sounds would change as we passed from trees to fields. This simple observation shook the dust off the dawn chorus. Suddenly I could see it more clearly and from a fresh angle. The *dawn* chorus reflects the space around us. It is more than a calendar and a clock; it is a map.

I played with this idea as I walked with Mya, asking her if she ever saw it that way. It was far from the first time I had asked a naturalist to pick up a telescope and look down the wrong end.

'I guess, going from woodland where you hear chiffchaffs, great tits, blackbirds . . . then, if you get a little patch of scrub, some brambles, gorse, you'll hear whitethroats. In places like heathlands, you'll get warblers, and in the heather, stonechats,' Mya said.

Most naturalists think along the same lines as natural navigators, but approach the challenge from the opposite direction – if they want to find a particular species of plant or animal, they head to the habitat they know the organism prefers. But natural navigators let the organism tell us about our habitat and this makes a map for us. Mya and I talked about the simple clues to landscape that bird sounds contain and settled on a bird that summed up the concept.

'What bird would you expect to find in a clearing in the woods?' I asked.

'I spend a lot of time watching spotted flycatchers. They like glades. They like to perch on the edge of trees, fly off and catch flies and other invertebrates from open areas. So I'd hope to find them in a clearing.'

'So, the sound of flycatchers deep in a forest would make you suspect that you were approaching an edge or clearing?'

'I guess so.'

I smiled and we continued our walk.

To me, this was a fresh way of thinking about the dawn

chorus, but mapmaking with animals is an ancient concept. Hunters look for animals in the places where animals look for food or water. All animals sense their chance of finding food spikes in certain places – it's why the flycatcher perches where it does. White-tailed eagles and flamingos live in different climates, but both are found near the shallow water where their dinner lives.

Dawn singing is territorial, which makes a map. If we can identify the singer, we can paint its territory around that song. But what shape is the territory? Is it a circle, with the bird at the centre? It depends on the species. Many birds, like yellowhammers, sing from the centre, but others, like some warblers, sing at the edge of their territory. Birds vary their position, approach and song depending on the aim and urgency, which is logical. They have a slightly different song for when they sense a rival neighbour and move towards the edge of the territory, the avian equivalent of 'Come and have a go if you think you're hard enough.' Many birds, like the wren, will start earlier and sing for longer if they have heard a rival in the area.

I have tried to sketch a simple map using birds for many years, mostly by identifying an individual bird and its habitat. The drumming of a greater spotted woodpecker told me I was getting near the grand old oak in my local woods. The coal tit, which has a sharper bill than other tits and is better at prising seeds from conifers, tells me I've climbed high enough to expect to see the trees change soon from broadleaves to conifers.

The only times I can recall using a chorus as a map are when I'm finding my way out of dense woodland. After a difficult natural navigation exercise across the brutal coniferous plantations of Kielder Forest, the sounds of birds signalled I was nearing the edge of that dark and damnable thicket.

I wanted to focus on these ancient maps so I climbed into the

Land Rover and drove north, roof tent on top. I knew that camping in Scotland in May would mean that the birds would remind me each morning of my aim. I would be 'up with the lark' so that I could study my alarm clock.

My first sample was taken by the banks of a river in Lanarkshire. The very early robin was soon joined by the chiffchaff, blackbird, wren, song thrush and a jackdaw, none of which would surprise me if I heard it floating through the bedroom window at home. Actually, that's not quite true. I rarely hear the jackdaw at home. It can be thought of as a suburban specialist. I don't see it in truly wild places, or in town centres, because it thrives at the edges of human habitation. I was in a beautiful natural setting, but not far from the village of New Lanark, a UNESCO World Heritage Site, famous for the approach of the mill's manager, Robert Owen: he recommended treating workers fairly and looking after them, a revolutionary innovation for an industrialist in the early nineteenth century. The jackdaw likes to perch at the edge of human stories.

With a little walking and patience, a few differences shone through. Much to my delight, I spotted, but did not hear, a dipper, which is a white-water specialist, not a bird I would see or hear within many miles of home. In truth, the white water itself made it a tough environment for tuning in to the sound of birds, and even though birds are known to raise the volume of their song to overcome background sounds, I struggled to make a map.

I continued driving north, entered the Loch Lomond and Trossachs National Park and stopped for lunch by Loch Lubnaig. A pair of ducks launched away from me and landed on the glassiest patch of water. That tranquil stretch mapped a wind shadow, offering calm away from the steady marching ripples that marked the windier areas. The ducks had read the map and settled on the placid water.

North, north and west. A long road and a short ferry, and I squinted as the sun set north of west over a beach on the Isle of Mull in the Hebrides. As the Land Rover's front wheels touched the sand, I pulled hard on the handbrake and knew I was ready to hear a different map.

I woke early to the gentle rocking of a sheep butting the Land Rover and the larks singing high above. It was a classic camping moment, which blended the pure delight of nature's embrace with the ridiculous temptation to get grumpy about it. Soon the oystercatchers started their racket and were joined, perhaps half an hour later, by a cuckoo, a Canada goose and some crows. The chorus was completed with a curlew and the always surreal, almost artificial sound of a lapwing. It was 5.40 a.m. and dawn was done, this was daytime.

A natural navigation exercise on Mull gave me the framework I love: a tempting goal of a distant wild beach and enough wide-open spaces between my start point and destination to roam a little. I threaded my way across rough pasture. Sheep trails and plants offered tips on the best routes to avoid the soggiest areas. The animals are not infallible, though, and as I picked a tricky route through some low wet ground marked by rushes, irises and marsh marigolds, I saw the rotting carcass of a sheep that had breathed its last in a bog.

My walk that day took me through varied terrains so the birdsong and alarm calls changed with the shifts in the landscape. As soon as I headed inland, I lost the loud oystercatchers and constant squawk of the gulls, although I did see them wheeling overhead. The coastal birds were replaced by those happier in the scrubland, small trees, grass and hills: warblers, wrens, whitethroats, cuckoos and many more. There is only one bird I remember keenly from that day's walking, because it conjured up thoughts of a very rare indigenous technique.

I return repeatedly and unapologetically to the same core concept: there is no randomness in the places where we find plants and animals. Each species must be revealing something about the habitat and therefore our location. But many years ago I came across a refinement of this philosophy that elevated it from a simple approach to something almost mystical in its precision.

Ibn Mujawir, a businessman travelling in southern Arabia in the thirteenth century, hinted at this technique as he offered tips to other visitors. The birds, he assures us, could act as a local guide:

> If a traveller in this [Arabian] Sea sees seven birds right out to sea, he knows he is opposite the island of Socotra. Any who travels in this sea and comes across the island will see the seven birds, night and day, morning and evening. From whatever direction ships approach, the birds receive them.[*]

The sight and sounds of birds signal land after long periods at sea. Pacific Islanders and Arab navigators referred to this broad map frequently. The Vikings, too, favoured this technique, and I had gone to some trouble a decade earlier to prove their methods worked; gulls, kittiwakes, skuas, terns, gannets and fulmars painted a picture of land over a North Atlantic horizon.[†] But Ibn Mujawir's account alludes to something different. This is a reference to an exact number of birds

---

[*] Staples, E, 'Indian Ocean navigation in Islamic sources 850–1560 CE', *History Compass*, 2018.

[†] Please see my 2012 paper, 'Nature's Radar', published by the *Journal of Navigation*.

indicating an exact place. This is not the same as a general prediction based on probability – we expect the number of people we pass on a path to increase the closer to a town we walk. Mujawir hints at a deeper, more precise relationship between animals and place.

Mau Piailug, a Micronesian navigator from the island of Satawal, passed on some of his knowledge to successors within his home region, as well as Western researchers, before his death in 2010. There was a very real risk that a wide range of natural navigation skills would have been lost with him if the world hadn't recognised his extraordinary experience and knowledge before it was too late. Mau Piailug was a master in the traditional techniques of using sun, stars, waves and animals to navigate. But he also passed on one animal technique that is extraordinarily rare: the idea that some animals perform a service to the *palu*, or navigator, by dependably appearing in certain locations. Piailug explained that certain fish, sharks or a pod of whales would be sighted reliably in precise locations relative to specific islands. He was referring to very particular animals, not a species in general, and there is no doubt about this, because he talked of identifying marks on them, including those on the skin of an individual shark.

There is a cultural difference between this traditional Pacific view and a Western scientific one. We may be comfortable with the idea that a particular fish frequents a zone near a reef so expect to find the species there and deduce the proximity of the reef. But the Pacific Islander perspective is that something more profound is at work, as the writer Stephen Thomas reported after interviewing Mau:

According to legend, [the animals] were placed in the sea by Fanur and Wareyang, the two sons of Palulap, father of all navigators, to aid *palu* when lost. When one creature dies, another one of the same species and markings takes his place.[*]

Mau Piailug called this peculiar technique *pookof.* Ever since I came across it, it has stuck with me and shaped my view of new places, sometimes in a light-hearted way. On holiday in Greece years ago, my family and I were searching for a hard-to-find turning to a beach that we kept missing. We resorted to talking about how we had to 'pass the Orthodox priest and turn left at the bin with a cat on it'.

My route across wet ground and through dwarf willows on the Isle of Mull took me past a collection of hollow, ruined buildings. I descended into a wide scrubland that rolled gently towards the sea. It was on this wide damp plane that I heard the unmistakable call of a stonechat, a bird that earned its name from its call, which sounds remarkably similar to two stones clacking together. The stonechat's call rang out across the bland scrubland, which held few notable landmarks. That made the bird's call stand out more proudly. It is unlikely we will reach for birdsong to help build a picture of a terrain if there is some striking landscape feature – a jagged summit, a shimmering lake, a solitary mighty tree – to hang our view on. Once the land loses distinctiveness, we grow more grateful for every unique feature that reaches our eyes, ears or nose. (This is one reason why we remember the smell of the sea creeping into the car after long journeys as children – from the back seat, the world can seem very samey until, suddenly, it isn't.)

The stonechat's call was my landmark. I didn't hear the bird before or after that. Its call was the feature that singled out that

---

[*] Thomas, Stephen, 'The Sons of Palulap: Navigating Without Instruments in Oceania', *Oceanus*, 1985, p. 85.

broad stretch of scrub. Unknown to me, when I first walked past the bird, my brain was filing this auditory landmark alongside other features I had passed. On my way back from the beach, I heard the same stonechat. My brain pulled up the relevant file and reminded me that I'd be passing ruins soon. *Pookof!*

Many animals, including birds, need to protect their young and their food sources and are at their most territorial at this time of year. They will often be at their most visible and audible at this time too – you can't defend territory by hiding silently in the undergrowth. This makes it the perfect time of year to practise the strange art of mapmaking through *pookof.* We can do this in wild places or by noticing the unique pattern on the pigeon that greets us as we sit for our lunchtime sandwich on the park bench.

I planned to camp for the night on a different beach and, on approaching it, I saw a gull defy the laws of physics, which is always a nice feeling. The bird was suspended about thirty feet in the air, facing the sea, wings outstretched and not flapping, and it was very slowly rising. It was creating energy, breaking rules, rebelling against textbooks and having a mellow fine time of it.

The gull was riding on 'ridge lift': the wind was coming off the sea and hitting the small hill behind the beach. This forced a current of air upwards and the birds were happy to rest on it. May is a good time to look for this. It is common near beaches, cliffs and other coastal features, but I see it inland too and in cities. As the wind hits any ramp – a hedge, a woodland edge, a building – we can expect the birds to sense the ridge lift and ride it.

A buzzard wheeled above me. The birds tune to another air freebie, the thermal – it's especially popular with birds of prey, which 'orbit', flying in tight circles over areas of rising warm air. There is a seasonal aspect to this behaviour because it reflects the strengthening of the sun in late spring and summer. The bigger the bird of prey, the heavier it is and the stronger a thermal must be to lift it. These patterns include a calendar and a clock. We tend to see smaller birds orbiting earlier in the year and the day, larger ones later in the year and the day, when the sun has had enough time to heat the land and generate a stronger thermal.

If you spot birds circling in the sky above you, there is meaning in that pattern: they are either climbing or fixing their gaze on something on the ground or both. Vultures are notorious for signalling death on the ground with their sky circles, but no birds can defy the mathematics of the circle. The only way to keep flying forwards and remain at a constant distance from an object on the ground is to fly in a circle.

Water Colours

I caught a ferry from Mull to the compact island of Iona. It is only about three miles long and a mile and a half across, with 170 permanent residents, but its fame as the cradle of Christianity in Scotland draws visitors from across the world.

I made my way along the coastline, between golden sands and characterful homes, some lived in and loved, others abandoned, all wearing their sea faces. After turning inland and uphill, I found a spot to pitch my tent, zipped my rucksack inside, then turned to explore the island.

There is an old Gaelic saying, *Am fear a thèid a dh'l thèid e trì tursan ann*:

'Those who come to Iona come not once but three times.'

More than one stranger told me I'd return; Iona gets under the skin of visitors, whether they care for Christianity or not. It taps into something deeper even than religion. I was amused to notice dark columbine flowers thriving among the ruins of the old nunnery, a botanical wink: St Columba arrived in 563 and set up the abbey, a more recent and grand version of which dominates the skyline and remains active to this day.

I've written elsewhere about the many ways in which churches make compasses (aligned west–east, with altar at the eastern end, highest point at western end, door on southern side, etc.), but it delights me that every year, without fail, I uncover a new gem. A sign by Iona Abbey informed me that most abbeys have their cloister (the covered stone path around an open square) on the south side of the church.

From the highest point, the island shrank and changed; the grand abbey and other scattered chapels could no longer claim the sky. The elements reasserted their dominance – the wind tugged at my collar and pressed the long grasses flat. The sun shone through high clouds and allowed me to organise the more distant lands in my mind. I walked down to the most northern part of the island and saw a rare treat. A tombolo is a thin strip of sand that connects an island to the mainland or, as in this case, a tiny island to a small one.

The colours were heavenly and made a map of land and water – white sands, turquoise shallow water turning to a deeper, darker blue with each inch of depth. This is the time of year to refresh our water-colour charts. After months of low suns and leaden skies, the sun now injects enough light into the water to reveal its secrets.

No navigator in Columba's time would have dared to set out to sea from new lands without first gaining height to study Nature's colour chart. We know the sea changes colour as we look from white waves breaking on the shore out to calmer darker blues. But there is so much before our eyes that we don't see unless we choose to. Cling to a simple mantra: every colour we see in the water must be caused by what's in, on or under it, or the journey of the light. Only four ingredients, but infinite colours and clues. A simple approach gives us the confidence to question anomalies. Gazing out from above the bright sand of a place called 'The White Strand of the Monks' (Traigh Ban nam Manach), I wondered: Why the lighter patch of water off the tiny island to the north? It is reflecting the sky better than the water on all other sides . . . It's flatter, calmer. If they ask my advice, that's where I'll send the landing party of monks.

This is the game with the sea. It wants to trick our brain into thinking two things simultaneously: that it's all the same and that there is too much variety for us to decipher what's happening in front of us. But we can tame both tactics, by looking for one small difference and quizzing it, wrestling it into the bag and remembering that each shade must be caused by what's in, on or under the water, or the journey of the light.

On my walk back towards the tent I noticed another lighter patch, this time halfway between Iona and Mull. After quizzing it, I could see that the water was slightly rougher, there were white flecks among the blue, but only in a narrow strip. The wind was accelerating through the channel between the islands and blowing against the flow of the water: wind against tide, a sailor's antagonist, as it leads to steeper waves, chop and churn.

Before reaching the tent, I passed a grassy hill and heard a sound I have rarely heard before, that of a corncrake, a migrant that winters in Africa. I was very unlikely to hear that bird anywhere else on the island, or the mainland, as its numbers have declined so dramatically. I heard it a few times from my tent that night also. It was a sound I can only describe as somewhere between a slipping ratchet and an electric shock. Each time it floated over from the same patch of distant scruffy grassland, marking it like a beacon, making a map. *Pookof.*

The Naivety of Youth

The plan was to cross back to the mainland on the ferry to meet a friend called Lupi, whom I have known for almost forty years. Our eldest sons are now good friends too. He is an inimitable blend of Italian and Scottish blood (I've never been certain, I forget each time I learn the truth, but believe 'Lupi' stems from Louis-Piero). Our appearances have changed plenty over the decades, my hair beating a retreat, his flourishing into a wild leonine mane, but neither of us has lost our appetite for schemes. Lupi's latest endeavour has been a passion project of building three bothies by a loch, in a place called Inverlonan, and offering guests 'rough luxury'. I was looking forward to catching up with him, experiencing a bit of rough luxury and no less keen to meet a lifelong colleague and friend of Lupi who knew the land in the area better than any other person alive.

The prospect of meeting those who know any land intimately always excites me and I met Ivan over a table covered with fresh local seafood Lupi had cooked. Ivan has worn many hats during a life of working on the local estates, which currently included water bailiff, gamekeeper and deerstalker.

We discussed the smolt activities of some fish at this time of year, an intriguing seasonal habit in which trout finish their juvenile freshwater stage of life and head out to the sea to become sea trout. 'The full moon in May, that's when they go,' Ivan said, with the soft accent that reflects these lands as much as a person's voice can. He was born here and has been absorbing it ever since. Full moon was only two days away and Ivan explained that he would be drift netting over the coming days, to check the health of the fish, before releasing them.

Ivan's voice takes on a hushed conspiratorial tone as he tells us he came close enough to red deer to hear them breathe, 'to see their eyelashes, you know?' He was proud to have done that with Red, his stocky, venison-reared Labrador, at his side. All it took was a hand signal to tell Red to stay calm and soon they were among five more deer.

The conversation moved on to the naivety of youth at this time of year and we shared stories of our observations of young animals doing daft and dangerous things that older, wiser animals never would. A young bird will drop down to a stream for a drink, but it will never grow to be an old bird unless it learns that this is a risky habit. Streams are dangerous to birds. The land drops steeply in a narrow gap and there's too much cover, too much vegetation close to the water to see any predator swooping. The wiser, mature birds drink from open areas, where they can see all around and ambushes are impossible. Nine out of ten young birds die in a tough season, from predation or weather. Those that survive combine fast learning with a little luck to form better survival habits. We see different patterns of behaviour in young and old, and in May the differences are great, because the young still have so much to learn. Wild fox cubs are naive enough to approach humans at this time of year; the wiliness comes later.

Lupi brought hand-ground coffee to the table and talked of a lamb that was taken recently by a fox; others had been lost to sea eagles. Ivan's voice turned downbeat as he spoke of a decline in wildlife in recent years. Lupi challenged his pessimism but Ivan answered, 'There's nothing out there, brother.'

We talked about the numbers of migrating birds dropping and Ivan said they were pickled in jars. We laughed, but he was serious and talked of the hunting that takes place in the many north African and southern European lands the birds fly over on their way to Scotland. 'They're waiting for them each year to fly over their shotguns. They're killing millions.'

I mentioned the countless cuckoos I had heard since crossing the border into Scotland. It is a rare happy sound across much of England now, but Lupi said it was too much for some of the locals, and the neighbouring farmer was complaining recently about the relentless din made by eight cuckoos lined up on a wire. This brought us on to the old country rhyme:

> The cuckoo comes in April,
> Sings the month of May,
> Changes its tune in the middle of June,
> And in July he flies away.

Blossom

After strong coffee, we set off into the hills, and as we followed a path that mirrored the edge of the loch below us, the sky changed and clouds began to fill the blue. Lens clouds, the saucer or UFO-shaped discs, appeared in growing numbers and size, indicating mountains beyond the land we could see. Ivan's dog was panting now – charging up and down the steep slopes had warmed him on a mild day. Dogs don't sweat much and panting is their main way of cooling down; it's a sign of a hot body, not being out of breath as it is for us. It's more common at this time of year, and by midsummer dogs in the sun are panting without running.

The sound of willow warblers drifted down from a young forest and we tracked the edge of the loch, discussing, inevitably midges, the biting insects that can blight experiences in damp northern temperate zones, like much of Scotland, through summer. I noticed the grasses were darker in the shade of some trees. Shade makes many green plants darker and we can often spot a dark tint in the grasses on the north side of trees and walls.

We dropped down to the loch's edge where Ivan and Lupi pointed to a mustard yellow pollen bloom that had gathered on the surface of the water. It had been shepherded into thick

blankets at the downwind edge of the loch. I looked for feathers among the dust – they gather at the downwind edges of
lakes and can reveal the resident waterfowl.

A skipper butterfly danced past. We talked about the territori-
ality of butterflies. I see a speckled wood butterfly regularly, a
species they also see in those parts, which paints two very different scale maps for us. As the name suggests, it is common at the
edge of woodland, so if we spot it when we're among the trees,
we're nearing the edge. But on a much smaller scale, it will
drop down from the canopy to a sun fleck on the forest floor
and defend it against intrusion by other males as part of its
mating strategy. It would be an extreme form of *pookof* to identify not just a part of the woods from a butterfly but individual
sunspots.

We were mystified by the lack of insects. Lupi believed there
was too much of a breeze and suggested a different bay. We
decided to head there, climbing back up on to the higher path.
On the way we passed a hawthorn tree in magnificent white
blossom.

I offer up the old saying: 'Ne'er cast a clout till May is out.'
'May' refers to the tree, not the month, and 'cast a clout' means
'take your jacket off'. In other words, don't cast off your coat
until the may tree, hawthorn, is in bloom. The saying captures
the capriciousness of the weather in late spring and early
summer. We can look out in the morning and see a blue sky and
bright sun, only to find ourselves battling sudden downpours or
cold winds a few hours later. The tradition is that the white blossom marks the moment in the year when we can have confidence that the sun's warmth will last the day. It marks another
step, after the steam and hail of March, from spring to summer.

Hawthorn is a common tree and the blossom is worth looking for at this time of year, but there is, of course, nothing magical about this flower. The hawthorn gauges the contraction in

the length of night and the bumpy rise in temperatures, as do the other plants, but it has no secret ability to predict the weather. But I like the saying as it's a prompt to tune into this moment in late spring. The sun's passage north nudges higher pressures and warmer air towards us and improves the outlook each day. There is value in sensing this moment and pairing it with flowers, although the blossom of another local plant in your area may give you as good or perhaps a better sense of this moment. If you feel that the cold has lost its grip until autumn, I'd encourage you to look at the blossoms that catch your eye.

I was discussing this with Lupi, when Ivan, who was sitting on a grassy knoll near the hawthorn, recited Siegfried Sassoon's poem, 'The Hawthorn Tree', from memory. It was enchanting and I asked him if he would do it again and he was happy to.

Ripples and Rises

We worked our way around the loch, shadowing it from a higher track that gave us an excellent view down over the water. There was a crannog, a small man-made island that had been built centuries ago. Lupi pointed to the stone causeway linking it to the shore, the stones now covered by water. I noticed that the wind-driven ripples were marching in a different direction from what I'd seen near the start of the day – the wind had backed. Looking up I saw white wispy cirrus clouds massing far over-head. A backing wind and mares' tails in the sky: the good weather would break. Blossom or none, tomorrow I would take a waterproof with me.

Away from the island, I saw a 'cat's paw', the darker patch of water formed when a gust of wind touches it. The water appears darker because the wind ruffles the surface, breaking up reflections of the brighter sky on the far side.

Lupi pointed to the sheltered bay where he had higher hopes

of finding life. We could see from the glassier water that there was a wind shadow, a patch of water sheltered from the breeze. We worked our way down the steep bumpy slope, brushing through pleasing scents of water mint and bog myrtle. We found a colony of yellow meadow ants and I showed Ivan the anthill compass. The ants' home, a small mound, like a grass-covered molehill, was not a perfect circle but flatter on one side. Yellow meadow ants construct a dome with a flat side that faces south-east, catching the early sun and warming the nest after the cold of the night.

Whenever we see a colony of insects gathered in one spot, we will be rewarded if we consider temperature. If we spot beetles on one side of a tree only, there will be a compass and a clock in their story. In cool weather, the sunlit southern side is popular, especially near the middle of the day. In hotter weather we might find them working their way around the bark, staying in the shade and one step ahead of the sun.

As we picked our way across difficult, clumpy ground, Ivan described a facet of deer behaviour that helped him. Ivan was paid to find deer for clients *reliably* – some of the visitors may have travelled thousands of miles for that experience. He explained that you can predict where you will find deer at a later time, ironically, by scaring them off.

'If you do your homework beforehand, you get a sense of the deer's territory. If an area is well populated with roe bucks, then scaring off a buck doesn't mean you've lost him. No, the opposite: he must return. It's too dangerous for that buck to linger in a neighbouring buck's territory. By scaring him off, we force him back to us at a later hour, if we wait patiently.'

This reminded me of a behaviour I see in birds at this most territorial time of year, a habit I call the 'rebound'. When approaching any territorial bird, it is likely to retreat and it does so in stages, flights that become shorter and shorter until it has been pushed all the way to the edge of its territory. If we keep pushing, it stops fleeing, takes off and flies over us, landing at the heart of its territory behind us – it rebounds.

Within a minute of reaching the water's edge we were seeing dragonflies and felt and heard a hundred tiny flying insects. The conditions were now perfect to find the treasure I had hoped for and had talked about many times during the day. The three of us gazed out over the water's surface, letting our focus skip across, like a skimming pebble. Seconds passed before we had all spotted many glitters from the gold. In May, the insect numbers explode and there is a frenzy of activity at the water's surface, making it the best month for spotting a 'rise': when a fish comes to the surface to gobble an insect and sends out ripples, which tell a short story.

A small dead insect is a small meal and it is going nowhere in a hurry. The fish knows this and will not waste energy propelling itself into a mad dash for such a small reward. It takes its time and plucks the morsel from the surface of the water with a gentle nibble. This creates a simple pattern known as a 'kiss', a series of circular small ripples emanating from the spot where the fish's mouth broke the surface. Imagine dropping a dried pea onto the water.

If, however, a fat juicy insect alights on the water, the situation is very different – a decent meal may take off and disappear at any moment. The fish knows this too: it will accelerate and thrust itself at the insect, sometimes with enough vigour that its head and tail break the surface. This creates a more energetic rise pattern that looks and even sounds very different. It may resemble a kidney-shaped pair of splashes, followed by bigger ripples. Imagine dropping two stones from one hand onto the water.

Each rise is a tale of wind, sun, water flow, insect and fish behaviour. The patterns on the water tell us the story. The ripples are not the subject but the narrator. We enjoyed a sublime half-hour reading rises as dragonflies patrolled the water's edge.

We worked our way along the damp ground at the edge of the loch, pausing only to sniff the top of a rock where there was otter spraint, the territorial marking of an otter, complete with tiny white bones.

After a long, blessed May day, I retired to my bed for the night, a high and wide bunk in a luxury bothy. Before drifting off, I pulled out a book I had bought in a small shop on Iona and read it in the late light of the long day. It contained the following quotation: 'Attentiveness is the heart's stillness, unbroken by any thought.' It is attributed to St Hesychios, who was a fifth-century priest and clearly no fool, but I'm not sure about this sentiment. We can encourage ourselves to notice more, to be more attentive, if we nurture the knowledge and, in turn, confidence to believe we will understand what we see. Thought and attentiveness can feed each other.

9

June

Butterfly Poses

—

Clear Water

—

Night Shining Clouds

—

Solstice Sun and Moon

—

Blocking Highs and Welcome Breezes

—

The Navigator's Triangle

—

Sand Stories

Butterfly Poses

The butterflies are busy, but when they rest, they choose their spots carefully. If we disturb them in sunshine they fly to another sunny spot; evict them from a shady perch and they fly to more shade. Look closely at the poses they adopt when still.

The lower the wingtips, the more wing-surface area is open to the sun; the colder the butterfly is, the more urgently it will try to warm up. Many cold butterflies will rest with their wings wide open, in the 'dorsal basking' position; some go even further and push their wingtips down until they touch the surface beneath them, the 'appression' position, which helps trap heat.

On warm days we will see more butterflies with their wings held up; the warmer they become, the more likely they are to align their bodies to face the sun as this offers the narrowest profile. On hot days, butterflies cast thin shadows and, odd though it sounds, I think of them as making shadow compasses and clocks at this time of year and their wings form a gnomon. (A gnomon is the part of a sundial or sun compass that casts the shadow.) On sultry summer days we find thin butterfly shadows pointing north in the middle of the day, turning to north-east as afternoon progresses.

Clear Water

June brings a surprising clarity to water. What we see when we look at it is rarely water. It may be a reflection of the sky, if we're looking across it, or the bottom of a shallow pond if we peer down into it. It could be the bubbles on the surface after a wave breaks or the rainbow colours formed as a drop of oil spreads across a city puddle. But none of these is water, because pure water is transparent and acts like a window or a mirror. We notice more dirty windows than clean ones.

If you spot shadows on water, that is a sign that the water isn't pure. Shadows appear on water only when light reflects back off particles suspended in it. The next time you walk over a low city bridge on a sunny day, look down into the water with a high sun on your back and you will see the shadow of the bridge as well as your own shadow in the murky water below you. City rivers are full of particles, not always bad ones, often just mud and silt in suspension, but you won't see pure water under a town bridge. The sunlight bounces back off these particles into your eyes giving a bright colour that contrasts with the darker, duller shade where there are shadows. If there were no particles at all in the water, if it was 100 per cent pure, the light would keep going until it hit the bottom and create a very different effect. It would appear odd, strangely pure, and everyone would comment on it. We have a strong sense of when we are look-ing at clear and impure water, which doubtless stems from our ancestral need to gauge the health of water sources. (Transparent water can be pure or dangerous, as some harm-ful things, including viruses, are too small to be visible to the naked eye; cloudy water is obviously impure and contains something we might not want in our stomachs.)

If you watch the same body of fresh water through the seasons, you will spot something interesting happen in June. The water turns clearer. In the depths of winter, the water in ponds, rivers and lakes can look pleasingly clear because sunlight is weak, and cold limits life. As winter turns to spring, temperatures and light levels rise and this stirs waterborne plants and animals into action.

Algae is a major cause of cloudiness in water. It starts to thrive in warming well-lit bodies of water in spring. The water turns slightly cloudier and this is part of a healthy freshwater ecosystem: algae are the food of many microscopic animals (and some large ones) so a little cloudiness in late spring is a good thing.

At this spring stage, the algae are doing well because they have warming water, plus plentiful nutrients and light. Microscopic animals, zooplankton, now start to flourish and feed on the algae. If the system is balanced, neither side dominates: the algae multiply and the animals keep them in check by grazing on them. The numbers on both sides fluctuate as temperatures and nutrient levels oscillate and the scales tip up and down in a healthy way.

Sometimes, however, the scales tip over. If nutrient levels shoot up in summer, the algae can bloom and overwhelm the ecosystem, leading to ponds that look like pea soup. This is most common in the warmest months, typically August, and happens when nutrient spikes create unhealthy 'eutrophic' waters. These algae are typically shades of green, but can be many other colours too, including, amazingly, pink.

Algal blooms stand out, but most people miss the scales tipping the other way. In June, the algae numbers plateau as they have maxed out on their available nutrients, but the microscopic-animal numbers grow rapidly and exhaust their food supply, the algae. This causes a crash in algae and a swing towards much clearer water, which means we see the water go from clear in winter to a little cloudy in late spring to clear again in June before turning murky again later in summer. The June clarity is known as the 'clear-water phase' and is easy to spot, but very few do. Bringing two pieces together, we can now understand why we see our shadow in fresh water in spring and late summer, but not in winter or midsummer.

I spoke to Dr Stephen J. Thackeray, an ecologist from the UK Centre for Ecology and Hydrology about the clear-water phase, which led into a fun broader discussion that shone a light on the strange, challenging but fascinating place where we are in our relationship with nature. Stephen explained that clarity of water is important for scientists to gauge, but hard to put a precise number on. One method is to lower something called a Secchi disc, a small black and white circle, into the water and keep lowering it until it disappears. All scientists dislike too much wiggle room for results and Stephen was no different: 'You could see this as quite a subjective thing, couldn't you? It's down to somebody's eyesight really. But whenever I've done this I've found that the differences among observers aren't that big, not really. We might disagree over a few centimetres on how deep it is, but when you compare that to how much it changes over the course of a year, it's not much.'

He explained how this low-technology method was available to pretty much everyone and how it had spawned citizen-science initiatives; individuals were monitoring their local waters and collecting data across the world.

'We've got a citizen-science app called "Bloomin' Algae" – its founders were dead pleased with that name,' Stephen told me.

At the other end of the scale, satellites are monitoring the colour of water in zones across the globe and feeding it into computers, which are now using AI to assess and predict developing issues. At this point, our conversation turned in an unexpected direction, but one I encounter increasingly frequently.

We talked about how looking for something in water,

properly looking, changed something in *us*. And that seems to be true, whatever our method and whatever draws us to do this.

'A deep observation of water leads to a presence in the moment. There's a mindfulness that comes with it, I think, which is really powerful.'

I was delighted to hear Stephen say that, because it resonated with my own experience. Something profound seems to happen when we look properly, but we are more likely to take the time to do so if we know at least one meaningful thing to look for. It is more powerful as a practice than a theory, so I encourage you to look for clear water in June.

Night Shining Clouds

Each time we touch down in a foreign land, the sun follows a new schedule. The time of sunrise and sunset depends on the date, your latitude and longitude, and your height above sea level. This is true on the smallest scale: the sun sets later for the taller person standing to the west of you, but we will catch the last glimpse by standing on a chair.

Look east towards hills at sunset and the shadow rises up the hills as the sun falls behind us. It is still sunny at the top after the sun has set, and it sets about a quarter of an hour later at the top of Mount Everest than it does at sea level; it rises earlier by the same amount, making the day last half an hour longer. The day is longer in a second-floor bedroom than in the ground-floor kitchen (and longer near the ceiling of that room than the bed; at the end of the day we can watch shadows climb the wall). We can play the tape of sunrise or sunset forwards or backwards by running up and down bumps within a landscape, giving us a free low-tech time machine.

Once the shadow has risen all the way over the highest ground, it continues up into the sky and a band of shade rises against a blue sky in the east. This dark band is Earth's shadow. If there are any clouds, the shadow continues its upward journey and their tops stay in sun the longest. On tall clouds we can look for sunset colours as stripes: the top of the cloud is bright white, below that yellow, then orange, red and finally dark and all these colours march slowly upwards. Sometimes you may catch the flash of the sun's reflection off an aircraft flying over you minutes after the sun set where you are.

These patterns are true all year, but there is a rare effect that we can start to look for in June and will only catch in summer. The very highest clouds we will ever see are about 200,000 feet above the ground, more than six times higher than the highest clouds we normally see. They are called 'noctilucent clouds' – night shining clouds. They are rare, peculiar and wonderful, and form only in summer because of the circulation of very cold air at high latitudes at this time of year. At night, when the sun is below our horizon, its light can still reach us if it bounces down from ice crystals in the mesosphere. There is a natural navigation aspect to these super-high clouds, as we see them only when we're looking towards the northern sky.

Solstice Sun and Moon

St Bede, the Anglo-Saxon scholar-monk also known as the Venerable Bede, argued that the summer solstice should fall on 20 June. This was one more example of someone trying to pin human conventions on to nature's rhythms. Each time we think midday is the moment when our watch says twelve o'clock, we fall into a similar trap because the middle of the day is halfway between sunrise and sunset, when the sun is highest in the sky and due south, regardless of the numbers on our watch. The sun and the planets don't tell the time: they *are* time and will remain so for ever, unbridled by monks or clocks. Bede wanted to reconcile the sun's habits with his understanding of Christian landmarks.

In the Middle Ages the religious thought that the sun's patterns must align with the births of St John the Baptist and Jesus, six months apart. Dr Eleanor Parker explains this yearning for symmetry in her book, *The Winters in the World*:

> Since John was born six months before Christ, their births are celebrated at the four key points of the solar year: just as Christ was said to have been conceived at the spring equinox and born at the winter solstice, so John was conceived at the autumn equinox and born at the summer solstice.[*]

We find echoes of these ideas in the yellow wildflower, St John's wort, which earned its name because it flowers at this time of year. It's an extraordinary plant, surrounded in myth. It contains compounds that have been shown to exert a better-than-placebo effect on treating depression. And yet it is toxic to many animals, including sheep, horses and cows, and can be lethal to humans when taken with other medicines. The Latin name for St John's wort, *Hypericum perforatum*, hints at the perforated character of its leaves and can help with identification. Hold a leaf up to sunlight and, if you have the right plant, the holes are clearly visible to the naked eye. Anglo-Saxon herbalists believed that plants gathered near the solstice had greater

---

[*] Parker, Eleanor, *The Winters in the World*, Reaktion Books, 2018, p. 174.

power and efficacy, which is not such a fanciful notion: more energy is available from the sun at this time of year than any other.

A long tradition survives to this day that the summer solstice is celebrated on a particular day, between 20 and 22 June, which has led to the belief that the solstice lasts a day. It does fall on one of those late-June days, but it doesn't last as long as a day. In astronomical terms, the solstice is shorter than a day, shorter than a second, in fact. It is a precise moment. Put another way, if you say the word 'solstice' at the time of the solstice, the first syllable of the word would fall before and the second after it.

The June solstice is the exact moment that Earth's orbit reaches the point where the North Pole points as much as it ever does towards the sun. It is also the exact moment when the sun is over the most northerly part of Earth, a line 23.5 degrees north of the equator that we call the Tropic of Cancer. This has many interesting practical consequences, especially for the natural navigator.

At the summer solstice the sun will rise as far north of east as it ever does and set as far north of west as it ever does. The further you are from the equator, the further north it will rise and set at this time. I have been teaching this for two decades and have noticed that the first time anyone learns this they are tempted to try to balance things, which leads to confusion that we should nip in the bud.

'If the sun rises north of east, then . . . surely it will set south of west?'

The sun always rises and sets on the same side of east and west each day. When it rises north of east, it sets north of west. When it rises due east (on only two days, the equinoxes) it sets due west. And, as we will see in December, if it rises south of east, it sets south of west. Knowing this can help avoid the

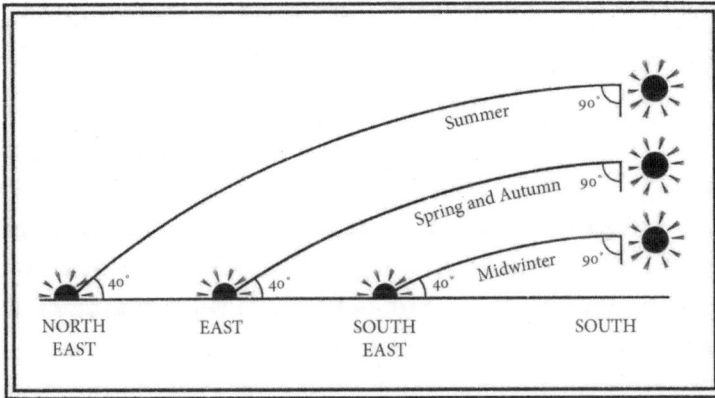

The sunrise to midday journey as seen over the seasons. The angle the sun rises will be close to 90 degrees minus your latitude, in this case, Latitude 50° N

pitfall, but there is another, more experiential, way to think about it.

However disconnected someone is from seasonal patterns, everyone notices that the days are longer in June than in December. Most give this no further thought, but if we question it, we find it is a helpful part of the jigsaw. The sun follows a much longer arc across the sky in summer than in winter. In June the sun rises near north-east and keeps rising as it tracks from left to right, arcing across the sky until it reaches due south in the middle of the day. Then it starts dropping as it continues its journey from left to right, but it has a very long way to go until it reaches the north-west horizon. That's the biggest arc and longest journey of the year. In December, it rises near south-east, moves left to right (as it always does in the northern parts of the world) and climbs a little until it reaches due south, then it starts falling on its short journey down to the south-western horizon. A very long arc from north-east to north-west in June leads to very long days. A short arc from south-east to south-west leads to short days in winter. In March and September we have the equinoxes, a middling arc and days that are twelve hours long, neither short nor long.

The sun is highest in June and this leads to another common misconception. Try asking people in summer where the sun is in the middle of the day. It won't take many tries before someone says, 'Overhead,' which is only odd when we think that it has never, not for one second, been overhead for anyone north of the tropics.

The sun reaches its highest point of the year at midday on the June solstice, but it is still not overhead.[*] The closer we are to the tropics, the higher the sun will appear at this time, but for anyone north of the Tropic of Cancer, the sun will be lower than overhead and due south in the middle of the day, even in June. And for every day after the solstice, the sun drops lower until it is 23.5 degrees lower at the September equinox and 47 degrees lower in December (2 x 23.5 degrees).

It follows that we get our shortest shadows in the middle of the day on the summer solstice and that they point due north. A simple exercise helps us reconnect with this moment in the calendar. During a sunny lunch break, go to an open area and walk until the shadow of your head just touches a fixed line, like the edge of a path. Note where you're standing. If you repeat this exercise a few times throughout the year, two things will happen. You will find yourself drifting away from the path and developing a relationship with the sun's seasonal habits.

---

[*] At midday on the summer solstice the sun is 90 degrees, minus your latitude, plus 23.5 degrees, above the horizon. I live near 50 degrees north, so the sums are 90 − 50 + 23.5. The sun is 63.5 degrees or six and a bit extended fists above the horizon, quite high, but definitely not overhead.

More than a thousand years ago, Aelfric of Eynsham noted the way the sun headed northwards until it was in the constellation Cancer, at which point it stopped, at the solstice. He described how the days then grew shorter until the winter solstice, when it changed direction and banished the winter cold with its warming rays. The word 'solstice' derives from the Latin words for 'sun' and 'standing still' and reflects how the sun appears to stop moving at each end of its journey up and down the eastern and western horizons.

Imagine a year of clear skies. Each morning we stand on the same spot, look out over a flat landscape and wait for the moment when the sun peeks halfway over the eastern horizon. At that moment each morning, we take a photo. Now we develop those photos on paper, giving us a stack of 365 photos of a sunrise over a landscape. If we flick through those photos, we'll see a basic animation and notice two things.

First, the sun moves along the horizon between its two stops, the left, north-eastern end, and the right, south-eastern end. The next thing you'll notice is that the speed changes dramatically over the year. The sun races through the middle (east at the equinoxes in March and September), then slows right down and appears to stop at each end (north-east and south-east at the solstices, in June and December). The ancients took great interest in this pattern, hence 'solstice' and the Anglo-Saxon 'sunstede' – sun in a fixed place.

Many cultures celebrate the summer solstice. Before electricity, the longest day was a boon, a time of plentiful light, warmth and food so these have always been festive times. However, the summer solstice was also tinged with anxiety . . . What goes up, must come down. We find stories of druids lighting bonfires at the summer solstice to encourage the sun's light and heat to linger – please don't leave us!

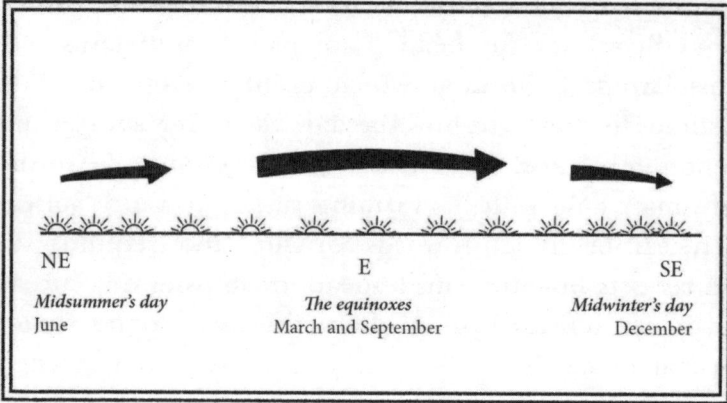

NE   E   SE

Midsummer's day   *The equinoxes*   *Midwinter's day*
June   March and September   December

*The seasonal change in sunrise direction. From a standstill at the
summer solstice, the sunrise moves south and accelerates until it is
changing at its fastest pace at the September equinox, before slowing to
a standstill at the winter solstice again. The same pattern repeats in
the opposite direction*

Solstices are extreme times for the Earth–sun relationship,
but there are extremes for most other celestial observations
too. Planets appear highest, on average, as they move across the
southern sky in June and lowest in December.

It leads to interesting patterns for any full moons at these
times too. Notice how any in late June behave in a very different
manner from the sun at this time, rising in the south-east at the
end of the day and setting in the south-west at the end of the
night. They follow a short arc and are at their lowest as they
cross the sky at this time. Full moons behave as the sun will in
six months' time. For a fuller exploration of this, please see *The
Moon and the Seasons*, in the Appendix.

Blocking Highs and Welcome Breezes

The solar energy hitting the northern hemisphere reaches a maximum in June and this has lots of big and small consequences. We'll work our way in from the large to the surprisingly small.

The sun heats high and low latitudes at different rates and land faster than water. This leads to warm, rising and expanding air, which creates low-pressure systems. In other regions, cooler air descends to create high-pressure systems. The systems are nudged around Earth's atmosphere by air currents set up by its rotation.

Low-pressure systems lead to turbulent air, clouds, rain and sometimes storms. High-pressure systems are drier and make blue skies more likely; they can be stubborn – they sometimes sit over areas for long periods and block other systems from moving along their normal tracks. This gives us a summer phenomenon to look out for: the blocking high.

The June sun is trying to pour huge amounts of solar energy down onto the northern hemisphere, but it is often stopped by cloud cover. We can think of the midsummer sun as constantly trying to overheat us, but failing much of the time. If, however, the dry, stable air of a high pressure moves over us and sits there stubbornly for days or even weeks, we have the ingredients for a heat wave. There are warm air masses and cooler ones, even in summer, as their temperature is shaped by their travels – so blocking highs lead to either manageable temperatures during a cool high, or serious heat waves with warmer air. Summer blocking highs lead us also towards drought.

We have been looking at the summer sun's effects on a massive scale, one that features on regional and even national weather forecasts, but if we zoom in a bit and drop down to ground level, we start to sense patterns that only feature in very detailed local forecasts. Let's imagine we decide to cool off during a summer high by heading to the sea or a large lake for a swim. The same solar heating that caused the massive high- and low-pressure systems is also working on this much smaller scale.

As we have seen, the sun heats the land faster than the sea and the land then warms the air above it. The warm air rises over the land leading to lower pressure there, but the sea remains cool for many hours after the land has warmed, leading to higher pressure there. The high-pressure air over the sea moves towards the land, which sets up a 'sea breeze' that strengthens during the day as the land warms.

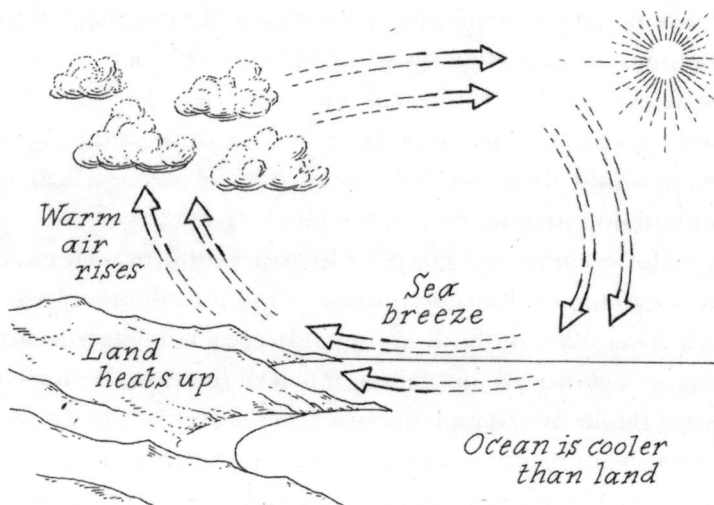

Warm air rises

Sea breeze

Land heats up

Ocean is cooler than land

The sea breeze

At the end of the day, the land cools rapidly when there are no clouds as the heat escapes quickly to space. By the middle of the night the land is cooler than the sea, because the sea cools as slowly as it heats. This turns the tables: there is now higher-pressure cool air over the land and lower-pressure air over the sea. A land breeze flows down towards the sea.

We reach the coast and decide we'd like a drink in a coastal café before heading down to the water. Often a busy coastal road runs parallel to the shore and we are likely to find a good pitstop along it – but should we go for a café on the sea or land side of the road? If it is late on a hot afternoon, we'll find that the sea breeze has kicked in and the wind is carrying pollution (and noise) from the road inland, reducing the air quality of anything on that side. If it is early morning, we might find the last of the land breeze blowing from the land towards the sea and the air quality on the sea side of the road will be worse.

Both land and sea breezes are caused by warm air rising, which leads to a line of fluffy white cumulus clouds that runs parallel to the coastline. Sea-breeze clouds will be well over the land, and land-breeze clouds will be over the sea, but the giveaway is a line of puffy clouds that mirrors the shape of the coastline.

The same effect happens on a smaller scale whenever land warms faster than a neighbouring body of water. It's unlikely that we'll notice it by a small pond or thin river, but it's common at large lakes, as summer visitors to Michigan's Great Lakes will know.

Sea and land breezes are examples of winds set up by changing temperatures leading to pressure differences. Whenever something causes one parcel of air to be warmer or cooler than its neighbour, a breeze will follow. Since the sun lies behind many of the changes, June is a good month to tune into them. When the sun warms a mountain slope, we find warm air flowing gently uphill and an 'anabatic wind'. If a mountainside cools faster than the land below it, a cold 'katabatic wind' rolls downhill. They can be calm breezes or terrifying blasts. I was hit by a robust katabatic wind once when sailing off the coast of Iceland in June: the cold air rolled off the snowy mountains and pushed the boat over. These winds are regular seasonal characters and often earn local names, like the 'Böhmwind' or 'Bohemian Wind' in Bavaria, Germany.

Dark surfaces warm faster than light ones as they absorb

more solar energy and reflect less. It's one reason why so many outdoor restaurant tables and chairs are white. Towns and cities are normally darker than their surroundings and they also generate their own heat, making them as much as 12 degrees centigrade warmer than the rural areas nearby, creating an effect known as the 'urban heat island'. We see more cumulus clouds bubbling up over urban areas, and as the warm air rises, cooler air flows in from outside the town, creating a 'city breeze'.

The city breeze

The Navigator's Triangle

The longest days of the year limit our stargazing opportunities, but eventually the sun falls below the north-western horizon and, when we know what to look for, some treats are on offer.

As we know, the sun's light slides into twilight and, as it sets so late at this time of year, there is a high chance that we will share our first stars with some remnants of the day. It's helpful to know the brightest to look for at this time.

As soon as it feels more like night than day, look halfway up the eastern sky and you will spot a pinprick of white light. This is Vega, a star more than twice as massive as our sun and a lot further away. Light from the sun takes a little more than eight minutes to reach us; light from Vega takes a quarter of a century.

If you look east after sunset for a few nights in June, you will come to know Vega well. It is our midsummer early-evening anchor star and we'll use it to find two other bright stars. To the north and a little lower than Vega you will spot Deneb; to the south of Vega and a little lower than Vega and Deneb is Altair. Deneb and Altair are bright, but noticeably less so than Vega. These three stars are each the brightest in three different constellations, Lyra (the Lyre), Cygnus (the Swan) and Aquila (the Eagle).

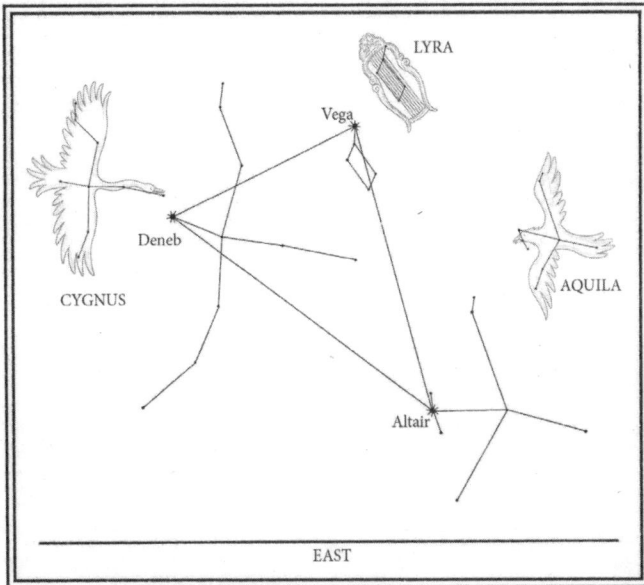

The Navigator's Triangle after sunset in midsummer

There are enjoyable and helpful ways of enlisting these three constellations as individuals – Cygnus, for example, is useful for finding the North Star (as we will discover in November) – but in midsummer we'll focus on the shape that the bright three form, known as the Navigator's Triangle (also known as the Summer Triangle). June is a great month to get to know it, but it is also visible at other times of year.

The Navigator's Triangle rises in the east, arcs up until it is very high, then rolls down towards the western horizon. It points towards the South Pole. Imagine a line from halfway between Deneb and Vega that runs to Altair and splits the triangle in two. The line rolls across the sky, and when it reaches a vertical, it marks a north–south line. Extend it to your horizon and you'll be looking due south. This happens at an unsociably late hour in June, but since the stars rise four minutes earlier each night, it appears earlier as the year progresses and before bedtime by early autumn.

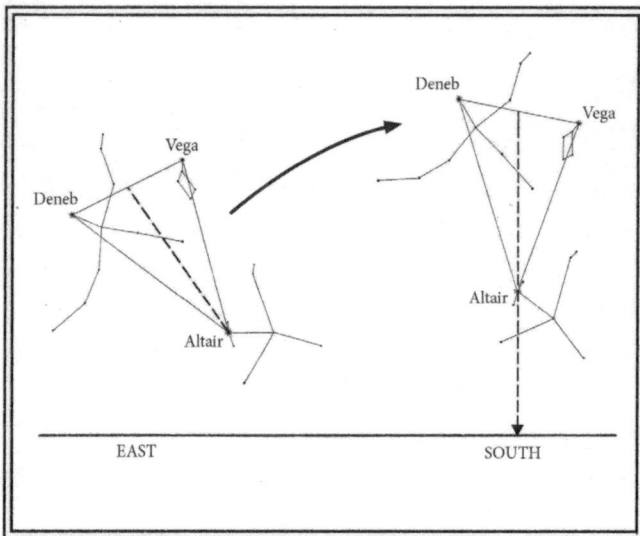

Finding South with the Navigator's Triangle

Our galaxy, the Milky Way, takes its name from the light of many billions of stars, which reaches us as a faint, milky glow against the darker backdrop of space. We see the Milky Way when we are looking through our neighbourhood. Imagine looking out from a skyscraper in a big city: when you look across the city at night you see the glow of a cityscape, thousands of tiny individual lights making up the scene of a busy urban landscape. But when you look up or down, you don't see the same lights. When we gaze across our galaxy we see the milky light of our neighbourhood stars, but when we look in other directions it is much darker.

The Milky Way runs across the sky and is bright enough that we'll sometimes spot it even when we're not actively looking for it. But if you're up when it's properly dark in June, this is a good time to search it out. One part runs in a band that goes through Deneb and Altair in the Navigator's Triangle.

By a strange quirk of the rhythms of the sun, moon, Earth and stars, if you look at a full moon in June, you'll be looking towards the centre of the Milky Way.

Sand Stories

The wind leaves its mark on every surface on Earth, from the ocean to the city, and other planets with atmospheres, like Mars, where there are wind-sculpted ripples and dunes. The wind's footprints are well worth learning to interpret, and one of the best schools for this is the beach.

The author Richard Grant resisted the temptation to join me as I lay on the sands of my local beach and lightly prodded both sides of a small ripple, no higher than my finger. 'The sand is very slightly firmer on this shallow side and softer on the opposite steep side,' I said.

Richard squatted, touched the sand and agreed he could feel the difference.

'It's firmer on this, the south-west, side because that is the direction the wind has come from. And can you see how the sand is different colours on each side of the tiny ridge? It's darker on the windward side and lighter downwind.'

Richard was spending a couple of days with me on a writing assignment for an American magazine. He was jetlagged after a journey from Tucson, Arizona, but fortified with strong coffee from my flask and cooled by a sea breeze, he coped with the energy I feel on sharing these patterns.

Summer beaches are covered with holidaymakers, their noses buried in books or tablets, but they miss the stories in the sand. Sand ripples are analogous to the waves that march over the ocean and they are miniature models of the dunes we find in sandy deserts across the world. This makes the beach a great laboratory for understanding the fundamental patterns we see on many scales across the world. Over the years, I have trained intrepid explorers, gnarly warriors and happy campers to read global patterns using local beaches.

We walked along the beach and I scanned the ripples until I noticed a disruption. Dropping to my belly once more, I pointed to the pebble. 'Can you see how this minute boulder has broken the airflow? The clean ripple pattern looks as if it has snapped. And see here . . .' I pointed to the tail of white sand that ran down and away from the tiny rounded stone, then to the small stub of darker sand on the windward side. 'Whenever anything slows the wind, a ridge, a pebble, even a piece of seaweed, we find that sand falls out of the airflow. The darker sands tend to be heavier and fall out on the windward side. The lighter coloured sands are lighter in weight too and don't drop out until they hit the wind shadow on the far side. This creates these little tails pointing downwind and the two colours we saw on the ripples.'

Each time a gale or storm goes through, all these patterns

reset and stay consistent until the next blast. Seasonality plays its part. During winter, the trains of gales that hit coastlines reshape whole beaches; by late spring the weather patterns settle and the beach holds its shape until the next winter. On the much smaller scale we find the patterns last longer too – a sand tail might last weeks in summer or a day in winter.

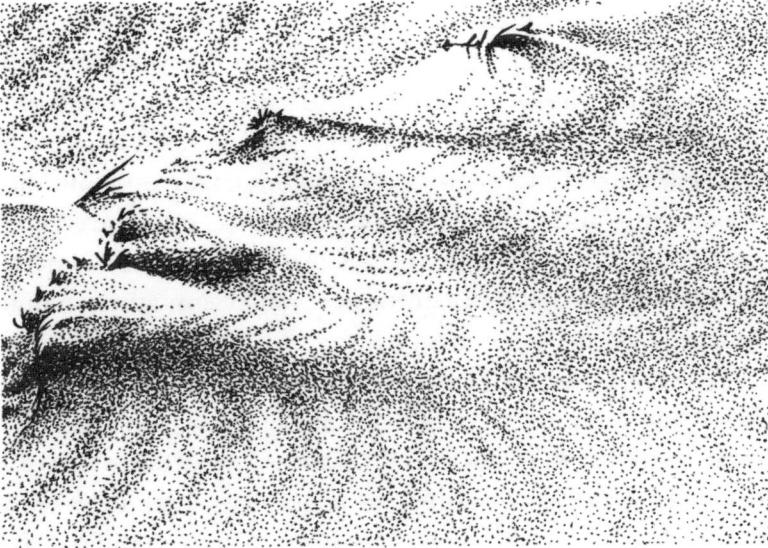

Sand tails

Once we recognise these forms as familiar characters, they pop up to meet us wherever we find loose particles on the ground. Similar patterns can be found in snow, leaf fragments and even dust in cities. The wind always deposits things in the places it can't reach: the wind shadows. I once saw a scattering of wrappers, crisps packets and other light rubbish by a laurel hedge in a city park. It wasn't the scene of a messy picnic, as I first guessed, it was a wind shadow, but I might not have worked that out if I hadn't watched a piece of cellophane whirl over the hedge and land in the same spot. Paper and other light rubbish behaves like sand or snow: it hitches a lift on the breeze and falls to the ground wherever the wind slows. Flotsam on water gathers where the water slows.

We soon passed a similar but different pattern. When strong coastal winds have blown in a consistent direction, they sculpt a series of much firmer skinnier forms in the harder damper sand that lies beneath the dry light particles. This leaves rows of thin lines in this much darker sand. I don't believe there is a formal name for them, but think of them as 'baby yardangs'. In deserts across the world, winds scour rocks for centuries and shape them into streamlined forms: yardangs. They come in sizes that range from a few metres to kilometres long. But they all point into and are aligned in the direction of the prevailing wind. The skinny dark sand lines are not yardangs, but the processes and resulting patterns are similar enough for me to see them as baby beach versions.

We walked past the marram-grass dunes, a familiar feature above the high-water mark of many sandy beaches. The dunes stabilise the beach and build as the grasses slow the wind and sand is deposited among the plants. They form perpendicular to the wind, creating banks that face the onshore winds, with a hard face on the sea side and a softer slope towards the land.

Heading further into the nature reserve at East Head we reached the water's edge. I pointed over the sea to the clouds bubbling up above the Isle of Wight and showed Richard how they mapped the land below them. The island clouds were taller and a different shape from those over the sea – they always are. An ancient navigator approaching the island from the open ocean would spot those cumulus clouds rising above the warm land and recognise them as significant, long before the island became visible.

We took a few steps back up the beach over a different family of beach patterns. In the places where the water of the last high tide had washed over the sand, we found a series of hard wet ripples. The sand was still waterlogged and much darker than any we had met so far, but I recognised many familiar shapes and old friends. The ripples were shallower on the side the water had flowed *from* and steeper on the side the water flowed *towards* on its journey to reunite with the sea. And there were the steep ridges where, hours earlier, waves had broken overhead, creating a washing-machine effect in the water and carving pointed ridges in the sand below.

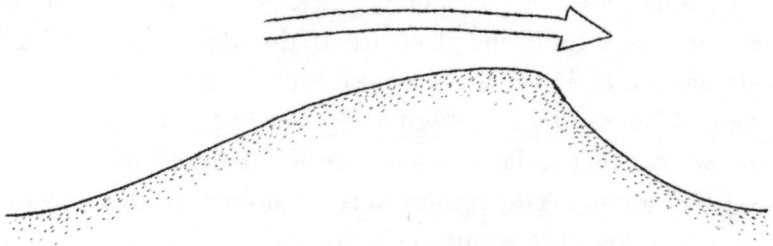

Water has flowed from left to right

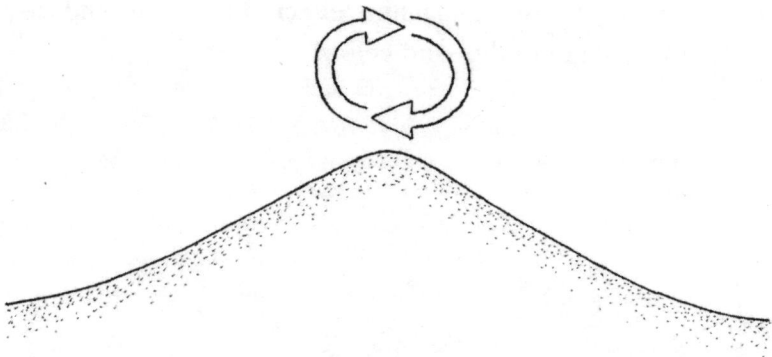

Water has oscillated, probably formed under breaking waves

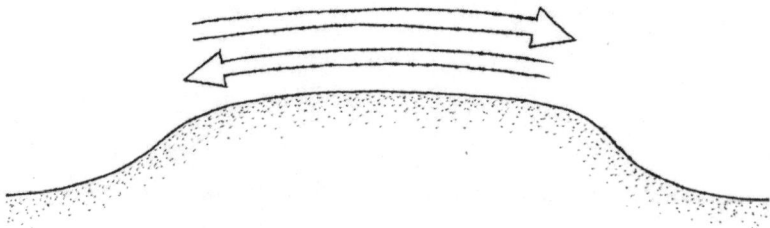

Water has flowed one way with the tide, then the opposite way

10

July

Colours and Scents

—

Grass Stories

—

Storm Signs

—

Beach Clues

—

Time Stamps

—

Rising or Falling?

—

Scorpius and the Delta Aquariids

—

Arcania

Colours and Scents

With so much light and warmth, we might expect a little more entertainment from the plants and animals, but July sits between the verdant explosion of spring and the bounteous fruits to come. We need to use a little guile to savour it.

Resident birds can be quiet, but some migrants are already packing their bags, ready to leave, which may lead to displays as they gather in the departure halls. Swifts swoop around our pond. Dragonflies are on patrol and we may spot a trend if we have been following them over the months. Many insects, including dragonflies and damselflies, reflect the seasons in a change of colour. Darker colours absorb more solar energy and are more popular in the cooler months of spring and autumn. Bright colours reflect more of the sun's radiation and are fashionable among the dragonflies that are busiest during the hot summer months.

The size of insects we see also changes over the course of the day in summer. When you're looking for this, keep in mind one of the basic rules of flying insects: the bigger they are the less they like summer lunchtime. Large insects are more likely to overheat near the middle of a summer day than small ones, which means we tend to see them nearer the start and end of the day. Flying insects get smaller as the sun rises and larger again as it sets.

Many amphibians have left the water, so it's calmer below, but the surface is still a riot of micro-ripples as whirligigs and many others leave patterns that interplay with the breeze's ripples.

It's time to sense subtle changes in the plants. This morning, I picked up the exquisite scent of wild marjoram (oregano) on a breeze and spied it lining only one side of the path. Wildflower scents come from energy-rich oils and the energy comes only from the sun. If we smell a flower, it follows that it will most likely be in a sunlit place and on the south-facing side of any trail or path. This is where we find the nectar-hungry butterflies and bees on patrol. On the hottest July days, pedestrians will cross to the shaded side of city streets, but insects patronise the energy-packed flowers on the sunny side.

If we pick up the scent of flowers, it is well worth using it as a prompt to sniff the air at different levels. We have a tendency to smell the world at two levels: macro and micro. We either sense general whiffs as we go about our day or we zoom in to savour the scent of a garden rose or a freshly baked loaf. Watch mammals for any period of time and you'll notice that they sense the world of smell in dozens of thin layers, lifting and lowering their noses to build a scent picture of their surroundings. Some prey animals, like deer, lick their noses to sharpen their sense of smell when they're at their most alert. We can lift and lower our head to sense that the world of smell is multi-layered.

We won't fail to notice fruits once they have turned bright reds and purples, but there are many small green ones swelling at this time. And there is a lot of satisfaction in spotting the places where the early colours show first.

Our neighbouring village, Slindon, could not be more 'English village' if it tried. It was listed as having thirty-five homes in the Domesday Book in 1086, which was considered a substantial settlement at the time. It is now more commonly referred to by visitors as 'sleepy', even though it has a quirky energy and sends gentle eccentric waves through the local area. For many decades it was known as the pumpkin capital of the world, thanks to a retired market gardener called Ralph Upton, who built up his plot until in 2008, aged eighty-seven, he was planting up to twenty thousand seeds of fifty varieties.

On the first hot July day of the year, I bought a pasty at the village shop, the Forge, which was set up by residents after the blacksmith downed tools a few years ago and remains community-owned. Outside, I turned left and walked uphill, pausing at a wooden gate to read a sign that reveals the hidden Slindon energy. Its words might act as a tonic and a beacon for our times:

The Jubilee Orchard was planted by the Slindon community in 2012 with a mixture of apples, pears, plums, medlar and quince. We manage the grassland as a meadow for wildlife and have benches and a mown path so that everybody can come and enjoy this special place. Ten years on, the trees are now bearing enough fruit to address a picking and gathering policy.

We are happy for you to pick an apple, plum or pear to supplement your lunch and we are also happy for you to take a bowl of fruit to turn into a pie, tart or crumble. We ask that you don't take any more than that at a time, so that everybody might have the opportunity to have their share.

Next to the sign, a map of the orchard showed the twenty-eight varieties of fruit, with a simple key. A small rosy apple next to its name meant the tree bore eating apples; a metal pot signalled it was a cooking variety. A mown path snaked between the tall grasses and led me between some old favourites, Bramley and Golden Pippin apples, towards a fruit utopia of names I didn't know: Merryweather damsons, Doyenne de Comice pears, Golden Sphere plums . . .

I ate my pasty sitting on a bench, quite overcome by the love-liness of the place. And then I continued to explore, keen to pick an apple to follow the pasty, but I resisted: it was not yet the season of ripeness.

Many fruits start to ripen following a hormonal trigger from gases within the fruit, like ethylene. If it is too windy, they are whisked away and the fruit fails to ripen. The gas fires the start-ing gun, but the speed of ripening is determined by many other factors, especially temperature. Most chemical processes accel-erate with a rise in temperature, the ripening of fruit included. The red colour in apples comes from anthocyanins and their formation quickens in ultra-violet light – sunlight. Direct sunlight falling on one side of an apple increases the rate of change on that side and leads to it turning red before the shaded side. The red side of the apple is more likely to face south than any other direction.

I continued my walk around the Slindon orchard, threading my way among a hundred apple compasses. The fruit on the trees appeared red when I walked towards my shadow and green when the high sun fell on my face.

On the walk home from Slindon, I spotted a couple of splashes of interesting colour. July is a good month for tall wild-flowers that include red in their palette. The perfect pink-purple of foxgloves lined the edge of the woods. The flowers point the way out of the woods as they face towards light. The flowers at the base open before those higher up. The pollinat-ing bumblebees, drawn to the flowers by the colour, shape and patterns on their landing lip, work their way up from the base towards the top, spiralling as they go.

(Foxglove flowers are bisexual. The stamen (male parts) matures first, releasing pollen before the stigma (female parts) is ready. As the flower ages it turns from functionally male to female. The oldest flowers in a foxglove are at the bottom of the spike so, effectively, male flowers are at the bottom and female at the top. All the flowers have male and female structures, which mature at different times.)

A similar pink-purple colour shone out from a wildflower colony beside the path and reminded me of the herbal tea I'd enjoyed with Miles in March. The tall spikes of rosebay willow-herb marked an area of upheaval and raised ground at the edge of a farmer's field, possibly where they had dumped some spoil. In North America it is known as fireweed and it thrives in areas recently cleared of other plants by fire. It's an enterprising and opportunistic plant, often the first colour on the scene after disturbance, but it rarely thrives anywhere for long periods and marks recent change. It earned the name 'bombweed' in the Second World War, thanks to its habit of springing up in craters left by explosives. It always prompts the question, 'What happened here?'

At the edge of a field of barley, there was a line of a deeper red, poppies, another flower that signals upheaval. They do well after a short period of mayhem, but are fussy about altitude, gradient, moisture and sunlight. If you see poppies thriving, you are looking at a dry, shallow-gradient low-country spot that gets lots of direct sunlight. If they are lining anything that casts shade, it is most likely to be the south-facing edge.

Heading to the other side of the colour spectrum, the observant may notice that the leaves on the trees have turned a darker green, the paler shades of spring and early summer long gone.

Grass Stories

I was one of a group of sixteen undertaking a one-day pilgrimage over the hills to Malvern Priory. The British Pilgrimage Trust organises many such walks and does it in an irresistibly inclusive way.* It encourages all to join their walks and to 'bring their own beliefs' or none. The idea is that walking with a goal and an intention of some kind is good for us: it promotes 'holistic wellbeing', which includes 'physical, mental, emotional, social, community, environmental and spiritual health'. And who couldn't use a few of those?

Our pilgrimage was led by Dawn and Gary, partners in life and walking. They were full of enthusiasm for their cause and keen to share their eclectic knowledge. Dawn couldn't have been happier to discover a nettle sting on one pilgrim's leg and proceeded to treat it with the sap from the ribwort plantains that grew along the verge of our path. There is real merit in this herbal remedy as the plant contains antihistamine.

I wanted to support the Trust by buying a ticket and joining a walk, but I was mainly there for selfish reasons – I had decided to treat myself to it as a follower, not a leader or guide. What an indulgence, to enjoy a walk in the company of a group without any responsibility for the route, the knowledge shared or even the experience or wellbeing of others. As part of this gift to myself, I wanted to keep my mouth shut about what I was seeing. A couple of things I thought might have been of interest to future pilgrims I kept to myself at the time, but I will share them here.

The ribwort plantain would have been helpful to ancient pilgrims for reasons beyond stings and medicine: being trampling-tolerant it would reveal the route of those who had passed before. It does not indicate trampling as clearly as its relative, the broad-leaved plantain, so it takes a little more skill to read. There are good clues in its leaves, which reach upwards in less disturbed places, but stay flat to the ground in busy places. Its numbers shoot

---

* Full disclosure: I am a proud patron of the British Pilgrimage Trust.

up as we approach civilisation. And it makes a compass too, being more common on south-facing slopes.

As we began a gentle climb up a hill, I looked down onto a field of wheat and found the lines I was looking for. Keep an eye open for animal trails in crops at this time of year. There is a perfect perspective for this: too low and we see only the waving heads of grasses; too high and we miss the detail. Gaze down on a field of wheat, oats or barley from a neighbouring slope and you will often spot the snaking lines of deer or other animal runs, dark squiggles against the pale crops. They are useful lines to follow if you accidentally find yourself trapped in a farmer's field – the animals lead us to gaps in fences. All day we passed tall and short grasses and each blade had a memory. July is the best month for reading grass stories.

In 2010, the popular American magazine *Outside* despatched the bestselling author Tom Vanderbilt from New York to meet me in Dartmoor. He would join me as I undertook a natural-navigation challenge. It was a simple plan: we would find our way to a wild part of already wild Dartmoor using fewer and fewer navigation aids, then camp for the night. The following morning we would set off with the aim of finding a pub five miles north of our start point using only nature's signs for navigation. I had never set eyes on any part of our route before.

A five-mile walk in good visibility with modern navigation aids might take an hour and a half. Our journey took us a day. We spent much of the time in thick fog and rain, which is never a surprise on Dartmoor, but these were exam conditions and it made my work a lot more challenging.

I never made it any secret, before or during the challenge, that I wasn't sure if we would succeed. I honestly didn't know. Natural navigation works: it is rooted in ancient skills and firm scientific principles and I felt I was the right person to attempt that short journey, but at times we could barely see a hundred yards in front of us. In natural navigation terms, a journey of a hundred miles under bright sun and stars is easier than five miles in thick fog. We were at the edge of feasible natural navigation and, as the mist swirled around us, I showed Tom how the wind had bent the grasses, creating the pattern that would act as our guide. It is a great one to look for in July, the month of tall grasses.

Reading grass compasses is about understanding that the shape of plants reveals a memory. Tall, exposed grasses have short memories: they flop over with every changing breeze. They will point a different direction at lunch than they did at breakfast. Shorter, firmer, less floppy grasses have a longer memory and reflect longer trends. They are combed over with the prevailing wind direction. These were the patterns I had shown Tom on Dartmoor, as my fingers jumped between the water-beaded blades. Lots of shorter grasses bent over from south-west to north-east, but many taller ones had been tipped from west to east by the more recent winds. We found our way out of Dartmoor and to the pub by trusting the memory of the grasses. Fourteen years later I was seeing the same patterns in the tall grasses outside a cave in Worcestershire. They are all around us at this time of year.

It's your turn. Look for any bobbing movement in tall grasses: you are witnessing the shortest memories being made. Look a little lower and you will find shorter, less proud grasses that don't move in a breeze but would in a gale. The key is to find grasses that are just tall enough to let the wind leave an impression, but short enough that they are not fickle.

I use a particular technique to demonstrate this when out teaching. Huff and puff. Can we change the direction of the grass using only our breath?

If the answer is 'Yes, easily,' we are looking at floppy, exposed grass that has a short wind memory. It is reflecting the breeze you feel on your face. If the answer is 'Not easily,' we are look-ing at longer trends, the footprints of prevailing winds. If the answer is 'No, not at all,' the grass might be too short and stub-born to help us. We are looking for grasses that are just tall enough that we can bend them ever so slightly by blowing hard. If they flex a tiny bit, then return to their original lie, that's perfect. Look for all three and tune into the way in which they have different memories and offer different clues. Some reveal a long-term compass; others have a needle that swings with the last wind. When it clouds over and the wind dies, every blade's story will pay back earlier curiosity.

Longer grasses reflect the most recent winds, shorter ones reflect longer trends. Both can be used to navigate

Storm Signs

A heavy shower started as soon we reached the highest ground in the Malvern Hills. This was no coincidence. High ground

forces air upwards, triggering the processes that lead to showers. As soon as the first cleared, I scanned the horizon again,
looking for certain signs. I wanted to know if there was a risk of
lightning, as thunderstorms and high ground are a dicey
combination.

July is an interesting weather month that likes to lurch from
one extreme to another. On warm, humid days, energy levels
build in tall, rising clouds until, like a rubber band stretched
too far, there is a snap and the energy is released. For long periods we may experience hot, sultry, calm airs that the peasant
poet, John Clare, captured so well,

> Noon gathers wi its blistering breath
> Around and day dyes still as death
> The breeze is stopt the lazy bough
> Hath not a leaf that dances now . . .

Then it's all change and we find ourselves fleeing thunderstorms. We may be glad to know the signs to look for.

There are two types of thunderstorm: isolated and frontal. In
July we're mainly concerned with the isolated storm that sometimes seems to appear out of a blue sky. They are the July bogey-
men. (As we'll see in November, some storms arrive in waves
when the violently unsettled weather of a cold front goes
through. They rarely catch us completely off-guard because
they are part of large weather changes that we sense and are
heralded by forecasters.)

Anything that makes the surface warmer than its surroundings or triggers moist air to rise is likely to be a hotspot for
storms. The Alps are bombed by thunderstorms in July. Hot
land next to cooler seas leads to warm moist air rising – the
ingredients for a storm – and any high ground downwind of
coastlines fizzes and crackles with violent electricity on July

afternoons. We get more storms over hot cities than in the cooler countryside that surrounds them. It is very common to find late-summer thunderstorms over big cities when no rain is falling a few miles away. But how can we tell if storms are likely?

Storm prediction is an energy and probability game. The chance of a thunderstorm over low-lying land during cool clear weather in summer is low, but never zero. If the sun heats the dark tarmac of an airport sufficiently and the atmosphere is moist and unstable enough, a cloud may tower up and lightning may follow. But we will want to be most alert when we sense the air has stored plenty of energy and moisture – those times when it feels both unusually warm and humid and visibility is poor. This is when the balance of probabilities swings: the gunpowder is waiting for a spark.

Look for any clouds that grow taller than they are wide. This reveals an unstable atmosphere and is a clue that the conditions are right for showers and possibly storms – the earlier in the day, the stronger the sign. If July clouds grow tall before midday, this is a particularly strong warning sign: they are towering up before the land has reached its warmest.

If we spot a tall cloud, we'll want to keep checking it to get a sense of its plans. Is the wind blowing it towards us? It's a good idea to study the tops of these clouds carefully – it can be helpful to label shapes creatively as they make it easier to judge changes. If we see a fish's tail or castle turrets in the top of the cloud, we'll notice any significant changes to that shape. We're trying to gauge whether the cloud is reaching a stable height or entering a runaway phase. Judging the height of the top of clouds is difficult, which is why shapes help us to notice if it is still growing upwards.

If a cloud towers ever higher, we are primed to expect a possible storm. And now we look for specific changes at the top of the cloud. If the top of a tall cloud holds its shape and definition, like cauliflower florets, it is still made up of water droplets and isn't a storm cloud yet. If, however, the top turns to wispy candyfloss, it tells us that the water has turned to ice. Storms form after ice falls from the top of the cloud and generates the friction needed for electrical charges to build up. If there is no ice at the top, it is not yet a storm cloud.

Once the wispy cirrus clouds that mark ice form at the top of this tallest of clouds – the cumulonimbus – the stage is set for a thunderstorm. Soon after you may spot an anvil shape forming at the top. This is ice spreading under a ceiling of warmer air and marks a mature storm cloud. If a finger is pointing from the anvil it maps the winds at that level and the direction in which the storm is heading.

The storm is about 50 km away and moving from right to left

Beach Clues

Last July I went on holiday with my wife, another couple, our two pairs of sons and eight of their young friends. We drove to

Polzeath, a coastal resort in north Cornwall – the teenagers love it for reasons that include breaking waves and broken hearts.

The gradient of beaches determines the shape of the waves and the experience we have on land and in the sea, and this is what lays the foundations for resorts. Steep beaches lead to steep, fast-breaking, inhospitable waves. Stepping into the water for a swim is not a relaxing activity and there is no point in learning to surf in those conditions.

Sandy beaches normally have a gentler slope to the water than stony ones, which lead to waves that break more gradually. Breaking waves follow simple rules: they steepen as the water gets shallower and break when the depth is 1.3 times the height of the wave. The shallower the gradient of the sand, the longer this process takes, the steadier the rise and fall of each wave. It follows that very shallow beaches combine two things that make for great family experiences: large open sandy areas and friendly, slow-breaking waves that are pleasant to swim or surf in. Change the gradient by a few degrees, the resort would disappear and the teenagers would find a different spot to animate by night.

Watch any wave bump into a stone and it will transport you to the Pacific. Waves are well-behaved: they march across the water in the direction that the wind has pushed them, with no plans of their own and showing no deviancy . . . until they meet the land. The moment the water becomes shallow, waves will bend towards the shallowest side, which is why they always bend towards the land. Look out from the top of a headland that juts into the sea and you'll see waves bending towards the headland and fanning out into the neighbouring bay. This is why we have crescent beaches – the waves continue straight in the deep centre, but fan out at the shallow edges.

The ripples passing over a pebble do exactly what the ocean swell does on meeting an island anywhere in the world and these are the patterns to look for:

1. The orderly parallel lines of open-ocean waves.
2. The slightly rougher patch where waves bounce back off the island and mix with the incoming waves.
3. There are some subtle patterns on either side of the island where there are weak reflections.
4. The waves bend and wrap around the island, meeting again on the far side, forming a cross-hatch pattern.
5. There is a wave shadow, a small calm zone where the waves can't reach.

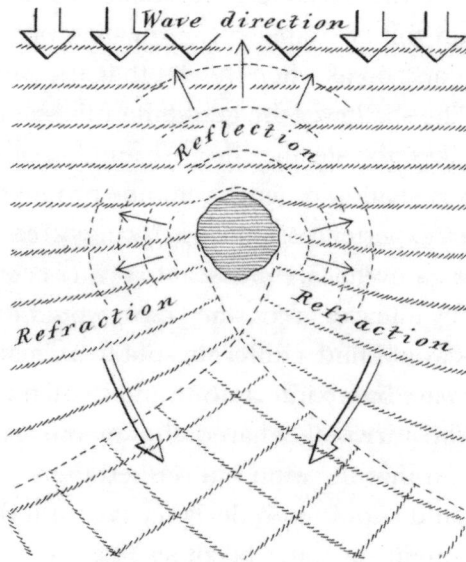

The ripples around a stone resemble
the waves around an island in the sea

Once we know these patterns, we can look for them around stones on a beach, plants in a pond, small islands in rivers or larger ones at sea; I have even seen them in puddles. The only thing that changes is our perspective. On the smallest scale, we can hover over the ripples and watch the patterns unfold with a bird's-eye view. Approaching an island at sea, we cannot look from above, but we can sense the changes in the rhythm of the waves we feel. Pacific Island navigators would concentrate on the change in rhythm in the waves by lying on the deck of their outrigger canoe, closing their eyes and feeling the change in their bodies. Some even sensed it in their testicles.

During a walk on the Cornish beach, I saw the unmistakable prints of a long-departed dog that had been enjoying its trip to the seaside. A sandy beach is the best possible environment for a fast, deep immersion into the world of tracking. The golden rule for fast learning is to remember that the prints we see in the sand or on the land are a story of behaviour more than identity. With a little practice we might learn to differentiate between the more rounded pads and prints of heavy, stocky dogs versus the longer thinner prints of the faster, slender breeds, like the greyhound, but we learn so much more if we focus on the story instead of the individual.

Instead of expending time and energy on the beach trying to identify the exact species of a track's owner, we can use common sense and uncover a narrative. The webbed feet reveal that the bird is an aquatic species, but working out exactly which one might spoil our lunch plans. Instead, we can ask the tracks to tell us what the bird was *doing*. Watch a bird land, walk or hop a few times, then take off on sand that is not too wet or too dry, just moist enough to hold the patterns, and we find a cheat sheet. From then on, we can piece together the story from similar tracks from the moment the bird landed and walked a few steps, a dog ran towards it, and the bird took off.

The dog was doubtless disappointed that the bird was not in the mood for playing, but its tracks contain their own story. We see the sand thrown back as the dog accelerated, the ridge at the side of the print as it pushed off and changed direction, and the steep ridge at the front as it juddered to a halt. When any animal changes their speed or direction on the beach, it leaves telltale patterns in the sand. There are the physical reactions of the sand, the Newtonian equal and opposite reaction to the force of the animal's feet. But there are also rhythm changes and some are easy to spot. The walking and trotting patterns of a dog are very different. When walking, dogs' paws all land separately, but as soon as they start to trot, the rear paws land on top of the front paw prints, a pattern known as 'registering'.

Moist sand is the kindest of teachers, but at first it helps to work backwards. If you notice a person or animal doing anything interesting as they cross the beach, head to that spot and look for the story in the marks. Our brain is extraordinarily good at pairing patterns with meaning* and none of us would exist if that weren't true because it has been a core part of our survival toolkit for thousands of years. The next time we encounter the same pattern we sense familiarity and the time after that we might find that the story of the horse swerving around the dog rises off the beach without us asking for it.

Developing a habit of pairing the actions we witness with patterns on the ground takes a conscious effort at first, but it yields rewards so quickly that we soon find ourselves doing it without thinking. As I brushed my teeth this morning, I watched a green woodpecker hammering the lawn with its beak, hunting for ants most likely. A couple of minutes later I enjoyed looking down at the simple stipple pattern in the earth and added it to my mental collection. If I take the time to note that pattern a couple more times over the coming weeks, my brain will soon see woodpeckers in the land without the bird ever coming into view.

---

* We are too good sometimes: we encounter conspiracy theories, which are nothing more than a brain trying too hard to attach meaning to a pattern or see a pattern where there is none.

Each high tide wipes part of the whiteboard clean and this becomes part of the timeline. As a wave retreats, we have the simplest of tableaux: there are no fresh animal or human tracks, only those left by the sea. Now look above the highest water mark, above the dark strandline furthest from the sea, and you will notice a confused picture – old and new tracks layered on each other. Between these two extremes we find a more stimulating story. We can pinpoint an action to its relationship with the tide and therefore fix it within a time window. The bird's footprints that head towards the sea and disappear at the last high-water mark must be older than the nearby ones that continue over that line. This is one of the oldest sciences, but far from complex. It's common sense, yet invisible to many.

Time Stamps

We can add one more layer to our picture: the weather. A rain shower or a gale will leave marks on the sand and add another time stamp. Rain leaves telltale pockmarks and they can't fall on a footprint that isn't there – any track with this patina of rain points to a creature that passed before the rain; a smooth surface points to action after the rain.

Without much effort, we can recognise the walkers that fall into several clear groups. First we spot those who were here before and after high tide; in the group that were here after high tide we have those who walked before and after the rain shower.

The shorter the time window, the easier it is to read the story but, just as we graduate as children from picture books to text, so we can move from the bottom of the beach uphill in stages. From the fresh smooth board below the recent high-tide mark, through the intertidal zone, all the way to the highest, oldest stories. If a strong easterly went through a week ago and there have been no strong winds since, we will find sand tails that mark the moment: any print that lies under a tail must be more than a week old.

Rising or Falling?

We will step off the beach now and I will leave you with a puzzle for your next visit. Is the tide rising or falling? Spend half an hour on a beach and the answer becomes obvious, but trying to resolve it in a few seconds is more challenging than it might seem.

If the sea was ever perfectly calm it would be easy – if there is a wet zone above it, the tide must be falling; if it is dry it is rising. But the constant tiny fluctuations in the height of the sea and wave actions can make it hard to compare the current height with any wetness or dryness above it. Sometimes it gives up its secrets, but not always. It helps to have another method.

Animals behave differently on a rising and falling tide. A falling tide leaves a new larder of possibilities for scavenging birds and other animals. A rising tide is a less exciting prospect so animal activity tends to be more intense and frenetic on a falling tide.

Water follows many routes back to the sea on a falling tide. We see it running down the sand with the retreating waves, creating some of the broad ripple patterns we met earlier. And lots of it seeps back under the sand, invisible to us. A third route mixes the two.

Some seawater emerges part of the way up the beach, well above the waves, and continues its journey as small streams down to the sea. They start as narrow channels before fanning out to become wide, shallow deltas of thin strands. This creates signature patterns, called 'rill marks', that look like tree roots or strands of hair. If there is a steady flow down these tiny deltas and fresh rill marks are forming, it is more likely to be a falling than a rising tide.

Never arrive at a new beach without trying to gauge whether the tide is heading up or down, especially if you're there to enjoy yourself.

Scorpius and the Delta Aquariids

July is the month for hunting scorpions by night. From northern latitudes, the southern constellation Scorpius can be seen after dark by looking south. It will be low in the sky and, depending on how far north you are, you may find half or more of the Scorpion's body below the horizon. Fortunately, the head and pincers are visible even from quite far north.

When looking for constellations low in the sky, we are often wrestling with light pollution. If searching for Scorpius in testing conditions, we are most likely to lock on to the bright red star Antares first. It is not only the brightest star in this constellation, but fifteenth brightest in the whole night sky and has such a distinct reddish tint that it has been nicknamed 'the rival of Mars' since classical times. (Ares was the Greek god of war, Mars the Roman equivalent.) Antares is the heart of the Scorpion and is high enough that it can be seen from southern Alaska.

To the right (west) of Antares there is a fainter star, Alniyat, and then three others, Acrab, Dschubba and Fang. Those three traditionally form part of the pincers, but once we have found them, we can use the Scorpion to make a compass.

Dschubba is due north of Fang so we can think of these two stars sitting on an imaginary north–south line in the night sky. As they roll across the southern sky, there is a moment when they appear as a vertical line, with Dschubba directly over Fang. Extend the line down to your horizon and you will be looking due south.

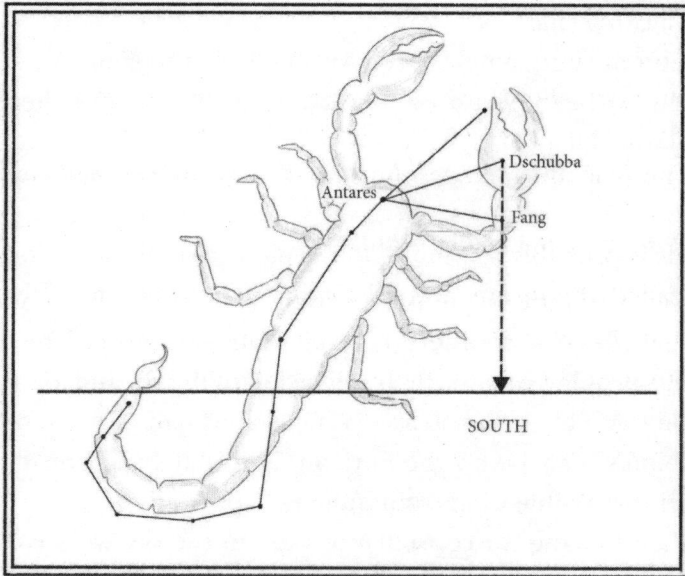

The Scorpius Method

The Scorpius constellation and method are a summer boon: a pleasingly brilliant red star, a satisfyingly recognisable shape and a practical natural navigation compass. Remember that it is ephemeral, gone by autumn, and you are more likely to seek it out – we value beautiful things that make themselves unavailable.

The Delta Aquariids meteor shower starts in the second half of July, normally peaks near the end of the month and continues through much of August. They are not the most dramatic or sociable of shooting stars, as Aquarius is low and best seen past midnight at this time of year. If you are up at this time and under clear skies, the constellation and shower radiant – the point in the sky where the shooting stars appear to emanate from – rolls up from south-east through south, from first dark to the early hours. We can think of the Delta Aquariids as a warm-up act for the Perseids, which really know how to entertain, in August.

Arcania

Time for a couple of arcane tips as we find ourselves in holiday season. There is a basic rule in biogeography that the larger the island, the more plant and animal species live there. The ecologist Tim Blackburn makes the case strongly in *The Jewel Box*:

> This is probably the most robust pattern in all of ecology – called the *species–area relationship*. For example, Great Britain has around 2400 species of moth recorded. Ireland just 1400. The Isles of Scilly off the western tip of Cornwall, perhaps 500. The same pattern is found in more or less every group of organisms counted on more or less every group of islands.*

So, if you find yourself torn between two island holiday choices, go for the bigger one: you'll see more variety in nature.

On a new island, you may experience a strange but not unpleasant sensation as your inner compass adjusts. In landlocked parts of the world, many residents like to combine a general sense of cardinal direction with major inland landscape features, like roads or towns – 'Head south till you hit the main road, which will take you all the way into town.' On islands, our mental map is redrawn to take into account the prominence of the coast and central high ground. North, east, south or west are much less significant on islands and we are likely to find ourselves thinking along the Hawaiian principles of *makai*, meaning 'towards the sea', or *mauka*, towards the mountain.

---

* Blackburn, Tim, *The Jewel Box*, Weidenfeld & Nicolson, 2023, p. 216.

11

August

Lammas Leaves and Harvest Suns

—

Ascending Seeds

—

Heliacal Rising

—

The Perseids

—

The Sagittarius Method

—

The First Narrowing

—

Petrichor

—

Ripening

—

Hidden Colours and Strange Shapes

—

Galling

Lammas Leaves and Harvest Suns

August 1 is Lammas Day, celebrated gratefully as a moment of plenty in traditional Christian and pagan calendars. It occurs at the same time as a second growth in tree leaves. Insect numbers spike early in the growing season and strip trees of foliage, denuding them at a time when they want to be harvesting as much sunlight as possible. They combat this with 'Lammas growth', a second spurt of shoots that replenishes the canopy. Look for a paler flush of young leaves in trees including oak, beech, ash, hawthorn and some conifers too, like Scots pine, yew and some spruces. A flutter of fresh leaves compensates for the quietness of the birds at this time.

The combine harvester has charged out of the farmyard and begun its pendulum swing across the large wheat field by our home. It stores the wheat for a few runs then offloads it into a shadowing grain cart. The straw is laid in lines on the field. After ploughing or harvesting, lines in the fields change the world we see. Look along them and you may pick up small animals at a distance, but look across them and the wildlife disappears. Poachers have used this quirk for centuries to get as close to their prey as possible before they're detected.

The harvest tells us to look towards the western horizon near the end of the day. The sun may appear muted, thanks to high humidity at this time of year, but you will also see extraordinarily rich colours. The warm dusk air is filled with dust* and pollen that scatter some of the light at the blue-green end of the spectrum, enhancing the rich reds and oranges of the setting sun. Sunset colours are seasonal.

Sunrises may be impressive at this time of year also, but the air is clearer at the start of the day, so the August effect is strongest at sunset. By chance, I write this under a redder-than-normal sunrise on the morning after a night of a rising red moon. Wildfires have scorched the land, pushing ash and smoke particles high into the atmosphere, leading to even redder suns and adding a tint to the moon and even the stars.

Ascending Seeds

At the edge of the pond, the willowherb is shrouded in a gossamer veil of fluffy white seeds. On the wilder, far side of the hedge, the thistles have also gone to seed and their prickly green stems have puffy white crowns. I had the perfect view as the seeds took to the air and crossed the hedge in either direction with shifts in the breeze. The dark backdrop of the woodland highlighted every motion of the white airships and I tracked their flight. We are in seed-tracking season.

It was the perfect day for it: sunshine and light breezes, classic high-pressure weather. If the wind is too strong, the seeds whisk past us without pausing to reveal any secrets. If overcast, we lose the intrigue of the thermals. The sport is most fun in the afternoon when the sun has had a chance to warm the land properly.

---

* The drier your part of the world, the more intense the summer dust and the redder the sunsets. An intrepid seventeenth-century German traveller, Johann Wild, observed camel riders in Egypt carrying water up from the Nile in goatskin bags. They dampened the streets of Cairo to stop the dust taking over the air. Nile sunsets are fabled.

I watched the seeds float over the green tendrils of bindweed that poked out of the top of a hedge. Sometimes we're most relaxed when focusing on something that doesn't demand our attention. I watched every motion of the airborne seeds, and an hour later, I had their secrets.

Several wind characters helped them on their journeys. The first was the main breeze: it carried the small puffy cumulus clouds a thousand feet over my head and moved the airborne seeds from right to left, west to east. The second was a horizontal eddy wind: the main wind was wrapping around the woodland ahead of me, leading to an intermittent breeze that blew in the opposite direction. The seeds would float past with the main breeze, then pause and retreat when caught by the eddy. The third was the lifting effect of the hedge: as the wind hit it from either direction, it was forced upwards into a rollercoaster up-and-down wave motion and the seeds had to go along for the ride. The fourth was a small vertical eddy, as the lowest part of the breeze snagged and somersaulted over the hedge. The odd seed fell out of it, dropping in the wind shadow on my side of the hedge, lying on the grass there until plucked up again by another small gust from the other direction.

My favourite journeys began when the breeze died down to near stillness. Now a seed would hitch a lift on a thermal, soaring vertically upwards for several seconds and stopping when they drifted to the edge of the thermal elevator. The dark soil of the field was clearly warmer than the lawn on my side of the hedge because all lift stopped if a seed drifted over the hedge towards me.

The most intriguing puzzles formed when the currents convened. A seed would rise up, then move horizontally for a few seconds, check itself and head back the other way, fall with gravity, then find itself sucked into the bottom of another thermal and rise again. One such seed bobbed and danced against the dark woodland backdrop for several minutes.

Heliacal Rising

The chirping grasshopper sits in a tree and pours down his shrill song continually from under his wings in the season of wearisome heat, then goats are plumpest and wine sweetest; women are most wanton, but men are feeblest, because Sirius parches head and knees and the skin is dry through heat.*

These are the translated words of Hesiod, the ancient Greek poet thought to have been writing about 2700 years ago. Here, he mentions Sirius, the brightest star in the night sky. It can be found by sliding down the belt of Orion, the hunter, and dominates at certain times of year, but not in August. Orion and Sirius command the winter evening sky, so why does Sirius have summer associations in so many classical references?

Stars that are over the tropics – near the equator – are seasonal and disappear behind the sun for certain parts of the year. The stars rise four minutes earlier each day relative to the sun, so if they are behind the sun one week, they will rise earlier enough to be visible just before sunrise a few weeks later. The ancients were keen observers of the moment when stars overtook the sun and thought of it as the 'heliacal rising' time of stars. It had great significance as a seasonal marker and is referred to widely in ancient sources. The heliacal rising of Sirius told the ancient Egyptians to expect the flooding of the Nile, their lifeblood.

The Greeks noted the heliacal rising of Sirius and paired it with the hot, dry days of late summer. Sirius is part of the 'Greater Dog' constellation, Canis Major, and is known as the

---

* Hesiod, *Works and Days* 582–96, in Starr, Chester G., *The Origins of Greek Civilization*, W. W. Norton and Company, 1991, p. 10.

'Dog Star'. Hence the expression 'the dog days' refers to this hot late-summer period. The ancients believed that the sun's energy combined with that of Sirius when the pair were aligned, which led to this oppressively hot period. We now know that Sirius is not responsible – late summer can be swelteringly hot because of the cumulative and lagging effect of the sun's heat, but the expression survives.

At the first hint of dawn, look for Sirius rising over the south-eastern horizon from August onwards. It gets easier the later in the month we look and the higher our latitude.* When you spot the brightest of all stars, expect thermometers and the Nile to rise sharply.

The Perseids

Adolphe Quetelet was a Belgian astronomer, mathematician and many other things in the nineteenth century when excellence in more than one field was still fashionable. He noticed that crime wasn't sprinkled randomly over regions, but spiked in certain neighbourhoods, leading to a key tool in crime analysis and policing, known as the 'cartographic school'.

Quetelet's work ranged from sociology to meteorology, but a common approach underpinned his curiosity. He was a statistician, brilliant at spotting clumps in data and realising there must be a reason for them. Quetelet noticed that shooting stars, thought by many to be the most unpredictable of events, were far from random. Some months were a lot busier than others and he observed, then predicted, correctly, that August was the best of all months to see them.

---

* At the equator, you can catch it from late July, but head up to the Arctic and you'll be waiting deep into September.

August is a mighty month for shooting stars. There is a sharp spike in numbers and a graph of hourly meteor rates against months of the year shows a Matterhorn of activity in August. We still have a steady trickle from the Delta Aquariids, which started in mid-July and continue until about 23 August, but the real cataract comes with the Perseids, a shower that radiates from near the constellation Perseus.

The Perseids can be seen from the second half of July until 24 August, but they reach their peak normally around 12–13 August. Perseus can be found low in the north-eastern sky soon after sunset and we can follow him as he climbs higher in the sky until he is nearly overhead. The show often improves the later we look and can be at its best before dawn. (This is true of many meteor showers: the later we look at the night sky, the closer we are to looking 'forward' as Earth passes through space. We see more raindrops hit the car's windscreen than the rear or side windows.) However, it's well worth heading out at any time between sunset and bedtime, because the Perseids are strong, dependable and sociable, happy to entertain in the often pleasant evening hours at this time of year.

Each meteor shower is unique because it forms as Earth passes through the dust and debris of a comet or asteroid and no two are identical. The Perseids pass through the wake of the Swift–Tuttle comet, which has some slightly larger pieces in its wake, leading to longer, brighter trails for many of the shooting stars. The frequency, brightness, colour, trail length and dependability make the Perseids a marvellous meteor shower.

If you want to improve your experience, try to reduce light pollution in the direction you will be looking. If you are south-west of a big town, the stars over the north-eastern horizon will wallow in that glow. A short journey can change a skyscape dramatically: light pollution drops impressively if we walk a few hundred yards away from any nearby source.

The top of a hill can lift us above the worst light pollution and it is a good time of year for forays to local summits. Academics have found evidence of many historic gatherings and festivals at the tops of hills in early August, including seventy-eight separate hilltop examples in Ireland, where locals would head to celebrate the harvest.

The Sagittarius Method

Scorpius is leaving us and Sagittarius is now rolling across the low southern sky after sunset.

In Greek mythology, Sagittarius is the centaur archer that hunts the scorpion, who is now sensibly fleeing the scene to the west. Sagittarius is better known as 'the teapot constellation' and this is a more helpful and familiar image. There are a few things we can note about the position of Sagittarius in the sky. First, this is the direction in which to point a rocket if you're hoping to head towards the centre of our galaxy, the Milky Way (and where we find full moons in June). Second, this is where the sun will be at the winter solstice.

The modern observer may not take a keen interest in the stars that sit behind the sun as it obscures them, but the ancients were obsessed by this. Before Copernicus, the sun was seen as passing through the constellations, which had great significance for our ancestors. The most southerly constellation that the sun reaches on its journey across the stars is Sagittarius in late December. We can't see the constellation then, but August is our chance. Come Christmas time, you may or may not be warmed by the idea that you have seen and know what lies behind the sun.

If you are struggling to find Sagittarius, try sliding down the left side of the Navigator's Triangle, from Deneb to Altair, and keep going down until you find the teapot. Look just above the spout and, if stargazing conditions are kind, you may spot a white smudge. This is the Lagoon Nebula, a giant cloud of dust, plasma and gases – think of it as the steam from the spout.

Now to turn the teapot into a compass. The method sounds more daunting than it is. Have a quick read through, then check the illustration below.*

Imagine a line that runs from the bottom left of the teapot (the bottom of the handle) across to the top-right star: we have an east–west celestial line. When the two stars are at the same height, picture a vertical line that cuts them in two and extend this down to the horizon. That gives us south.

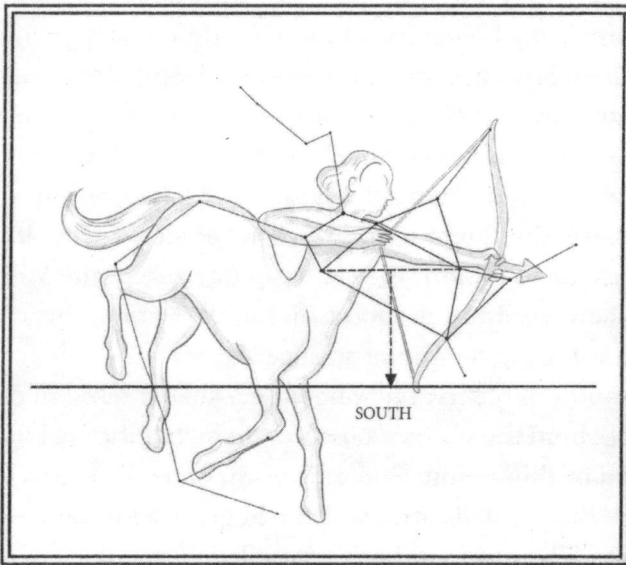

SOUTH

The Sagittarius Method

---

* If you are living in the northern regions, you will only spot Sagittarius low in the southern sky and will not need a method to find general direction. It can be helpful, though, if you travel south and need its help. As with all natural navigation methods, it is knowledge that is satisfying and enjoyable to possess, beyond necessity.

The First Narrowing

A couple of years ago I went for a walk in Oman with a local man who knew the old ways. Winter in desert regions can teach us a lot about late summer closer to home.

I learned much on that walk with Ahmed that is not relevant to our gathering of seasonal wisdom – did you know that camels can act as a compass? Hot camels, like butterflies, face the sun so that it heats less of their body. They tend to face east in the morning and west late in the day. This was not something I had ever noticed, even though I'd spent plenty of time with camels in the past. I went through my photos of Arabian and African deserts, and can't verify it, but Ahmed assured me it is true. (I don't know how it fits with something the British author Robert Twigger once told me over lunch in Dorset: 'At the end of the day, camels turn to face their starting point.')

My Omani walk shines a light on our experience of August.

By August, the cumulative effect of the sun's time over the northern hemisphere is taking its toll. The land dries, which changes everything from now until the autumn rains arrive. Late summer can be a challenging time for all organisms and life narrows its focus towards water. My time in dry Oman rekindled my understanding of this key relationship. Almost everything Ahmed pointed out could be tethered back to the availability of fresh water.

'The dragonflies face the water,' Ahmed said, pointing to some ground water a dozen yards away. We followed a trail of goat droppings: they revealed the tested route over that ridge to water in the neighbouring valley. A line of date palms announced that water was available near the surface and acacia trees showed where it could be found by digging deeper.

'Don't be lazy. My grandpa taught me to move is to learn,' Ahmed said, as he led me up steeper ground. From the ridge, we looked down on a dry valley, arid brown rocks broken by a handful of white buildings and scattered goats.

'Farm animals face the sea near the coast and the mountains when far from the sea. For the cool air.' The animals were clearly familiar with the sea and the katabatic breezes we met in June. Ahmed pointed to the farm below us. I asked about the washing-line; something about it looked odd to me. 'Those white shirts are to scare the cougars and foxes away.'

The goats roamed over a huge area and I asked if they ever lost any. I should have guessed the answer: 'If they have not been taken, they find them at the places the water collects.'

I asked Ahmed about seasons in particular. He pointed to the date palms, 'When in flower, brown snapper is ready.'

Head off the beaten track, or back in time, and we find seasonal pairings move centre stage, sometimes literally. Aristophanes, the comic Greek playwright, had one of his characters tell another that the song of the cuckoo signalled that it was time to harvest wheat and barley. Aristophanes being Aristophanes, the whole passage actually alluded to sex, but he was able to assume his audience would understand the seasonal pairing of bird call and farm rhythms. (Later in the play he expands on the theme of seasonal pairings. The cranes departing for Libya mark when farmers should sow crops and sailors stay ashore; the kite rings the bell for sheep-shearing, and the swallows' arrival heralds the switch from winter to summer clothing – like our 'Ne'er cast a clout, till may is out'.)

Ahmed told me his grandfather could divine the location of water from the shape of the rocks within the cliffs – smooth and rounded were strong signs of water. We can see the same patterns near seasonal watercourses at this time of year: dry rounded stones in summer mark where water will flow strongly in a few months' time.

'When the pigeons fly low, there is water,' Ahmed said, as we began our descent and a flock passed below us in the valley. We can practise the same skill: note how birds follow lines that take them over the high ground and any trees or other obstacles. Any dip below a line is a clue to a nest, food or water.

Towards the end of our time together, we passed a graveyard and Ahmed confirmed that the graves were aligned perpendicular to Qibla, the direction of Mecca. He then showed me how flushes of green in the hills mapped recent localised showers. We will also see green flushes and new flowers blossom after late summer rain breaks a dry spell.

Before we said goodbye, I told Ahmed I had heard about someone in a nearby village I might visit and asked if he knew them. Ahmed said he did and asked, 'Will you be having coffee?'

I said I wasn't sure and noticed intensity in his expression. He revealed that the person I was talking about was traditional and I should know the language that surrounds coffee-drinking. If I placed the small tumbler of coffee down when half full, I was silently requesting more, or dates, if they were being offered. If I shook my cup from side to side when I put it down it meant I had had enough. If I put it down empty but without any motion, it was a sign I wanted to talk business. Ahmed had signalled to me that he understood and appreciated my love of signs and hidden meanings. I thanked him profusely and we said our goodbyes.

We will always notice more in late summer if we take inspiration from indigenous cultures in arid regions. The Kalumburu people of the northern Kimberley region of Western Australia have different terms for landscape niches that reveal a relationship with water. *Djindi* is the greenery that surrounds a freshwater source which lasts year-round. A different Aboriginal people from the Great Sandy Desert, another region of Western

Australia, have many names for landscape features that include water:

Djunu – a soak, revealing water below the surface, that can be found by digging

Waniri – a rock hole containing long-lasting water

Giligi – a river that runs occasionally but can leave water in holes

Walgir – a billabong, off-shoot of a main river

Baldju – temporary swamp

Waran – a claypan area that holds water after rain

Baragu – a salt lake that offers drinkable water in some seasons

The notable thing about these names is that they relate to water availability by place *and* time. Indigenous language maps not just the places where water will be found, but their dependability and how this relates to seasons and conditions. This same relationship to water and time can be found as echoes in the traditional place names in many parts of the world. 'Bourne' is an old English word meaning small stream; the town of Bournemouth is found at the mouth of the river Bourne. Water flows from a spring in a suburb called Springbourne. Winterbourne is the name given to streams that flow only after rain and dry up in summer to leave a line of rounded stones.

Indigenous tribespeople know that animal behaviour follows annual and diurnal patterns; the behaviour of birds at dusk can reveal which of these landscape features are worth exploring. Bees, wasps and ant trails provide a final guide when close. If humans are still sensitive to these patterns, we can be sure animals are too. That is why some prey animals avoid watering holes at dusk or night – if behaviour patterns are obvious, it's too easy for predators.

Late summer is when we taste these skills for ourselves. Try to tune into the places in your part of the world that hold fresh water permanently, those that hold it for some time after rain and places that dry quickly. These zones are part of your map of animal activity. The pond in our garden is one of the few fresh-water options for animals in the area in late summer. Dragonflies gather by day, pigeons and other birds swoop in at dusk, and the bats fly extraordinary lines as the last light fades. One of my favourite August dusk activities is to read by the pond as the birds swoop in for a drink. Then, a little unkindly, I time my standing up to catch them near the bottom of their dive, forcing them to climb steeply away before they have had a drink or touched the water. The prize I'm after is to catch the pairs of ripples on the water surface from the down-thrust of the wings. I love that water has a memory of the beats of the wings of a bird that never touched it.

Petrichor

This morning, I listened to an excitable presenter celebrating overnight rain on BBC Radio 4, this in a country that is teased about its wet weather – 'How can you tell it's summer in the UK? The rain is warmer.' Any change from dry to wet at this time of year can be emotional.

After any dry spell, rain releases actinomycetes bacteria spores from the soil and, with plant oils, this creates a signature scent known as 'petrichor', from the Greek words *petros*, meaning 'stone' (someone petrified has turned to stone), and *ichor*, meaning 'liquid flowing through the veins of the gods'.

The scent of petrichor seems to generate positive emotions and there may be scientific reasons for that. One theory is that our ancestors' lives depended on finding water after dry spells and sensitivity to it could save lives. Perhaps some part of our lizard brain still associates the smell with life itself and rewards us for detecting it with positive feelings. We can pick up surprisingly low concentrations of these airborne chemicals, and desert animals, like camels, are super-sensitive to the odour, allowing them to locate water from 50 miles away.

Many animals favour direct sunlight when the air is cool. That is why we find clouds of flying insects in sunbeams in early spring. However, by August, many animals are shielding themselves from excess heat and dehydration, which can lead to spikes in activity on cooler cloudy days at this time of year.

Gardeners often yearn for rain in August, but grumble when it spoils plans for a day out. They are not the only ones – there is an Islamic prayer for such times: 'Allah, please let the rain fall all around us but not on us.'

Ripening

Some birds have left already, others are preparing to migrate south with the sun. As the land dries, berries ripen and the resident birds switch from focusing on food in moist soil, like worms and grubs, to fruits.

An old bridge led me over a dry stream – a winterbourne. I doubled back and scrambled down the shallow bank until I was standing on the dusty silt of the stream's bed. Water-crowfoot thrived in patches, its pretty white and yellow flowers facing the southern sun. I clambered out and searched for a high point. I wanted to find a vantage point to survey the green fields that rolled to the base of the hills away to the south.

Colour had leached from the grass and it was now verdant in only two zones: in the lowest points of the valley and over the deepest soils of the fields. Elsewhere the green had given way to yellows and browns. We have reached the time of year when grasses yield secrets about the soil below them – archaeologists find ditches and stone-works by reading colours in grasses. Below drought-ravaged plants there are old walls or foundations, and below tall, green grasses the deep soil of old ditches. Those patterns shone out from the first ever aerial photos taken in late summer and led to many new discoveries of old settlements, but we can spot them as we explore on foot.

'I expected more colour to be honest,' one woman said to another, near the entrance to West Dean Gardens; there have been grand gardens on this site near my home in West Sussex for four hundred years. Like me, the two women had just arrived and were scanning the flowerbeds and lawns beyond. The gardens had lost colour from their peak earlier in the year but, as I was to discover, there was plenty still to be found: it had migrated from the petals to the fruits.

The walled garden is the jewel in the crown at West Dean and I made my way through an ornate metal gate to an orchard of apples and pears. Many apples lay strewn across the grass. A pair of gardeners stopped what they were doing and walked over to me.

Tessa and David introduced themselves. I explained my simple mission and they led me to the Sussex Mother apple tree.

'It doesn't look particularly attractive,' David said, over the apple bucket that hung from a strap around his neck.

'But it tastes fantastic!' Tessa added, handing me my own to try.

David continued, 'It's not pretty, with brown flush over yellow, but looks don't matter for a cottage apple. A tree that ripens in stages is good in a cottage garden, because you wanted a few apples each day. We've been picking this for three weeks now.'

'Commercial growers want the crop to be ready all at once,' Tessa said, and explained that the traditional way of harvesting apples for personal or local use would be to move with the season over the tree, plucking a few from the warm south side of the tree one week, moving to the cooler shaded parts of the tree towards the end of the season. I bit into mine and it had as good a flavour as any I can recall and made supermarket offerings taste as if they had never seen the sun. Tessa lamented that knowledge was ebbing with the generations, only the older visitors really understanding the richness of what they were looking at. 'The younger visitors might show interest, but they have no . . . nostalgia.'

We talked about the way the red colour revealed the southern sun and they grinned.

'For that you want the Red Devil!' David said, and led us towards it. 'It's so sensitive to light, you can actually stencil letters on it.' I asked if he'd done that and he said he had: 'WD for West Dean. But I couldn't find a satisfactory method of getting a stencil to stick on an apple.'

'Really you want to stencil "Mine, mine, mine" on it because it's so tasty!' Tessa added, handing me one from the ground. 'The windfalls are usually lovely and sweet.' I bit into it and was amazed at the flavour.

Taste marked the month. July had added a flush of colour to the fruits, but August brought sweet ripening.

Hidden Colours and Strange Shapes

I thanked them both, followed a tip from Tessa to check out the hydrangeas, and left the walled garden through another pretty metal gate. I passed the ladies from earlier, who remained cheerless: 'It's been the worst year for butterflies for many years. And they are indicators for all the other insects. Not good. Not good at all.' I stepped off the path as they passed me. A bee was working busily on the vibrant Mexican sunflower behind them.

In the shade of an oak, lords-and-ladies thrust up from a scraggly bed and made a fine traffic light. The berries ripen from top to bottom, bright red at the top, yellow-amber in the middle and green near the bottom. The head gardener would soon be despatching someone to that bed to assault the bindweed that ran over many bushes. I felt only goodwill towards the white trumpet flowers that pointed the way out of the darkness in the direction I needed to head.

The Sunken Garden was a few steps below the surrounding gardens but this was enough to cause problems. Chalk words on a blackboard: 'Due to disease and prolonged cold temperatures, a number of shrubs in this area have deteriorated to a point where a new approach was needed.'

New plants had been introduced to cope with the cold of this frost pocket, which also suffered 'extremes of drought and flooding'. Tough orpines and thymes were coping in the coarse sand, but there was a new problem. The sand beds didn't look like flowerbeds and people kept walking over them.

Over the following hour, I learned a new way to see late summer colours with the help of a mighty copper beech. The rich red-purple anthocyanin colour was deepest on the sunny southern side and penetrated only a little way into the leaves on the shaded north side of the tree, which is what we should expect. But a surprise had me snapping a series of photos with my phone: there were shifts in colour from the bottom to the top of the tree. I was not expecting that. The colour mix couldn't be explained by the north–south differences. I walked all around the grand tree a few times, then took off my hat to let my head cool in its shade. Eventually the puzzle solved itself; perhaps the cool helped my brain fit the pieces together. As with so many such conundrums, in hindsight the answer was wonderfully simple.

Whenever we look at any large tree, we view it from a series of quite different angles so we see a different collection of leaves depending on where we look. When staring at the lowest parts of a tree, we're looking close to horizontal and our gaze penetrates deeper into foliage – we see through the layers. When we look up towards the top of a tall tree, our eyes skim the surface: we see hardly any leaves behind the outer ones. In early summer, this doesn't change what we see dramatically, as there is less variety in the colour of the leaves at that time of year. But come late August, the colours at the extremities have changed and this is when the effect really kicks in. Try it: find a tall broadleaf tree, stand a few paces from the edge of the canopy and compare the colours you see when looking low and high.

I reached the hydrangeas and it was worth it. They were the 'panicled' variety – shaped like rounded pyramids – and their tips pointed south. But the real joy came in the colours. Tessa had explained that the fashion over recent years had been for varieties that segued from one colour to a different one over the season. There were 'vanille' flowers that changed from bright white to cream, 'limelight', which morphed from pale green to white, and those I saw in front of me, 'fraise', which turned pink with time.

My path through the gardens would madden a planner, snaking and swerving from one delight to another. There, the giant horse chestnut tree whose branches sagged a little with conkers in their bright green spiky cases. The leaves were a surprising brown, thanks to the mottled patchwork of the horse chestnut leaf miner – caterpillars that have invaded and devoured the leaves. They attack many trees in the *Aesculus* and *Acer* families and in such numbers that the effects are hard to miss and the discoloration at first tricks us into thinking autumn has leaped forward. Fortunately, the timing of the larvae of this moth is the saving of the trees: they do huge damage, but just late enough in the season that the trees do not suffer life-threatening consequences – the serious photosynthesis work has been done for the year.

Galling

I meandered back to the dry stream bed near the entrance and there found that another insect's progeny had left their mark on the oak trees. Galls were spread across one side. Galls are abnormal growths that can be found on most parts of plants, but are conspicuous at this time of year near the tips of some broadleaf-tree branches. They can be caused by fungi or bacteria, but the most interesting and recognisable forms are home to the next generation of insects. Oak trees are host to at least five hundred different insects and a great place to look for these knobbly protrusions. Some, like the artichoke gall, are easy to spot and identify, while others are more mercurial in their form and colours. All are peculiar and intriguing. I found a mix of galls on those oaks, many knopper oak galls, home to a small wasp. They were all on the warmer south side of the tree, none on the cool, shady north.

12

September

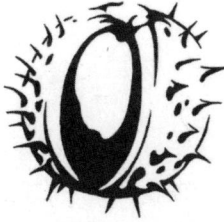

Senescence

—

Falling Leaves

—

Equinox

—

Mists, Dew and September Breezes

—

Kung Fu at the Lake

—

Equinoctial Gales

—

A September Smorgasbord

—

Late Harvests

Senescence

In September we start our autumn vigil, keeping an eye open for signs of senescence, the process of seasonal ageing. If we wait until everyone is talking about the leaves turning on the trees, we will have missed a hundred small changes. Brown leaves on trees tell us we're in the latter stages of plants' preparation for winter. Work has been going on behind the scenes for many weeks. Trees set winter buds well before any major colour changes.

Green plants constantly replenish the stocks of chlorophyll in their leaves through the growing season. We can think of the chlorophyll in leaves as a green mask. As the nights grow longer and temperatures drop, trees stop replenishing the chlorophyll and the mask slips, revealing the compounds – flavonoids and carotenoids – that are responsible for the yellows, oranges and reds we see. The trees that offer dependably strong yellow colours each year – birches, limes, sycamores and many poplars – are rich in flavonoids, for example. Each of these chemicals helps protect the chlorophyll from the harmful effects of solar radiation so we see stronger colours on the sunniest side of a tree, typically the south side, making a sublime seasonal colour compass.

It is harder to predict change in autumn by plant families than it is in spring. It works for a few trees. Horse chestnuts go early, whereas the leaves of beeches, oaks and poplars, are late to change colour and fall. But some families have members at different points of the spectrum: red maples go very early, sugar maples surprisingly late.

We can expect a general progression from high to low. Spring moves upwards, but autumn flows downwards from the top of the canopy to the forest floor. However, there are a few subtleties to this top–down idea, and once we know them, we see a more intricate picture.

Understorey trees tend to be slightly later than canopy trees for changing colours and falling leaves, but the differences are smaller than in spring and there is a lot of variability from year to year. The understorey trees are more sensitive to temperature than the canopy trees, and small trees can be some of the earliest and latest to turn in the same year. Small trees in bright areas – in the open, at edges or in gaps – turn before the understorey trees of the same species in shady places.

It is not the height of the tree that is critical but the distance of the leaves from the roots. Autumn accelerates with thirst. The tops of most trees have leaves that are furthest from the roots so this works well as a general rule, but notice how any very broad trees, individuals that are wider than they are tall, have leaves that turn at their widest points as early as any of their top ones.

If roots struggle to access plentiful water, a tree will turn before nearby well-quenched trees. I pass a tall beech regularly with roots that are boxed in by a road. Its leaves turn a couple of weeks before the beeches in the roomy soil of the woods behind it and fastest on the roadside. If a tree is stressed by drought, disease, harsh winds or hungry herbivores, autumn comes early. Any tree that turns before neighbouring trees of the same kind is unhappy about something.

Look for any trees that have busy paths over their roots, especially trails that run over the 'drip line', where fine roots harvest rain water that runs off the edge of the canopy. The leaves over the path will change colour early or the branch may fail altogether. Many trees pretend to be in good health in June, but reveal their worries in September.

It is time to think about shapes and neighbours. If you are looking at a wood of climax trees, a broad high canopy of foliage of even height, you can expect to see the colours change near the top and work downwards. Canopy trees rise on a bare trunk to a good height, then spread out at the top. They have a very different shape from isolated trees, which are shorter and take on a more rounded, globular shape. If a large tree stands on its own, we will see autumn colours crowd in from the sides as well as the top.

Tall climax trees turn from the tops and outside in, but colonising trees, like birches, turn from the inside out. That is a simplification: it's not as neat as the leaves nearest the trunk turning first and a wave spreading outwards from birches, but we do find plenty of leaves near the heart of these trees turning at the same time as those at the outer edge. It creates a mottled, patchwork appearance.

Temperature has interesting effects. Cold snaps bring changes forward, but also intensify colours by trapping sugars in the leaves, which increases the production of anthocyanins; cold sunny spells set up the best shows. Prolonged mild temperatures delay autumn and lead to less impressive colours.

If we zoom in to look at the warming effects of sunlight on individual trees, we meet the phenomenon I call the '*Blade Runner* effect'. Near the end of the cult 1982 movie, *Blade Runner*, a character finds out that their time is up, they are about to die after a brief, but very intense life: 'The light that burns twice as bright burns half as long – and you have burned so very, very brightly, Roy.' The leaves in the warmest part of each tree will turn before the cooler parts and lead to trends that are helpful for natural navigation – the sun warms the south side of trees more than the shaded north side.

When light, warmth and thirst work together, the effects compound to create striking and helpful patterns. I walked across a park near Brighton on a sunny September afternoon and came to a clump of tall mixed broadleaf trees with a tint of brown in their highest leaves. Then I saw a magnificent Golden Rain tree that had indeed turned golden, but only in one place, the top right as I saw it. The highest southern leaves had received more light, warmed more and grown thirstier than all the other leaves and changed colour first – I could sense I was walking east.

Nearer home, there are four wild cherry trees that I see most days and, like most wild cherries, they are towards the edge of the forest. Near the middle of the day, two are in shade and two are open to the sun. On 24 September, I walked past all four: the shaded pair was well clothed in green, with only a handful of yellowing leaves. Roughly a quarter of the leaves on the sunlit trees had changed to yellow or pink. And the spread wasn't even over the individual trees. The tips of the longest branches in the sunny spots had few green leaves – almost all had turned to yellow, gold or pink.

Falling Leaves

Once the leaves have lost their greens and adopted their autumn colours, we can look for patterns in the way they fall. Some of the traits that help predict the marching order in spring break down in autumn. For example, age is more important in spring than autumn. For most trees, there is little difference in the timing of colour changes or leaf fall in juvenile and adult trees of the same species. There are a few exceptions: very young elms hold on to their leaves noticeably longer than the older trees. Keep in mind that trees are not a single age: they have old parts and young. New shoots can have a much later season – the sprouts around the base of lime trees appear a vibrant green in late October, many weeks after the leaves at the top of these tall trees have started falling.

Understorey trees do not stay in leaf significantly longer than the trees above them. This is odd if we think about it: logic suggests they should. As we have seen, the small trees come out earlier in spring to grab some light before the canopy throws shade over them, so why wouldn't they want to hang around after the canopy leaves fall to cash in on sunlight at the end of the season? It's because of the slow start and finish of the tall trees. If we focus on sunlight levels, we can see why the early strategy works, but the late one is too risky. In late March, the sun is over the equator and high enough in the sky that it is providing lots of solar energy. Critically, the canopy trees haven't got going, there is little shade and it's well worth the small plants making an early dash for light.

Fast-forward to the end of September and the sun is just as high and strong as it is in late March, but the canopy is still fulsome and casting deep shade. By the time all the canopy leaves have fallen, the sun will be much lower and, crucially, the risk of frost will have shot up. Small trees, shrubs and wildflowers can harvest equinox levels of light in spring, but not in autumn. If they wait late enough for leafless canopy, the risk of freezing is too great.

There is one more big advantage to early spring over late autumn photosynthesis – there is normally plenty of water in March but September can be cruel for thirsty plants. This explains why the smaller plants tend to shut up shop around the same time as the canopy trees. If you can't beat them, join them.

The wind plays a big part in stripping leaves from trees, especially as the autumn gales arrive. We find trees are stripped bare on the side the winds come from, which is often the prevailing wind direction in each region. In the UK, the exposed south-west side of trees is bare before the more sheltered north-east, and this starts near the top, where winds are stronger, and moves lower.

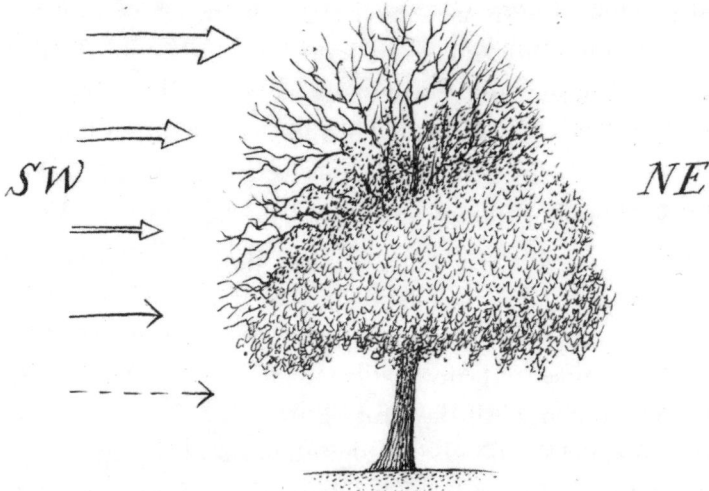

Autumn leaf loss patterns

Equinox

On 22 September (occasionally the twenty-first or twenty-third) we have our second equinox of the year. In some ways it mirrors the March equinox – the sun is once more over the equator and rises and sets due east and west again – but its direction of travel is the opposite to the March equinox. The sun has spent six months over the northern hemisphere, rising and setting north of east and west all of that time, and is now heading south quickly. It will rise and set south of east and west until the March equinox.

The sun is now falling precipitously in the sky. The midday sun drops at least ten degrees in September, more than an extended fist, which is roughly double the distance it falls in July. Shadows grow noticeably longer. From the end of this month, we will have to wait six months before we see the sun high in the sky again.

The rapid rate of change near the equinoxes is helpful to nature: it makes the key seasons more obvious. As we have seen, the plants and animals are gauging the length of the day, which changes little in June or December, but dramatically at this time. It is ironic that most organisms find it easier to get ready for falling temperatures by sensing the rapidly shortening days, not the cooling of the air.

Mists, Dew and September Breezes

I walked out earlier than the sun's first rays to enjoy the last moments of Sirius in the south-east. Then I felt the chill in my toes and cursed my choice of footwear: with a clear sky in September, I should have known to put boots on. Dew soaked into my socks.

I walked the walk of the soggy-shoed explorer, lifting each foot higher than normal. I must have looked like a heron, a big one. On reaching the fence that separates our garden from farmland and keeps most deer and some pheasants out, I gazed across the land. Squinting as the sun neared the crest of the hill opposite, I looked downhill. And there it was, the ribbon of cotton, a thin dense mist lining the lowest ground, hugging the dip in the land. Dew and morning mists are cousins and share some habits. For either to form, we need moist air, cool temperatures and clear skies.

Falling temperatures make dew and mist more likely. When the temperature drops, the amount of water that the air can hold as a gas falls and it turns to liquid – look above the spout of a boiling kettle and you'll see there is a clear gap just above the opening and the steam appears just above it. The water leaves the spout as a hot gas, clear and invisible, then cools and condenses to form water, easy to spot as steam. Dew or mist follows the same condensation process on a grander stage.

Mists and dew need cool air in the morning, and in September that is most likely when the heat has escaped from the land into space after a night of cloud-free skies. Clouds act as a blanket and the land won't cool sufficiently overnight under an eider-down of overcast skies.

The perfect sequence for mist and dew in September is for the dry weather to break with a period of heavy rain, then for that to move through, leaving clear skies and cool air. A cold front is tailor-made for this: it brings unsettled weather, often including storms, and is followed by cool clear air, known as the 'clear slot'. Let's split up the cousins and look at each in turn to see the maps they make of the land.

Walk across some dewy grass and you'll notice the dew is thick in some places and bare in others. For dew to form, we need cold ground – if the ground isn't cold, there is no way the gaseous water vapour will condense into dewdrops. But why are some grassy areas covered with dew and not others?

Notice how the dew stops under the cover of trees, bridges or anything else that acts as a blanket overnight and blocks the heat's escape. A single jutting low branch can create a dew-free strip in the grass.

Now notice how the dew doesn't cover all surfaces equally. It is thick on the open grass, but stops at the flowerbed. It covers the tabletop, but the stone terrace around the table is dry. In each of these cases, there is no cover and nothing blocking the heat's escape. The answer lies below the surface. Some mater-ials conduct heat from below better than others. Stone conducts better than mud, which conducts better than grass. Plastic is a poor conductor of heat. The stone terrace lets heat flow from the warmer ground below into the stone, making it too warm for dew. But the plastic table is covered with dew because all of the heat escaped upwards but none has flowed from below. The result is a cold tabletop, lots of condensation and dew in great fat drops. The cold grass has dew, but the warmer soil of the flowerbed has none.

After savouring Sirius and the sunrise, I walked back and saw my footprints in the dew as smudged lines of darker green. There were a few small dark patches where the birds had landed and hopped about. I once heard that rabbits won't travel over dew because it makes their bellies cold, and while I don't know if that is true or not, I do know that no animal can walk over dew without leaving a trace. For a laugh, try crossing a dewy lawn without leaving a footprint.

I celebrated the dew and mist of that cool bright morning by looking at my *Heiligenschein*, the bright halo that forms around the shadow of our head as the dewy grass reflects more sunlight directly back to us from that spot than anywhere else.

Morning mists in late summer and early autumn tell a slightly different story from that of dew. Mists also need moist, cool conditions and this is likely after rain has passed through and the sky is now clear. But mist forms in the air, not on the ground, so we find it in places where cool air gathers. Cold air is dense and flows downhill. Autumn morning mists congregate in low points; they are fond of forming thick bands in valleys and dips. If you walk down into them you will feel the temperature drop: they have mapped a chill zone.

Mists can also map the flow of the air. There are unlikely to be strong winds if you are looking at these types of mists as they form under calm clear conditions, but it is quite common just before sunrise to notice that cool air is still flowing downhill, mists creeping towards the lowest point in the landscape. The next stage is for the sun to rise and start to warm the land below the mist, which then warms the air, which rises, lifting and dissolving the mist. With patience we can watch mists move downhill slowly, then start lifting after sunrise. Once you have spotted mist on the move, you will feel ready to sense gentle flows and breezes on clear mornings without the help of the mist.

Kung Fu at the Lake

I joined a French anthropologist, Dr David Jaclin, for a short walk in Sussex. David is a professor at the University of Ottawa and was researching practices around the world related to bodies of water. He had got in touch to say he was currently travelling in Europe with his young family in a campervan; he would like to meet and discuss my approach to reading water. Less than a week later we were walking around Swanbourne Lake, near Arundel, under blue September skies.

We circled the lake and exchanged perspectives on topics that ranged from trees, through environmentalism to the water that was a constant presence on our left. I mentioned that non-randomness underpinned my approach to water – every ripple has a cause that we can divine, if we take the time to read and understand them. David smiled and told me that *kung fu* in China refers to the patience and dedication needed to master a skill, not specifically a martial art. Near the end of our short walk, he asked how I develop my own skills and I tried to answer, but realised that my explanation was neither particularly helpful nor insightful. I changed tack.

'I like to pick two things in the landscape and find the link,' I said, as we paused in an opening between waterside willow trees. 'And the less obvious the connection, the more instructive I find it. I will pick something that captures my attention, then choose something else, apparently unrelated, and try to find the deductive bridge between them. It is sometimes easy, sometimes difficult, but I hold on to the idea that it can never be impossible, because everything is connected if we look deep enough. Like these ripples.' I pointed at the ripples that spread across the otherwise tranquil waters before us. 'I've picked them. Now you pick something that grabs your attention, perhaps something that initially appears to have no connection to the ripples.'

'Anything?' David said.

'Anything,' I replied.

We stood in silence and I looked away to give him space to find something that worked for him.

'OK. That line there.' He pointed across the small lake to the rising hill on the far side. 'The line between light and dark on that side.'

'The line separating sunlight and shade?' I checked, as we looked at the line that marked where the shadow of the hill behind us was rising slowly up the hill opposite, to the east of us.

'Yes.'

'Would you agree that there is no obvious connection between that line and the ripples we're looking at in the water?'

He paused. 'Well . . . maybe, no . . . I think maybe it will take some steps, maybe three or four steps . . .'

It took me less time than it often does. Luck plays a part in this game, as it does in every other. I turned back to David, 'Can you feel that on the back of your neck?' I touched the back of mine. 'The coolness of the breeze?'

David took a moment, then said, 'Yes, I can.'

'We looked at the wind and the clouds earlier and that breeze we feel on our necks is not the direction the wind was blowing even twenty minutes ago. The line between dark and sun on that hill opposite is showing us the division between warm and cooling land – and therefore the line between rising and descending air. This is setting up new local winds and these are blowing across the water, setting up new ripples, on top of the ones formed by the waterbirds. There is a weak cool breeze rolling downhill from the steep shady hill behind us. This is a new breeze. It is the feeblest of katabatic winds and is leaving the faintest of footprints in the ripples we see in that water.'

David's face lit up and he explained that he lives in a country of mountains and water and was very familiar with katabatic winds and much stronger ones than we were feeling then. We first met them in June, but September is a good month for sensing these winds forming, weak or strong, as they are powered by differentials in temperature; this is an excellent time of year for dramatic contrasts. The September sun does good work during the day, heating the land to a warm temperature, before the rapid cooling that takes place once it falls below the horizon.

Dew, mists and breezes reflect a shift in power from warm to cool at this time of year, each in their own way. They make maps and tell us stories about the land, sky, water, sun, wind, clouds and animals.

Equinoctial Gales

In late September and into October, we may experience a sudden break in the weather and even storms. When this happens, the expression 'equinoctial gales' will bubble up in conversations. When reading seasonal signs, we must remain on guard, always sensitive to the difference between causation and correlation.

Does sunscreen cause shark attacks? Can ice cream turn us into geniuses? If we dug into the data, we would find plenty of evidence that sunscreen sales are highest near the times of most shark attacks. We would also notice that countries with a high consumption of ice cream produce more Nobel Prize winners than those with little taste for it. In each case there is, of course, no causal link between the two. Sunscreen sales are highest when most people are on the beach, which is when shark attacks are more probable. Nobel Prizes tend to be won by people in wealthy countries and those populations eat more ice cream. In these examples, there is correlation but no causation.

There is correlation, causation and a secret ingredient in the relationship between equinoxes and gales. We get more gales in late September and early October than we do in midsummer, but we get even more in midwinter. Strong winds are least common near midsummer in the British Isles, and most likely near midwinter. These are the times when the sun is lodged, briefly, at the extremes of north and south, which sets up air masses at their northern and southern extremes too. As the sun moves south from summer to autumn, some air-pressure systems also move south, which make gales and unsettled weather more likely. However, when we talk about equinoctial gales in September, it probably has as much to do with psychology as meteorology. The secret ingredient is emotion and the clue is in March.

We experience plenty of strong winds and storms in March but, in my experience, equinoctial gales rarely feature in conversation. I believe something historical, personal and very human is happening. Near the end of summer we are braced, already wary of the coming onslaught of winter and looking for clues that the gates are close to breaking down. Gales in March seem like more bad weather piled on top of months of challenging skies – no interesting shift for us to pick up on, no good or bad omens in more of the same. But a couple of days of blustery wet weather in September signify change, from easy to tough. Autumn is the outrider of winter.

The hardships of winter remain real to us today, but were existential to our ancestors. The pairing of gales with the equinox is not statistically sound, but we hold on to the idea and the expression as an echo of our forebears' seasonal anxiety.

A September Smorgasbord

On my way to Laughton, East Sussex, I took a break and stepped out of the Land Rover. The clunk of the car door disturbed the thrushes that were flitting about the rowan berries. In berry season, look at the leaves near the berries. You'll notice that those nearest a bumper fruit crop tend to show signs of age before others. As we have seen, stress accelerates ageing, and parenthood, even for plants, is exhausting. Each time my foot landed, I scared off more of the birds that were ravaging the wild fruit all around. Berries mean birds and together they tell us to be on the lookout for autumn arrivals from further north.

I've heard talk about a bumper rowan-berry display and how it is a sign of a harsh winter ahead. This is a myth: sadly, plants can't forecast the seasons. Good or bad fruit crops are a reflection of conditions earlier in the year. Kind temperatures, plentiful water and healthy pollinators over past months shape fruit quantities and tell us nothing about the winter ahead.

The blackberries I passed had gone over a little, but I couldn't resist plucking a few and comparing them as I walked towards the village church. I believed I could taste the sweetness in the south-facing fruit, but would I have noted that if I didn't know that south-facing fruits harvest more light and make more sugars?

Blackberries are a hedgerow vanguard, charging out ahead of many other fruits. Green turns to early red, which is still unripe. The following ripe black bounty is popular with birds and mammals, including badgers, foxes and, in wilder parts, bears. It is easy to overlook the leaves, which reveal much to those who tune in to them. The thorns scratch, but the leaves are astringent, used in traditional medicine to treat wounds and staunch blood.

When we see a bramble colony, we can be sure some light is reaching that spot as the plant does not tolerate deep shade. The leaves orient themselves to catch the light, like most leaves, but there is tutorial beauty in the way they do it. The art of reading the leaves lies in the gaze.

Do not stare at an individual leaf: instead let your eyes hop across them before settling into a broad gaze over the colony. At first you will see a sea of green, but with practice we learn to divine the collective shape of the leaves together and the direction they are facing. One or two leaves may have their own peculiar agenda, but the average is honest and tells us where most of the light comes from. If the area is fairly open this is likely to be south.

The brambles also map the activity of wildlife in the area. Grazing animals, especially deer, munch the leaves, and for every deer we might spot, there will be a hundred snipped blackberry stems hinting at eyes watching us.

September is a time of rapid change in solar habits. The sun's height and the time it rises and sets are changing as fast as they ever do. This leads to variety and messages in the clouds. The sky over Sussex was mostly clear, except for one corner where I spotted a high mackerel pattern in the clouds. Mackerel skies are much admired, but not widely understood. A mackerel pattern can be used to forecast weather, but it's not the easiest piece of weather lore to interpret.

A mackerel sky of any kind means change is likely. This is reflected in the associated weather lore: 'Mackerel sky, mackerel sky – never long wet, never long dry.' However, if you want to work out whether the change will be for better or worse, you need to know the difference between the two types of cloud that can create a mackerel sky: altocumulus and cirrocumulus.

An altocumulus mackerel sky has long thick white lines running perpendicular to the direction the upper wind is blowing, a little like waves in the sea. The clouds are substantial and opaque. This indicates that change is coming, but improvement is as likely as bad weather. We need a couple more clues to work out what is coming next.

A cirrocumulus mackerel sky is made up of smaller, wispier, patchier higher clouds. There are no thick lines and the clouds appear translucent. These clouds can run before a front and the accompanying bad weather. Cirrocumulus is often found with wispy cirrus, sometimes shaped like 'mares' tails'. Hence, 'Mares' tails and mackerel scales make tall ships take in their sails.'

The pattern I saw that morning in Laughton was formed of the thicker lower bands of altocumulus. They ran from south-west to north-east and confirmed that the higher winds were from the north-west, which matched the winds I could feel nearer the ground – if high and low winds agree, the chance of settled weather is much better than if they vary significantly. Blue sky, thick mackerel lines, high and low winds from the same direction suggested that the fair weather would hold.

I ducked into All Saints Church in Laughton, passing a splendid pine tree compass: all the branches were on the southern side and the top of the tree had been tipped over by winds from the south-west. Inside the church, I squinted at the stained-glass window from a pew. September and March are great months for dazzling early-morning displays through the eastern windows behind most altars because the sun rises east at the equinoxes. If your church alignment is off, if the altar is not neatly at the

A

Altocumulus mackerel sky

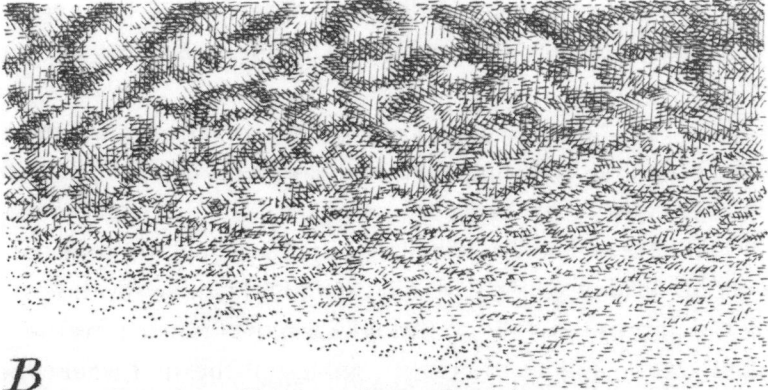

B

Cirrocumulus mackerel sky

C

Mares' tails (Cirrus)

eastern end, then look up the feast day of your local church's patron saint: one tradition holds that churches were built with the sunrise on the saint's day in mind. A church dedicated to St John, for example, is likely named after the Baptist and his birthday is celebrated on 24 June, meaning the altar may be aligned to sunrise on that day, much closer to north-east.

Leaving the churchyard, rushes and willows told me water lay ahead. A heron waited a minute, perfectly still, before leaping into the air. My feet crunched over the crab apples that lined the path and I stopped to admire the tree. Any reason to pause changes our relationship with and experience of our surroundings and leads to new and different observations, but I could never have guessed at the delightful idea that fell on me at that moment.

Near the crab-apple tree, there was an oak and I could tell at once that it was suffering: clumps of shoots burst out of its bark well below the lowest branches – a classic sign of arboreal stress – and looking up I could see that the branches high over the path were all dead or dying. This led me to look at the way the path passed over its roots – footfall was killing the branches overhead on the same side as the path. Looking at the spot where the roots rose to meet the trunk, I saw a compact 'fairy house', the dark hollows formed at the base of trees when disease, normally fungi, find a way in and devour the interior of the tree. It suddenly dawned on me that these portals, the dark doors to the fairy houses, are more likely to face the path – because footfall, damage and vulnerability are more likely on the side of the tree that humans or animals pass. The fairies face the path. It was too delightful a deduction to walk on.

I sat on a fallen tree limb, one more victim of heavy footfall over the years, and made a cup of tea, sending a rabbit scuttling down its own burrow. But this pause lit another fuse of curiosity – which way do rabbit burrows face in the woods?

The fairy house faces the path

As we saw in April, warren entrances in the open tend to face between south and west. But on pacing around three sides of that small copse, I found no consistent aspect to the rabbits' holes in the wood. It was clear that wind was not the dominant factor in their architecture. The trend I did spot was that many holes faced towards the edge of the woods, which makes good sense. When grazing in the open field, a rabbit could flee from a predator and head straight down their hole without changing direction. A handbrake-turn during a high-speed escape from a fox might be the rabbit's last move. Fairies point to paths and rabbits show the way out of the woods. It was proving a fruitful morning, without the need for the crab apples or acorns, which I could hear dropping through leaves around me with each surge in the breeze.

Rosehips thrived on the south-facing side of the path. The sun broke through the canopy and lit patches of the path with wobbling brightness. The rays caught a pair of silk threads that stretched across the path at chest height. We are likely to spot spiders and their webs at this time of year, when males are more active and on the lookout for potential mates. We can be on the lookout too, for the delightful sight of spiders' silk adorning grassy fields. These strands are crashed aircraft, remnants of the threads that many small spider species spin to catch a lift on rising air, thermals, a habit called 'ballooning'.

The silk threads are lifted by thermals, which is a clue to the weather pattern we'll see at the same time. We don't get thermals without sunshine. Very often, the webs are glistening with dew: these small spiders favour sunny weather and light breezes, conditions that favour dew overnight. Notice how the silky threads are so much easier to spot when looking towards the sun. If you walk with the sun to one side, the line of bright silk appears to follow you, moving over the grass as you walk. Of course we can hold on to a strong sense of direction, using the sun or its shadows, but for pure romance, working out which way we're facing from a shimmering line of dewy silk is a delight.

Late Harvests

One freshly fallen acorn was a polished pale green and reflected a tiny parcel of sunlight up to my eyes from the ground. I stepped over it and towards the huge white wind turbine that powered Glyndebourne, the opera house in the middle of beautiful nowhere. It was the arranged place for my meeting with Ruby Taylor.

Ruby has lived and worked in remote areas of Ethiopia and Sudan, experiences that inform her work as an artist and maker in Sussex. She forages for plants and clay, and has written a book on wild basketry techniques. She wore a nettle-fibre bag around her neck. We said our hellos as a kestrel swooped and fell from the sky in a vertical plummet towards some prey behind the trees.

Ruby's gathering season rises sharply with the sap in May, a time for nettle fibres and bast (inner bark) from other semi-woody plants. She collects willow and sweet-chestnut bark when the sap is full in the tree. 'The sap allows the bark to be removed easily.' She cuts from coppiced trees that will re-grow. 'I am always tending the trees I work with, looking after them for future seasons.'

The second part of the season that stretches from July to September is another intense period for harvesting grasses, rushes and reed mace for basketry. 'They have to be harvested at the height of their growth season, when there's maximum vegetable growth, then dried and stored. It's like being a farmer, you have a short window to harvest your crop. You can't gather it after that as it's not in good enough nick.'

We are near the end of the gathering and this is the last chance to bring in some wild-rose stems, which Ruby uses as the framework for bramble baskets – they're long, strong and without much of a taper. 'I'm looking for the long whips poking out of the hedges. By September, the hips are out, which tells me I must get to them before the hedges are trimmed or flailed. I want to cut them before the frost gets to them, because I have to bend them into a circular shape and set them in a jig.

'September is the start of bramble cutting. I'm looking for this year's growth, which will be long and flexible. The best ones are not in hedgerows, but under mixed woodland canopy where they're growing for light.'

'I got snared and tangled in some this morning,' I said. 'You would have liked them – you'd have got a whole basket out of the ones slowing me down.'

'Those are the ones, the ones that trip you up.' We laughed. 'Brambles are amazing. Every time a tip touches the ground it re-roots. In the height of their growing season, they grow four inches a day.'

'No!' I cried.

'I'm not kidding. It's an unusual plant because you can harvest from September to April. Ivy is the other that can be harvested then.'

We walked on and I noted that clematis was thriving in well-lit south-facing places. I asked Ruby if aspect was important when selecting sites and plants for her harvest. She revealed that plants exposed to the south-western winds were best if she needed dryness in the fibres. The wind was much stronger now we were higher up, and pale butterflies danced in the wind shadow by the woods.

We passed a dried puddle. All around it the tracks of animals, including those of dogs and pheasants, had set hard in the dried chalky mud. We talked about light and wind and how we had reached the driest moment in the year.

'The only plant I cut that grows in wet conditions is the reed mace, which is really good for twined baskets. I like to cut it at this time of year when the ground is drier so I can access it. People often call it bulrush, but it's not a rush . . . Sedges have edges, rushes are round, grasses are hollow to the ground . . . Reed mace isn't round like a rush. It's structured like a leek.

'Rushes have been used for traditional crafts and the reed mace is the same. It grows widely around the world in temperate regions. It's called cattail by indigenous American peoples and it's a traditional basketry material there. It grows plentifully in stagnant water and this time of year is perfect: where I cut it, which is in the clay pit, I can get to it. In July I can't really get in there – the mud is too wet and deep to be in waders but there's not enough water to be on a craft. If I wait until September, it's dried up sufficiently for me to get in and cut them. And any rush wainscot moths will have pupated and gone so I won't be interrupting their lifecycle, which is important to me.'

September is a time of low fresh water and warm seawater.

We admired the view of some Bronze Age barrows on distant hilltops and then began our descent. I asked Ruby if she sells the baskets she makes. She sounded a little sad and said she couldn't compete on price with makers from other parts of the world. But then her voice turned cheerier and she explained that, wherever they were made, they were all made by hand: 'A basket can't be made by a machine.'

13

October

Smoke and Frost Maps

—

The Second Narrowing

—

The Festival of the Dead

—

Leaf Litter Compass

—

The Pleiades

—

Orion and the Orionids

I had risen early near the Wiltshire town of Marlborough and headed into the Savernake Forest, home to ancient trees that were now raked by the sun cutting through the gaps. I was willing it to rise higher and warm me. Summer was gone.

The mosses were plumper, the soil darker and the leaves quieter underfoot, all signs of a wetter world. After an hour of slipping on mud churned by the cattle in the forest, I worked my way to the edge. The sound of birds greeted me as I left the trees, as it so often does, and the sun now hit me fully, but the air temperature dropped. I picked up the scent of smoke and then, moments later, saw steam rising from the east side of a dark thatched roof. The opposite, west, side was still coated with white frost. There had been no frost under the trees but now in the open my feet crunched over the white grass. It was a picturesque seasonal scene, smoke on the air, brown leaves and white frost on the ground, but our job is to decipher the patterns that hide in beauty.

Smoke and Frost Maps

The smell of bonfire smoke on the air in October is a happy seasonal marker, coming after the dry dusts of summer and then petrichor as rain slakes dry ground, but before the smell of rotting leaves. There is a difference between the strong punch from a nearby bonfire and the mellower blend of smoke that has travelled far and mixed well with the air. It reminds us to think about wind direction – smoke must hitch a ride on the breeze so its scent reveals activity to windward.

Desert nomads use a particular technique for navigating with smoke. The key is to put the wind on your cheek. We need to avoid walking upwind or downwind until we have picked up the scent. Otherwise we can walk parallel to any smoke trail indefinitely without ever smelling it. Instead, walk across the wind, with it on your right or left cheek, for as long as it takes, until you pick up the smell of smoke, then turn and track upwind, like a bloodhound, until you surprise a group sitting around a fire. Wherever you are in the world, light a fire only if you are happy to be found.

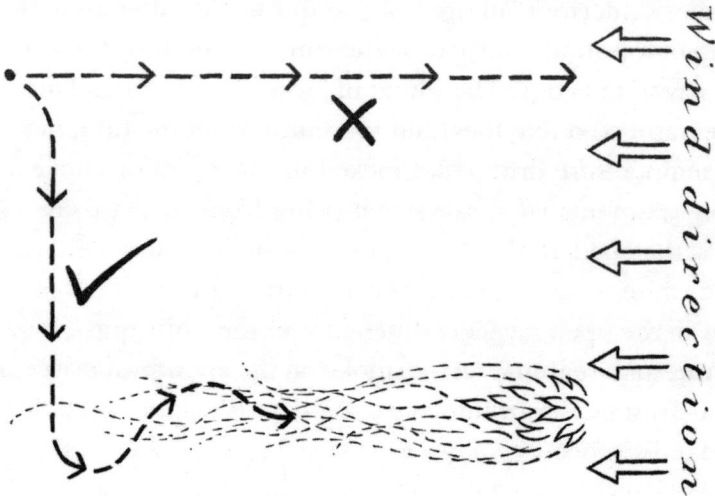

Navigating with smoke

A white tint covered the land, but not uniformly, and the ground was sprinkled with frost maps. Frost follows many of the same rules as the dew we met last month – it needs cold air touching the ground and this is a lot less likely under cover or with strong winds that stir the air. This is why the air temperature had dropped as I left the woods – the trees had stopped

some of the heat radiating to space and held on to a few degrees –
enough to feel, enough to stop the frost. We get frost after clear
calm nights in places where there have been no clouds, trees or
anything else stopping the heat escaping overnight. There are
a couple of additional layers to frost maps.

As I looked over the Wiltshire valley, I could see that the frost
was white and brilliant in many places, but not all. It had melted
in the morning sunshine in the east-facing spots and on many
different scales. A green east-facing field ran away from me
downhill until it met a white-frosted west-facing field at the
bottom of the vale. One side of the thatched cottage was white-
frosted, and steam rose from the dark, wet east-facing side. By
my feet there was frost on one side of an old cow pat and none
on the eastern side. The cows were facing north–south, having
turned side-on to the sun, offering their flanks to its warming
rays, a common habit in animals trying to warm up after a chilling night (and the opposite to hot camels).

As autumn slides towards winter and the sun rises further
south each day, try to notice how the line of frost thaw also
shifts. In early October we are near to the equinox and the sun
rises only a touch south of east. This creates north–south, white-
dark frost-thaw lines, but by the end of the year, the sun is rising
closer to south-east and these lines turn clockwise.

Like dew, frost avoids any spots where heat can rise from
below. However cold the air gets, it stays warm deep underground, even in Siberia. Mud and stone conduct heat from
underground and stay warmer than the nearby grass, which is
why the lawn is frosty and the soil of the flowerbed is not. Zoom
in and we notice that the lawn is not uniformly frosty: the blades
of grass that are lifted above the ground and facing upwards are
the purest white. The flowerbed soil is mostly free from frost,
but look at the fallen leaf that curls above the earth – it has a
frost on its topmost parts.

The Second Narrowing

I embarked on a short natural navigation exercise in Ashdown Forest, over boggy moorland and under turbulent skies. The sun gave me my bearings and I picked a target in the distance, a weather-ravaged pair of pines. Soon after setting off, a peculiar sound map started to take shape. I heard the constant dull hum of a road to my south, boring as a sound but vibrant as a clue; it's hard to feel disoriented when a constant sound acts as a beacon in the landscape. Then there was the intermittent rattle of rifle shots at a military range to the north. Least dependable, but most beautiful, a deer was barking to the east.

Flowers were sprinkled over the south side of the gorse and urged me on until I rested on reaching dry ground. It was firm enough under bracken, as it usually is, but soon things grew much more challenging. The colour map was stark: grey-green heather dominated in places where the moorland was drained and the ground firm, but the pale moor grass warned me that my boots would sink far enough for the water to pour in. The wet boots and deeper water weren't a problem – I hadn't imagined getting to the end of the day with dry feet – but the tussocks of moor grass were hard going and I fell over twice.

Ashdown Forest has earned the nickname 'Little Scotland' for its wide-open vistas of heather, pines and miles of moorland grasses. The open spaces are not what most expect from a place with 'Forest' in its name, but that word signifies only that it was once a royal hunting ground. It was one of the key iron works in England during Roman times and the trees were fuel for smelting iron ore. The Romans referred to the region as 'Anderida' and thought of it as a place that mixed wood, jungle and swamp. But that was before they started cutting down the trees in earnest. (We can map how the trees were cleared in the place names: any areas with 'field' or 'fold' in their names were the first to lose their trees to cultivation; place names with 'hurst' or 'holt' held on to their trees for longer. The word 'field' is related to felled, as in cut down.)

I reached high ground a few hours after setting off and Tom Forward was waiting for me. He laughed when I asked him what title he gave his job.

'Here we go . . .' he said. A broad smile under the black beanie hat broke into a chuckle. 'Erm . . . ecologist, wildlife guide, environmental educator . . .'

We had met at a place Tom knew well, called Bushy Willows. It offered fantastic views of the Forest in all directions. He told me he had listened to my audiobook, *The Secret World of Weather*, and we spent a few enjoyable minutes reading the way the clouds were mapping the ridges of high ground to the north and south of us. Tom then recounted an incident in which he had had to play the clouds with precision. He wanted to show a group of walkers a purple emperor butterfly, but to have any luck – and you always need luck with these magnificent but mercurial insects – he had to time the walk to coincide with the sun breaking through a narrow gap of blue in an otherwise cloudy sky. He kept his eyes on the movement above, leading the group like a conductor, and arrived at the sallow trees the butterflies call home, as the sun broke through. It worked a treat. A butterfly appeared onstage on cue and the group were delighted with their prize.

We set off to explore the Forest and Tom's eyes scoured the edges of the vegetation.

'I like to see my last reptile at this time of year,' he said, his eyes hopping along the ground near our feet. He explained that it was a good time to look for reptiles because they have to be very choosy about the spots they pick. Tom was scanning in the few places that hold warmth on cool days and they were very particular. He was tuned to the wind direction, the shelter offered by the gorse and the arc of the sun in his search for the few remaining warmth traps in the landscape. Earlier in the year it is easier for reptiles and harder for us to spot them, because they can afford to be less fussy when it is warm all around. (You may notice a similar trend at home: as the season turns colder, the room and even the seats people choose become more predictable – nobody will sit for more than a minute in the chair by the draughty door.)

'I love reptiles and constantly want to hone my "snaky sense",' Tom said, his eyes not lifting from the verge. 'When I'm in the right place, I feel the sun on the back of my neck and know there's going to be something.' He pointed to the small crescents of sunlit, sheltered warmth among the gorse where he'd seen a lizard the day before. But the temperature had dropped over-night and he wasn't getting the 'sense'. He may have seen his last of the season – a day is a long time in autumn. We were happily distracted by the sound of birds descending on the brilliant red berries that lined the southern side of a proud pair of holly trees.

We saw in late summer that there is a narrowing as animals are funnelled towards increasingly scarce sources of fresh water. As the temperature drops in autumn, reptiles seek out the last heat, and animals of all kinds work harder to find dependable food sources. The holly berries are a favourite of the thrush family, blackbirds, fieldfares and redwings, who know the value of a late feast. The funnelling towards warmth and food at this time of year is the 'second narrowing'. It makes life tougher for the animals and a little easier for us to know where to find them.

The Festival of the Dead

We walked on, past more holly berries, their rich red glistening in the low sun. This led into a chat about mast years, when trees ramp up production, littering the ground with a thick layer of acorns and other nuts. Tom told me that the oak mast year can change the appearance of the ground in unexpected ways. Its purpose is to swamp the system, to provide more food than will be eaten by wild pigs, giving the tree's seeds a better chance of making it to sapling. In the leaner years between, the pigs are forced to work harder to find their food and this means rootling around in the soil. Mast years mean fat pigs and neat, undisturbed soil; lean years mean thinner pigs and roughed-up soil.

The yellow tormentil flowers indicated that we were walking over acidic soil, reflected back in all we saw for the rest of the day: plenty of pines, moorland, heather, ink-dark oligotrophic ponds and bogs. We continued over the higher ground and passed an isolated pine tree that wore a long thin dark scar. It was a sign that we were on ground susceptible to lightning. I glanced at the sky, which was changing rapidly, and felt we ought to descend if the towering cumulus clouds started to build any higher.

Lightning does strike twice and more. If you can touch a lightning scar on a tree, you're in the wrong place to wait out a storm. The scars are fairly easy to identify: any long thin vertical burn mark on a tree that runs from above animal-grazing height to the ground is the fingerprint of lightning. If the tree survives, and most do, you'll often find the bark trying to grow around the burned area, squeezing in from the sides like fat lips. Lightning thins woods on high ground. In the stormiest regions, lightning is one of the most important natural factors in killing trees and enough are struck each year to reduce the density of trees on high ground.

The nature of storms changes at this time of year. In late summer we meet many isolated storms, but as autumn matures, the sun weakens and most storms arrive with new air masses, at weather fronts. Nearing winter, most storms come in waves. Waves of trouble.

After dropping off the highest ground, we enjoyed looking for and listening to the birds and making maps from their sounds; the coal tits signalled that there were more pines ahead. We passed the conifers and stepped into a magnificent grove of beeches. Their forms spoke of pollarding many years ago. A forester had cut the trees at head height, stimulating new life to start again vigorously above that line. That work was deep in the past century, but there was no mistaking the impact on the trees' form: mighty fat trunks that burst out into branches at about head height.

And then we met the festival of death.

Around the world there are celebrations that recognise those who have died and many take place at this time of year, most likely because the end of October and beginning of November mark the point that is halfway between the autumn equinox and the winter solstice. One of the best known of these festivals, the Mexican Dia de los Muertos, allows family members to celebrate lost loved ones with flowers and *calaveras* – decorated skulls. The joy stems from the belief that the deceased return to be with their family for a day before going back to the afterlife. Halloween is celebrated in many countries and marks the start of a Christian period of remembering the dead, not least the saints and martyrs. Samhain, an ancient Celtic festival, marked the end of the harvest but also when burial mounds offered a portal to the otherworld, a realm of deities and the dead.

Nature puts on its own festival of death at this time. As Tom and I made our way deeper into the beech grove and ducked under one of the lowest branches, our noses met the polished shininess of a hundred porcelain mushrooms. They lined a few of the beeches' branches, but were absent from most, and are a sign of death and decay, but not its cause. As life leaches away from a tree's branch and temperatures drop, the saprotrophic fungi turn the page from death to life and put on a show of fruiting bodies. The porcelain fungi were a glorious sight, a bright white sheen against the darkness of dying wood. This fungus is sociable with its own kind and found in clusters, but not seen with other fungi. It releases a fungicide, a natural chemical called strobilurin A. Studies of such chemicals led to the development of agricultural fungicides that perform the same role on a wider scale, protecting cash crops from fungal attack and mildew.

Like other fungi, porcelain mushrooms can sense gravity and use it to direct their growth. Under the branch stems arced from pointing at the ground to reaching for the sky. The fungi were a reminder that all branches will fail one day. The ground around us was strewn with dead limbs, some as thick as my thigh. Beech trees are famous for dropping substantial branches with no warning. I've seen or heard many hit the ground hard over the years. These are the 'widowmaker' branches: they seem to fall more regularly in spring and autumn as the big changes happen, although there is no foolproof way to predict when one will come down. That said, if you see any fungi on a tree, you may want to avoid long periods under its bigger branches. I don't give it much thought unless a gale is baring its teeth. A. A. Milne wrote the *Winnie the Pooh* stories in Ashdown Forest and, when assessing such risks, I defer to Pooh's philosophy:

'Supposing a tree fell down?' said Piglet.
'Supposing it doesn't,' said Pooh.

Leaf Litter Compass

The path dipped down to some dark waters and we crossed a bridge made from sweet chestnut timber brought down in the

October storm of 1987. The living chestnut woodland cloaked the hill and at its edge I spotted a perfect pattern. I showed Tom the leaf litter compass.

A million leaves, husks and twigs cover the ground of any mature woodland, far too many for us to observe them all as individuals, but the brain is good at sensing some order in apparent chaos. The base of the chestnut nearest us was free of leaves. It looked clean and we could see a thin carpet of green mosses lying over the roots. On the opposite side, the ground was hidden under a thick pouch of brown dead leaves. The wind had scoured one side of the tree, lifting any leaves that fell or collected there and carrying them downwind. On the opposite side of the trunk, there was a wind shadow, a pocket where the prevailing wind from the south-west could not reach. The leaves dropped out of the still air there, forming a collection and mapping the one spot that the winds struggled to reach. There were no leaves on the south-west side of the tree and plenty on the opposite north-east side. This is the leaf litter compass.

When we spot such a simple pattern, we can test our observation and its value: 'If we're seeing a dependable leaf compass, we should find a small pile of leaves on the far side of the base of those trees and that fallen trunk over there,' I said to Tom, and we set off to investigate. Sure enough, there were bare patches on the near side of each obstacle and a small but definite pile on the far side.

There are other leaf litter patterns to look out for at this time of year, but most follow the same rule: the leaves gather where the wind doesn't blow. Notice how any hollows or dips in the land quickly fill while any bumps or protrusions stay bare. In plantation woods there are alternating rows of higher ground and miniature valleys; the leaves form deep carpets in the dips and leave the higher rows naked.

The leaf litter compass

The Pleiades

In 1999, Mario Renner and Henry Westphal turned on their metal detectors and started sweeping the ground near the town of Nebra in central Germany. They knew their chances of finding something remarkable were better than average because they were searching on a hill within a palisade that dated back to the Bronze Age. Their lust for treasure had led them to a place that was illegal to search without a licence.

Their detector alarms signalled metal underground and they started to dig. When one of the spades stopped hard on metal, they doubtless suspected one more piece of rusting modern junk, but they had struck treasure and their worlds were about to change, albeit not exactly in the way they had imagined. They had found and damaged an ornate bronze disc that was at least 3500 years old. They sold their find on the black market and must have hoped they would hear no more about it.

Four years later, in September 2003, the Naumburg court in Germany found the pair guilty of looting. Renner and Westphal received prison sentences of four months and ten months. The judge had taken into account the plea bargain they had struck for leading police and archaeologists to the scene of the crime.

The Nebra Disc, as it is now known, is circular, about 30 centimetres across and decorated with intriguing gold symbols. Some we can recognise instantly and others are more ambiguous. Experts like to disagree, so the crescent shape is either the moon or an eclipsed sun, and the bright circle is the sun or the full moon. (I'm confident it's the former in each case.)

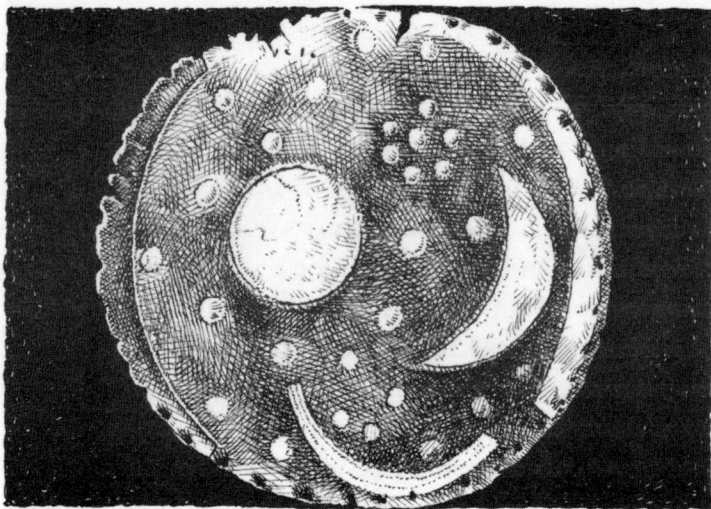

Nebra Disc

The smaller circles surrounding the sun and moon are undeniably stars and one pattern grabs the attention. There are thirty-two stars on the disc, but only seven that draw the eye. They stand out because they form a tight cluster. Given the cost in materials and craft needed to create this rare object, this must have been a deliberate attempt to portray a cluster of

seven stars in the night sky. It can represent only one astronomical formation.

The Pleiades, pronounced 'ply-a-dees', were easy to spot on
an ancient bronze disc and they are easy to recognise in the
night sky for the same reason: there is nowhere else in the night
sky where a tight group of about seven stars can be found easily
with the naked eye. And this is why we can find reference to the
Pleiades in almost all civilisations that left records, under many
different names. The Navajo considered 'Dilyéhé' to be one of
the few significant star patterns; the rest were scattered randomly
by the Black God.

'About seven stars'. *About?* Surely the whole point is that this is a
definite cluster of seven stars. Well, no, not quite. The cluster is
easy to spot, but the precise number of stars we see will depend on
the conditions – a veil of high clouds, light pollution and light
from the moon all have an impact – but also the time of night and
our eyesight. The number grows less definite still when we learn
that a variable star in the group, Pleione, fluctuates in brightness.

How many stars do *you* see? The act of trying to count them
sharpens our powers of observation and kindles a closer relationship. In 1961, the late astronomer Sir Patrick Moore put
this question to the audience of the popular BBC weekly TV
programme he hosted, *The Sky at Night,* and viewers wrote in
with their answers. The numbers varied: some saw fewer than
seven, others saw eight stars, nine or even, in one case, eleven.
But the average number was seven. The weird thing is that
seven is a fair average, but not the most likely number you will
see. If conditions are good enough to see more than six stars,
they are probably good enough to see as many as nine – because
there are three fainter stars of similar brightness. Light pollution may be worse now than it was in 1961 – it can be challenging in a city, but stars are often visible from the centre of parks –
but the number seven will stick. It's a sticky number, popular in

ancient times and considered lucky by many to this day. The number is further reinforced by the cluster's alliterative nickname, the Seven Sisters.

Stars appearing and disappearing in a whimsical way would present a problem for most constellations. The Triangulum constellation would shrink to a pathetic short line with the loss of a single star. But this doesn't cause any issues when identifying the Pleiades because they retain a unique appearance, despite fluctuations in numbers. Part of their distinctiveness comes from a bright smudge effect. There are lots of fainter stars, as many as five hundred, in the cluster that we don't recognise as individuals, but which contribute to the light from the group, adding a tinge to the spaces between the stars we spot. This effect is compounded because the light bounces off a dust cloud and gives the Pleiades a signature glow. This is the 'silver braid' that Alfred, Lord Tennyson admired:

> Many a night I saw the Pleiads, rising thro' the mellow
>   shade,
> Glitter like a swarm of fire-flies tangled in a silver braid.

If you see a tight pack of about seven blue-white stars, more likely fewer, that look a little smudged you have found the Pleiades. But now we will get a little more forensic about it, because that is where the gold lies.

The Pleiades are one of the earliest stars to appear in literature, featuring in Chinese works from 2357 BC and in Hindu writings from around 1730 BC. They pop up in Australian Aboriginal mythology, and villagers in the Peruvian Andes took note of them when considering their crop yields. The Vikings saw them as hens. I could list dozens more cultural references, but instead I'd like you to reread this paragraph and see if you can spot an astronomical clue within it.

Did you notice that the Pleiades are clearly visible to cultures from as far north as the Vikings and south to Australia? This is only possible if stars sit near enough the celestial equator. The Pleiades are 24 degrees north of the celestial equator, close enough to the equator to be visible to most of the world's population for part of the year. Further north and they would never appear in any Australian culture.

In autumn the Pleiades can be seen climbing above the eastern horizon soon after nightfall. In spring they catch up with the sun and we soon lose them again. These times marked important periods in many traditional societies so it was inevitable that the Pleiades should become an important seasonal marker. Hesiod wrote, 'At the time when Pleiades, the daughters of Atlas are rising, begin your harvest, and plow again when they are setting.'*

They mark significant moments well beyond the familiar patterns of northern agriculture, which is why we find the same cluster marking time in South Africa, where IsiLimela are seen as the 'digging stars', and Japan, where they signal the time for planting rice.

The Pleiades rise and set close to north-east and north-west from temperate latitudes. Like all stars that rise over the eastern horizon, they climb until they reach their highest point when they are due south – a moment known to astronomers as 'culmination' – before descending towards the western horizon.

There is always a seasonal aspect to the moment any star is highest and due south. If, for example, we happen to notice that a favourite star is highest in the sky at 11 p.m. one night, it will reach the same height two hours earlier a month later

---

* Hesiod, *Works and Days*, 383–384 in Ruggles, Clive, *Ancient Astronomy*, ABC Clio, 2005, p. 185.

(30 x 4 minutes). For most stars this sort of timing was not considered important by ancient peoples, but for the great characters, including the Pleiades, it was significant.

There is a belief in some circles that the Druids marked Samhain, the precursor of Halloween, using the culmination of the Pleiades at midnight, which is plausible. The night skies have shifted a little in the intervening years and the culmination is closer to 1 a.m. these days, but I find it a helpful and colourful prompt: they will still be seen high in the sky late at night near Halloween. Pumpkins mean Pleiades.

The Pleiades are not a constellation in themselves, but part of a much larger pattern, the constellation of Taurus, the Bull. The Pleiades are the early outriders of this constellation, more than ten degrees – an outstretched fist – ahead of the most familiar parts of Taurus, the V shape of his horns and burning red eye, the star Aldebaran. This means that the cluster rises earlier (more than an hour for mid-latitudes) than the recognisable head of Taurus.

From early October through November, the Taurid meteor showers mean we are likely to see good shooting stars in the region of Taurus, peaking near 10 November. The quality varies enormously from year to year, from underwhelming to frightening. The Taurids are two separate showers formed by debris from a comet and an asteroid, but they can be thought of as one long-lasting shower. Larger fragments burn spectacularly, leading to another nickname for this shower: the Halloween fireballs.

Renner and Westphal, the metal-detecting looters who unearthed and illegally sold the Nebra Disc in 1999, felt they had been harshly treated by the Naumburg court in 2003. They appealed their sentences of four months and ten months. The court weighed the evidence afresh and disagreed – their sentences were raised to six months and twelve months respectively.

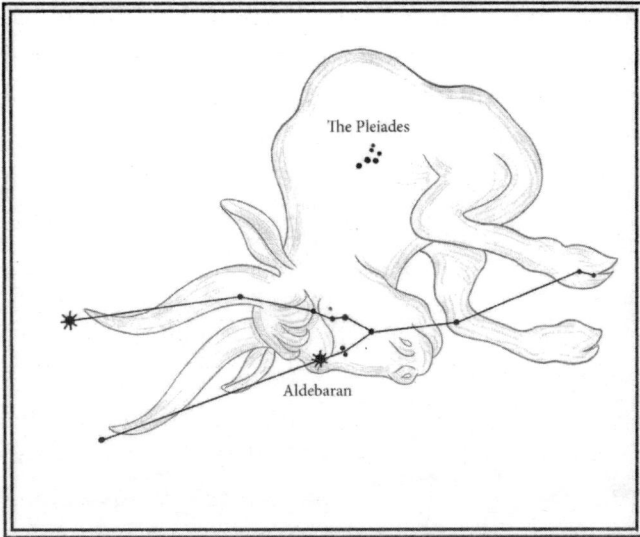

Looking east at Taurus and the Pleiades after they have risen

Orion and the Orionids

Orion holds some of the brightest stars of the night sky in friendly patterns, making it one of the easiest constellations to recognise and one of the most useful for natural navigation. It also hosts the Orionids, an excellent October meteor shower. Orion climbs in the east after Taurus and this is the month to befriend the Hunter.

Orion straddles the celestial equator, the imaginary line in space that sits over our equator. Any constellation that hovers over it will rise in the east, roll high through the south and set in the west; this is true of some constellations we have met already and some we haven't but may sound familiar:

Leo
Virgo
Aquila
Aquarius

Pisces
Taurus
Orion

These constellations are all seasonal – in some months they are hidden by the sun. Don't look for Orion in June: it's a thankless task, even with good sunglasses.*

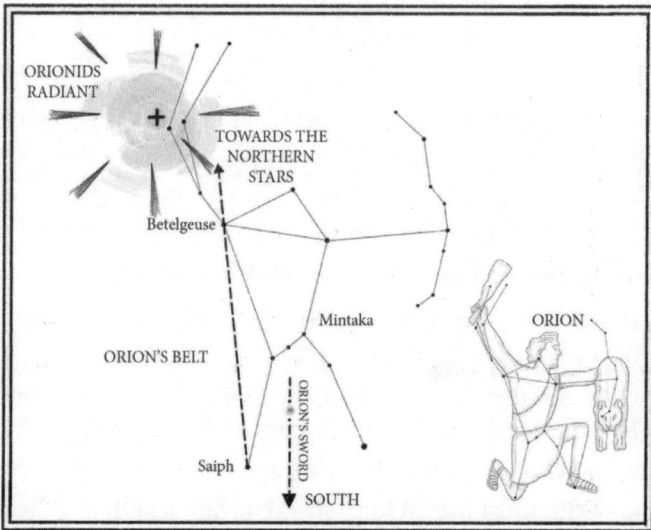

Orion

---

* Orion is described as a winter constellation, but this label can be constrictive and even misleading. Don't be surprised if you spot him at other times. When equatorial constellations are given a single-season label, it refers to the time of year when they are visible during sociable evening hours. It never refers to the full range of months when they can be seen. Stars on the celestial equator are hidden for about three months (the exact length depends on latitude), but are visible at all other times of year – if you are happy to lose a little sleep. It would be more accurate to refer to equatorial stars by the non-season: Orion is a non-midsummer constellation more than a strictly winter one.

Mintaka is the leading star of three in Orion's belt and rises and sets within one degree of true east and west. When Orion is high in the southern sky, we can use different stars. His sword hangs from his belt and when this is vertical it points down to due south on the horizon. And two of the brightest stars, the orange-tinted Betelgeuse – pronounced by many *Beetlejuice* – and blue-white Saiph form a large north–south line in the sky. Imagine a line that runs from Saiph to Betelgeuse and keep going. It takes you towards the northern constellations; head in the opposite direction and it leads you to the southern horizon.

In October, Earth travels through the dust left in the wake of Halley's comet. This creates the Orionid meteor shower, radiating from a point ten degrees, or one outstretched fist, to the north-east of Orion above the left shoulder. Shooting stars are worth looking for in this part of the night sky all through October and the first week of November, but the peak is normally close to 21 October. This is still in the unsociable part of Orion's year, which means viewing between midnight and pre-dawn. Good for early birds or late ravers.

14

November

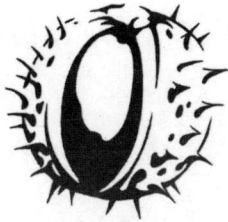

Sea Cumulus

—

Seasonal Sounds

—

A Fright and Scar

—

Twinkling Stars

—

Northern Stars

—

The Darkening

Looking out from the high ground of Shaftesbury, a market town in Dorset that dates back to Saxon times, I could see miles of Thomas Hardy country. Behind me, time stretched further back in the ruins of an abbey founded by Alfred the Great in 888. The first abbess was Æthelgifu, who was, not coincidentally, Alfred's daughter.

The town is impressively pretty and I paused to take in the rolling green landscape behind the weathered stone of ancient buttressed walls. One street is so eye-catching that it featured in a famous Hovis bread advert, directed by a young Ridley Scott, in the 1970s. Reality crept in: I saw buildings wrapped in ugly scaffolding and ducked into one where the shopkeeper told me, through deep sighs, 'They don't understand *our* seasons at all! They held off putting up this monstrous stuff until summer was past.' She waved a hand at the metal latticework surrounding her shop. 'They wanted to keep the town looking its best during the summer holidays. But we're well into November now, and the next six weeks are critical. The run up to Christmas is the make-or-break season for independent retailers like us.'

I could see her point. Seasons are subjective. Seasons are personal. Rain to the holidaymaker is not the same as rain to the farmer. Or the umbrella-vendor. The skies turn sombre in November and wetness creeps over the land, but spotting signs adds colour and banishes the drabness that others see.

Pannus

I layered up and walked out into the rain. We don't often look up at a raining sky, but if we have a view, it is worth looking across the lowest layer. It is here that we see the darker ruffled underbelly of the rain clouds. Colour is an obvious clue: the darker a cloud, the more water it holds, but shape and textures are important too. The clouds that have rain falling from them have a jagged appearance at the bottom, with fragments of broken cloud suspended beneath them, known as 'pannus'. Pannus forms when cold rain falls through warmer air below the cloud, cooling that air and causing water vapour to condense into mini-clouds. Clouds make rain, but rain makes clouds. It is a rare November week with no pannus clouds, and befriending them adds warmth and colour to a sombre sky.

The Greening

In November a green tint spreads in shady, but not too shady, places. Algae need light to photosynthesise, but water is critical: they die in sunny spots that dry out, but do well in damp places that receive indirect light – low on the north side of buildings, for example.

Stepping to the side of the main path to inspect a plant, I nearly slipped on the cobbles of Shaftesbury. Slippery algae act as a reminder to look for 'the greening'. The conditions the algae need to flourish are similar to those needed by other organisms, especially mosses, ferns and some lichens. The second we notice a hint of algae doing well, it's time to look for a change of colour in the woods.

Algae love the parts of broadleaf woodland where weak light creeps between the thinning trees, reaching the trunks without heating or drying them. After November rains, a thin coat blooms

Pannus clouds over Shaftesbury

on the bark. Glance into broadleaf woods in November and there will come a moment when you sense the green spreading. Rain causes the bloom, but the effect is most dramatic during a spell of finer weather after plenty of rain – all colours are more vibrant when well lit. Put a low sun on your back and enjoy the greening.

Most algae are too small to identify to a species with the naked eye. Sometimes the best we can do is say that a slimy green film, clammy to the touch, which lacks the structure of lichens and mosses, is most likely an algae colony. There is one exception that stands out, *Trentepohlia*, an orange-brown alga so sensitive to drying light that it can be a good indicator of north when found as vertical strips on only one side of trees.

I'm often asked if I have noticed shifts in nature due to climate change. Scientific data are much more reliable than personal observation when assessing trends in nature, but *Trentepohlia* is the best example I can offer from my own experience. It loves mild damp conditions and harks from tropical regions, but certainly appears to be on the march north. When I first started using it as a natural compass a couple of decades ago, it was common in the south of England but rarer up north. Now I expect to find it in north Scotland.

Reading Mosses

We can read mosses at any time of year, but late autumn is one of the best as moisture levels rise sharply.

Moss means moisture. Mosses cannot reproduce without plentiful water – female cells secrete a chemical to guide male sperm via a film of water – so any healthy moss colony is telling us that this area stays wet much of the time. That is the cornerstone of moss-reading and the only fast and obvious sign in mosses. However, if we pause to ask the mosses why their home is so damp, we find many interesting clues.

Mosses do well anywhere that rain is channelled or slowed. Mosses love shallow slopes – gradient is one of the most important factors in the moss world. Flat roofs have lots of mosses; steep roofs have fewer. Horizontal branches host many mosses; vertical ones have few.

Mosses thrive at the bottom of a fork in a tree, especially if there is a little flat area where water gathers. Coarse bark slows water and makes for a happy moss home. Watch any smooth trunk during heavy rain and you will see small vertical streams form as the water is forced to pick a route between the major branches. The mosses love these rivulets and form strips that the rainwater leaps off.

Now for the popular idea that moss grows on the north side of trees. The sun does most of its drying near the middle of the day when it is in the south, so the south side of any exposed object will dry faster than the north. Mosses abhor dryness, so the north side of a tree is a more natural home than the south side. But this rarely overrides the more powerful factors above.

Now we can start reading mosses in earnest. The air near the ground is wetter than that near our head, which is why mosses do well around the base of trees. In my natural navigation courses for beginners, I explain that mosses thrive near the ground as it is damper there – mosses below knee height are telling us only that the ground holds moisture. In my advanced lessons I show that although mosses wrap the base of trees there is a gentle slope, an angle from one side to the other. The mosses are very slightly higher around the base of the north side of the tree than they are on the south side. And there is a small spike: a place where the mosses shoot up one side of the tree where a rain channel has met a patch of rough bark.

Once we are focusing on life at the base of trees, we might notice that not all mosses are the same. In fact, there are at least ten thousand species of moss. Obviously, we won't try to identify every one we see, but notice how one form yields to another in bands near the base of tree trunks. Each moss has its own fussiness about moisture: some like to be sopping wet while others cope with short periods of dryness. The shift from one form to another shows us the moisture levels changing near the forest floor, wettest near the ground, drying as we look higher.

Now we are seeing the different factors at play in the moss story. The next time somebody tells you that moss grows on the north side of trees, you can nod and smile and decide whether you will share the richer picture.

Sensible Animals

Rain does not deter hungry animals and it softens the ground. Robins, thrushes and many other birds prefer full stomachs to dry feathers and peck at the ground during heavy rain at this time of year. However, the gales that tear the leaves from the trees make life uncomfortable for animals. Wild and domestic creatures behave differently, each looking for shelter, but employing tactics tailored to their environment. Look for the way wild animals, like birds, rabbits and deer, move to the sheltered, leeward side of woodlands as gales approach.

Farm animals range less far and come closer to the farmstead during bad weather. They also draw closer together: herd animals form tighter groups when they sense risk and that includes bad weather. Sheep, which are happy to spread far and wide over hilltops in sunshine, come down from the hills when the skies turn. I often see them clumped together under the trees on the lower slopes. Animals in fields with hedges often move towards the wind, gathering in the windward corner of the field as this nook offers some of the best shelter.

Birds can warn of weather changes – they make alarm calls when bad weather looms and go silent just before it hits. As the

winds pick up, notice how the birds fly lower. This is easiest to spot in any that are patrolling in circuits over an open area. They climb on the downwind leg, catching a ride on the strong winds, but drop lower as they turn into wind because the wind-speed drops near the ground. They land and take off facing into the wind.

The Leonids

We first met Leo the Lion constellation in April, and in November he plays host to an impressive meteor shower, the Leonids. They can be seen from about the sixth and through-out the rest of the month, peaking around the seventeenth or eighteenth. We are unlikely to catch Leo before we go to bed in November, as he rises so late. The good news is that longer nights mean we may spot him high in the sky to the south just before dawn.

The frequency of meteors varies greatly each year and there are occasional extraordinary storm peaks when thousands of shooting stars appear. This tends to happen about every thirty-three years, the period of the parent comet, Tempel-Tuttle. In 1966 the storm was so intense that it created an optical illusion: Earth appeared to be rushing through space and some stargazers felt the need to grip the ground and hold on tight. The last was in 2000 so we're not due another for a while, but the display is good enough in most years to warrant looking for if you find yourself awake in the early hours.

Sea Cumulus

If you spend any time near the coast, look for a shift in cumulus maps. In summer the land is warmer than the sea during the day, leading to thermals over land. We find cumulus clouds bubbling up, especially over hills, dark woods and towns, as we saw in June. As the sun rises further south each day and stays closer to the horizon, the land grows colder faster than the sea. This leads to a switch: thermals now rise over the warmer sea and cumulus clouds form in the moist air over water instead of land. The effect can be seen at any time of day, but dawn can offer the most dramatic differences. From my local hills, I often see a wall of tall clouds mapping the distant sea, which is especially satisfying when the sea is hidden.

In summer, cumulus clouds map the land. In winter they point the way to the coast from land. In autumn, we see an arm wrestle – any cold snap leads to sea cumulus and any unseasonably warm spell invites the clouds back over land.

Seasonal Sounds

I was able to take a dozen steps towards the roe deer before I made the sounds that raised its head and sent it away in pronking leaps.* This would have been impossible a few weeks ago. I had noticed the leaves and twigs growing quieter, less crunchy, in October in the Savernake Forest, but now the woodland floor was soaked, soggy and quiet underfoot. It was a thought that lingered and prompted me to reach out to those who spend time considering outdoor sounds professionally.

The composer Pascal Wyse was the first to get back to me. He had also noticed the sound of our footsteps changing with the months: 'from a percussive, tight thud to a sinking slop!' And he pointed me towards a community of people sensitive to the smallest changes. Sound recordists who work outdoors are tuned to every audible change and the huge dent we make on the soundscape.

Chris Watson was a founding member of the influential Sheffield-based experimental music group Cabaret Voltaire during the late 1970s and early 1980s. Since then, he has developed a passionate interest in recording the sounds of wildlife and habitats from around the world. As an award-winning nature sound recordist, he specialises in creating work that features a strong sense and spirit of place. He has worked on many BBC productions, including the globally popular David Attenborough series. I've been an admirer of Chris's work since I heard him speak at a festival in Cornwall many years ago. I asked him if any sounds marked seasonal moments for him. He wrapped things up beautifully and economically: 'The dry hiss of reed beds, the "seep" of migrating redwing overhead at night; dry, cold winter winds through leafless trees, the wind catching

---

* Pronking is an exaggerated bounding motion that prey animals display to deter predators. It is very common in deer and used as a signal of fitness, a way of suggesting to any predator that this deer is fit, fast and full of energy, that any chase will be a wasted effort and it would be better to pick another victim.

clumps of dry leaves, the muting effect of snow, the acoustic quality of being around and walking upon ice, temperature inversions, a breeze catching newly unfurled leaves, caterpillar frass falling from the leaf canopy, grasshoppers and crickets, the singing breeze through meadow grass, summer thunder.'

Temperature inversions are one of the most intriguing. After clear nights, a low layer of cold air becomes trapped beneath a layer of warmer air. Sounds travel much further than normal in these conditions as they bounce in the cold sandwich between the ground and the warmer layer boundary. It grants us the temporary superpower of hearing further than we can at other times. I remember it this way: 'Frost on the ground carries the sound.'

Smoke gets trapped in this layer too, so we can sometimes smell a temperature inversion from the musty scent of distant fires. And it changes how light behaves, stretching sunrises vertically and making distant objects appear to levitate.

The most interesting change in my auditory experience came from understanding something of our inner world and there followed a period of experimentation. It has changed my experience of all seasons.

The brain is constantly hit with too much information to process – the senses feed it as much as 11 million pieces of data per second – and one of its most important jobs is to sift and bin information as quickly as possible. It prioritises a very thin selection for our conscious minds to weigh. This leads to the 'cocktail-party effect', where we hear our name across a crowded room, even though we don't recall anything said by that person prior to that moment. Outdoors, the same automatic filter works all the time: we hear a branch snap but miss the subtler shift in sounds signalling that the wind direction has changed. But we do have some control over this process. When we concentrate or focus on something we are telling our brain to prioritise certain sounds – a manual override for the system.

The theory is straightforward, but it led me to an unpredicted place. Focus, by definition, is not broad. There is no point in stepping outside and telling our brain to concentrate on seasonal sounds. It shrugs: 'Too vague. Too much data.' And quickly goes back to its automated mode. We can pick any single sound and focus on it, listen intently, but on its own this is a blunt approach. Instead, I have found myself using an exercise that helps.

Interrogate sounds more specifically. Ask what qualities would be impossible at any other time of year. This morning, I spent half an hour in my local woods, eyes closed, casting an auditory net for interesting sounds. Rain had stopped about half an hour earlier, but I heard the familiar patter of raindrops falling from leaves as a wood pigeon took off from a nearby branch. Neither the sound of the bird's wings nor the raindrops was particular to the season. I could have heard them in any month. The sound that was unique was the sound the rain made as it hit the bracken around the base of a tree. The bracken had turned its November brown and looked, felt and sounded different from bracken in other seasons. The seasonal moment was there, hiding within the obvious, as it so often does.

A Fright and Scar

Halloween has passed, but November brings a fright during any dry spell. Walk alone along a country road under stars and you will sense an unwelcome visitation. Dry leaves fall on the breeze, then scratch along hard, dry ground, making an eerie, other-worldly sound. Each year I turn and brace myself before I realise that a few crinkled leaves are scuttling harmlessly towards me.

Once the leaves have fallen, we can look for the scar they leave behind. It is a signature and is unique to each species. The horse chestnut leaf scar, for example, looks like a horse-shoe with seven nails in it.

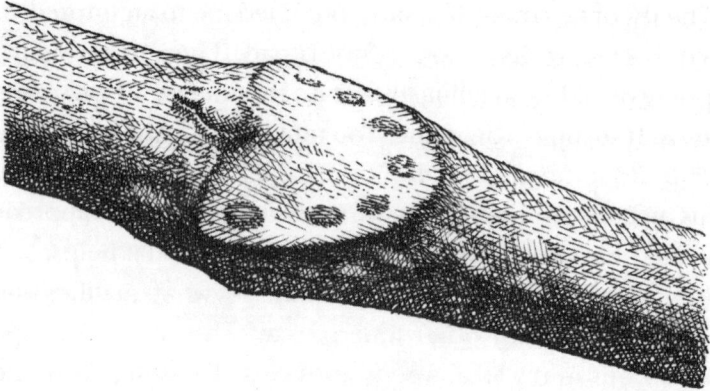

Horse chestnut leaf scar

Twinkling Stars

The nights are long, which makes this the perfect time for a deeper immersion in the stars.

Twinkling stars contain messages about the weather. They have a steady light in the vacuum of space, but when that light hits our atmosphere, it bounces off the air molecules and aerosols, which makes it scintillate and we see twinkling. On a clear night, notice how all the stars twinkle, but unevenly: those directly overhead fluctuate much less than those lower down and the lowest ones we can see, just above the horizon, twinkle most, because their light passes through more atmosphere on its way to our eyes than from the stars over our head. This is also why they appear fainter low down. We never see the weakest stars when they are low in the sky, only when they are overhead.

If you look for these effects during a period of settled cool, dry weather it will give you a good baseline – this is the night sky with the twinkling dialled down. Now keep an eye on the weather from day to day and watch what happens as rain approaches. Long before the first clouds arrive, the moisture levels in the upper atmosphere rise, which has a big impact on the light from the stars, making them twinkle more. The stars overhead start to twinkle as energetically as those near the horizon did days earlier, and the stars lower down twinkle more until they lose clarity and visibility deteriorates, especially in the direction from which the bad weather is arriving. Twinkling stars offer one of the earliest natural signs of impending weather change.

Northern Stars

In the northern sky, the stars appear to rotate counter-clockwise around a single star, the North Star – also known as the Pole Star or Polaris. This means that a collection of stars around the North Star appear never to rise or set and they are known as 'circumpolar stars'. Within this group, two patterns are supremely helpful in finding the North Star and many other astral patterns.

The word 'north' is shorthand for 'towards the North Pole'. The North Star sits directly over the North Pole, which means that if we can find and face it, we are looking north.

There are hundreds of ways we can find the North Star, but we'll look first at some fundamental pointers, then a couple of less well-known seasonal ones.

The Plough

The easiest method for finding the North Star is by using a group of seven stars known as the Plough in the UK, the Big Dipper in North America, and the Saucepan to many others. Next you find the 'pointer' stars, the two stars that a liquid would run off if you tipped up your Saucepan. The North Star will always be five times the distance between these two pointers in the direction that they point (up and away from the pan). True north lies under this star.

The Plough rotates anticlockwise about the North Star, so it will sometimes appear on its side or even upside down. However, its relationship with the North Star never changes and it will always dependably point the way to it.

The North Star is less bright than most expect and is never the brightest object in the night sky, but it has the advantage of appearing in a relatively dark patch of sky and having few close neighbours.

If we follow the pointer stars in the Plough in the opposite direction we reach the constellation Leo.

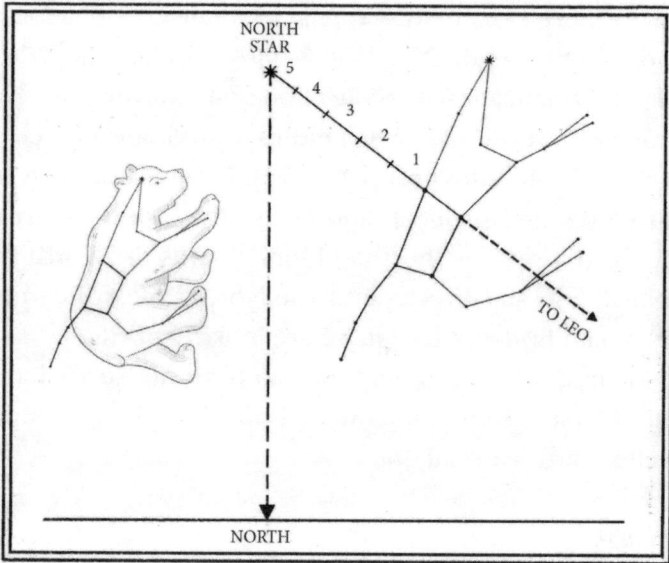

Finding the North Star with help from the Great Bear

Cassiopeia

The constellation Cassiopeia is helpful in finding the North Star: it will always be on the opposite side of the North Star from the Plough and therefore high in the sky when the Plough is low and obscured by trees, buildings or mountains. It looks a little like a flattened W, but since it rotates it can appear on its side or upside down, as an M.

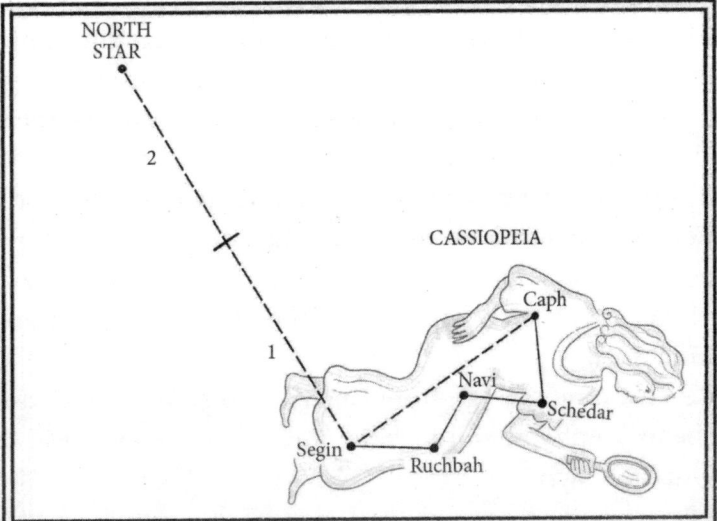

NORTH
STAR

2

1

CASSIOPEIA

Caph

Navi

Schedar

Segin

Ruchbah

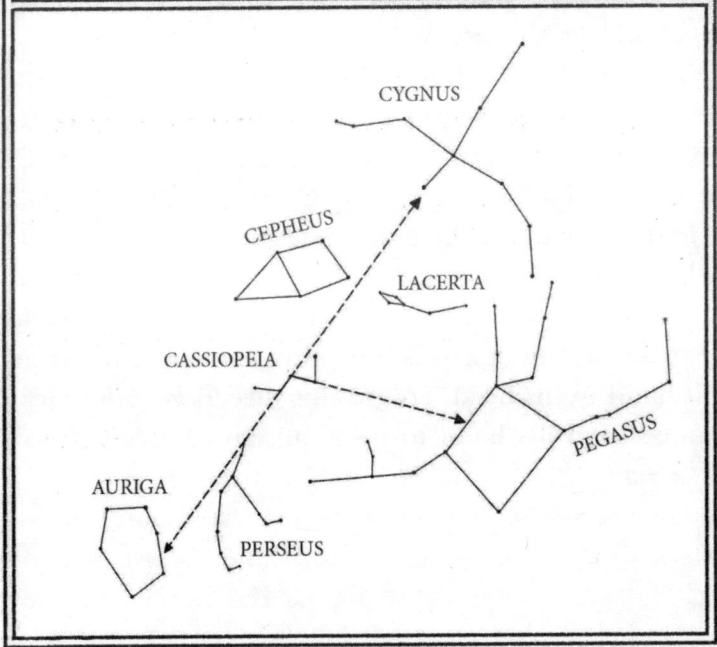

CYGNUS

CEPHEUS

LACERTA

CASSIOPEIA

PEGASUS

AURIGA

PERSEUS

To find the North Star, picture it as a W. Imagine a line that runs from the top left star to the top right one. Now rotate the line 90 degrees anticlockwise and double its length. This will lead you to the North Star.

Cassiopeia, the Queen of ancient Ethiopia and mother of Andromeda, is a useful guide in her own right, but she also points the way to other helpful patterns in the sky.

Let your eyes slide from the star Navi to Schedar and keep going until you find Pegasus. Head the other way, from Navi to Ruchbah, and keep going: you will find Perseus and then, next to him, Auriga.

Reverse direction: go from Ruchbah to Navi, head past her husband, Cepheus, and Lacerta, the Lizard, and you will find Cygnus, the Swan.

Cygnus and the Northern Cross

The constellation Cygnus looks, at a stretch, like a swan in flight. It rises in the north-east, rolls high and sets in the north-west. It contains an asterism (shape) called the Northern Cross that is very helpful for navigation. On clear early evenings, you will find it high in the sky at this time of year.

I have a weird way of remembering how to use this cross. The most famous cross in history was used to crucify Jesus and, macabre though it is, imagine Jesus pointing with *his* right hand to his head. Follow this direction, five times the distance from his hand to his head, and it takes us to the North Star.

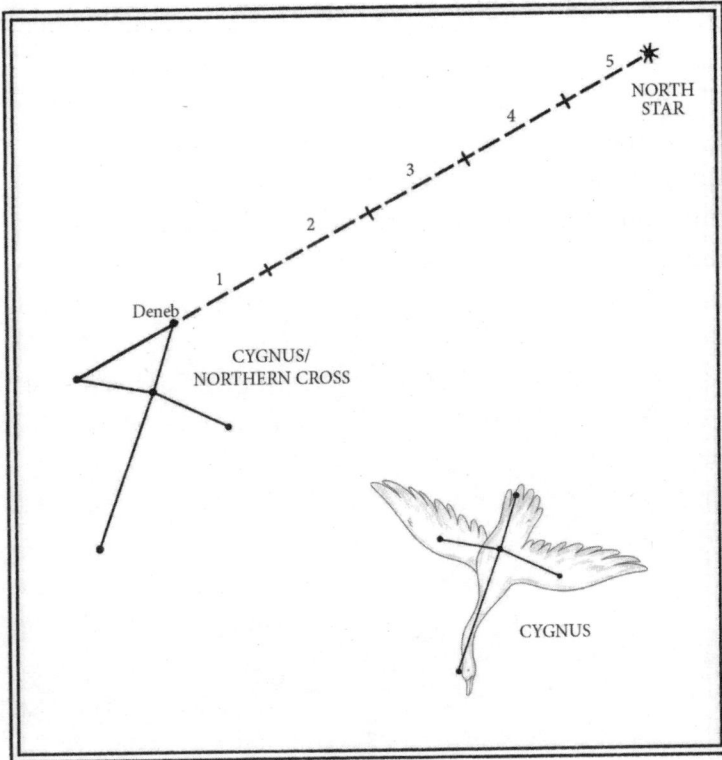

The Northern Cross Method

The Square of Pegasus

Pegasus is, in theory, a winged horse, but you could stare at the stars of this constellation for an hour and see neither wing nor horse in them. Fortunately, there is one easy-to-recognise shape within the constellation: a square.

The Great Square of Pegasus looks and acts a little like the pan of the saucepan shape in the Plough, above, and can also be used to find north. It is a lot bigger than the Plough and the

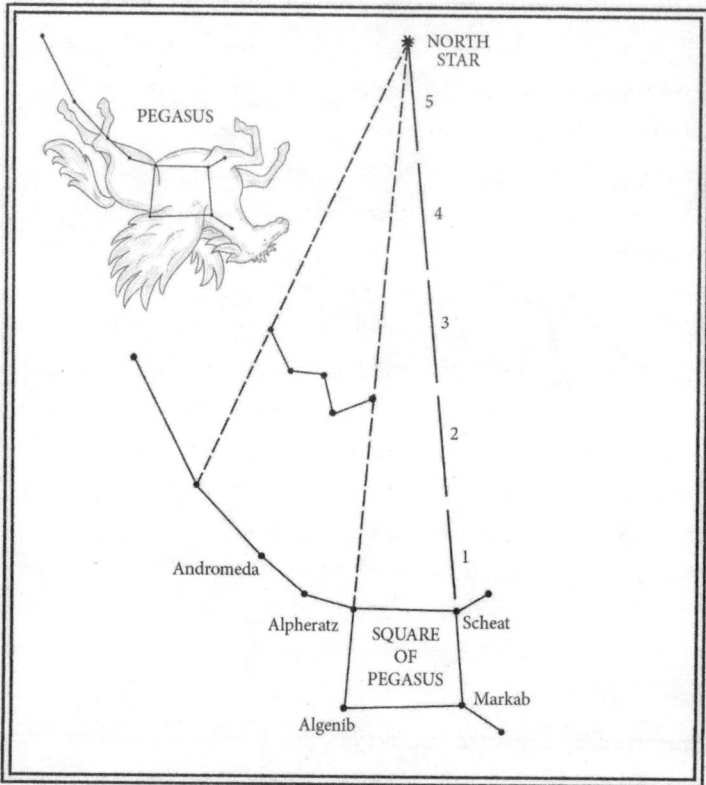

stars are a little fainter; the four that make up the square are of roughly equal brightness. You can test the stargazing conditions by looking inside the square; at first you probably won't spot many stars, but let your eyes adjust, then move them in small skips inside the square and a few faint stars will appear if light pollution is not too bad. Remember that it is much easier to make out faint stars when they are high in the sky. Try comparing Pegasus when it is low and high and you'll see a marked difference.

Imagine a line from the stars Markab to Scheat and keep going five times that distance and you'll find the North Star.

We are now far enough from the North Star that the stars dip below the horizon at certain times of year and night, making them seasonal.

The Northern Stars and the Seasons

The further from the North Star we look, the more likely we will lose the stars we see for part of the year.

We know that the North Star does not appear to move and the stars nearby rotate anticlockwise around it. Those nearest to it trace a small circle. As we move further from the North Star, the circles grow larger. When we find a star with a circle big enough to touch the horizon, due north of us, we can think of it as a guide to latitude and seasons.

The North Star sits over the North Pole, which makes it the same angle above the horizon as our latitude. If we are at 40 degrees north, the North Star appears 40 degrees (four extended fists) above the horizon. If we travel north to 50 degrees north, the North Star will be 10 degrees, an extra fist, higher in the sky. But this will also mean there is more room for stars to rotate in a circle around it without dropping below the northern horizon. The further north we are, the bigger the circle that can fit, and the more room there is for northern stars and constellations to stay above the horizon and remain circumpolar.

Lacerta, the Lizard, which we passed briefly earlier, is a seasonal constellation at 40 degrees north, disappearing below the northern horizon at its lowest point, but a circumpolar one at 50 degrees north. The lizard is seasonal in Denver and Madrid, but above the horizon all year in Edinburgh and Moscow.

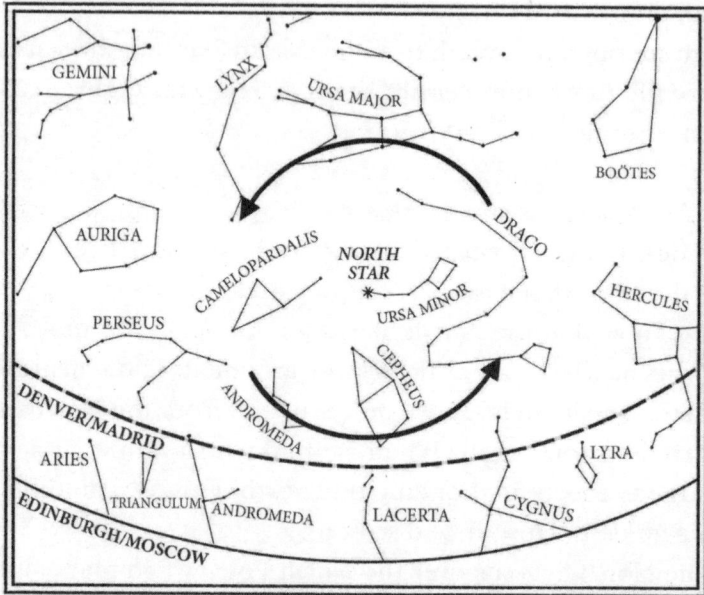

We lose some northern stars for a time when we head south, their season shortens

In a nutshell, if you visually gauge the distance of a star or constellation from the North Star, it gives you a sense of how seasonal it is. Once you are 90 degrees, nine fists, away you are looking at stars over the equator and, as we have seen, they rise due east, set due west and are all strictly seasonal – wherever you are in the world these stars are lost to the sun for a few months.

Head even further away from the North Star and you're now looking at stars over the southern hemisphere. Their seasonal window is short, as we have seen in July and August with Scorpius and Sagittarius. Further still and the stars remain underground all year – they have no season from the northern parts of the world.

Canopus is the second brightest star, after Sirius, but it is much further south, deep into the southern hemisphere and can't be seen by anyone beyond 37 degrees north, that is anyone north of Africa, Arizona or India. I mention it here because it is worth seeking out if you like to head south to escape the winter. It can be seen from Florida or anywhere south of there; the further south you head, the longer its season, and from the South Island of New Zealand, it is a circumpolar: its season fills the year. Canopus has been used by the Bedouin and Pacific Islanders to find direction, but never the Vikings.

The Darkening

Towards the end of the month, a foreboding accompanies sunset, a wariness of the long darkness ahead. There is a different, more energising and inspiring way of thinking about the dark weeks.

Emma Cunis grew up in the Devon countryside and spent a lot of her formative years in the fresh air; she remembers her mother ringing a bell outside for suppertime. After a corporate career that took her to cities around the world and her health to worse places, Emma returned to her roots and began leading nature walks in Dartmoor. We led one walk together a few years ago and I was struck by the way Emma's personality wove disparate strands together – a deep-rooted love of the rural life, a punchiness and confidence in communicating, perhaps nurtured in the rat-race, and interests that took in science, pagan folklore, traditional remedies and ancient Chinese thought.

Emma had much wisdom to share about foraging and she passed on one recipe for a hawthorn tincture that pulls many seasons into a single bottle. Collect the young leaves of hawthorn in the spring and put them in brandy for about a month. Let the flavour from the leaves seep into the spirit, then strain the liquid. Pick some hawthorn blossoms, put them into the flavoured brandy and leave for about a month. Strain again, and wait until the first frost. Pick some hawthorn berries, put them into the liquid for a month, then strain again. The resulting remedy is supposed to be good for healing the heart and regulating blood pressure. It was also recommended for emotional healing after relationship troubles, although Emma confessed that perhaps the brandy did that.

We shared many viewpoints, both taking inspiration from lore, but disliking factual untruths. We discussed the long nights at this time of year and Emma said, 'Everything starts in the dark. Babies, seeds, the universe. It's the most potent, fertile period according to Chinese philosophy. All ancient wisdom sees, in this time, the idea of the infinite. God, vastness, the darkness . . . which we're so afraid of in our modern Western world. It's the dreaming time, it's powerful, it's the night, it's when ideas and dreams come to you.'

15

December

Two Ices

—

Auriga

—

Gemini

—

Low Sun Lines

—

The Winter Solstice and the Lag

—

The Ursids

—

Stories Are Paths

—

The Taurus Compass

—

Sirius at New Year

Two Ices

There is meaning in a monochrome landscape. In December we look for stories in silver lands, black skies and peculiar places.

The fog lifted as I walked up the hill to the ridge of the South Downs. It had been a slippery morning: the Land Rover had lost traction on some black ice at the start of the day and now my boots were not giving me the grip I needed. The land was white. It was a day for reading icy patterns.

Black ice is one of the names given to water freezing on roads. It isn't black, it's transparent, but the road underneath is black, hence the name. It is also known as 'glazed ice', because the frozen water is a little like a glazed window. It has earned a malign reputation for causing road accidents. The ice is no more slippery than any other ice, but its transparency can make it 'disappear' and give no warning. That is what causes the trouble.

On reaching the ridge, I was met by a line of hawthorn trees, which brought me cheer in the form of many familiar patterns – old friends. The very tops of thorn trees have whip-like branches and there were layers of meaning in the shapes I saw. The top third of those short trees was sculpted by the prevailing winds, bent over from the south-west towards the north-east. On most days the very highest, whippiest branches will follow this trend, but not on that cold morning. The topmost whips were bent back over the tree, like spindrift blown off the top of a wave. This was a sign that the most recent winds had broken the long-term trend: northerly winds had brought in the cold weather and changed the form at the tops of the trees, giving them an awkward appearance.

There was a striking asymmetry in the colours of the hawthorns, too, so I stepped in to investigate. The colours would have earned a place on any Christmas card, rich fruity red haws (berries) and a generous dusting of perfect white set against thin black branches and a grey sky. But here was the charm. The red was so much stronger on one side, the white more brilliant on the opposite. Even from a few yards away, I could see that one side was all wintry white, the opposite all rouge and cheer, but the real fun was to be had by getting among the thorns, where I recognised an old favourite: rime ice.

Overnight the cold northerly winds had brought tiny, near-freezing droplets of water for a ride over the hills. Water can stay in liquid form, suspended in the air as freezing fog, sometimes as low as minus 40 degrees centigrade. On meeting obstacles that are themselves below freezing, the super-cooled droplets instantly freeze on contact.

The wind causes the ice crystals to layer on top of each other on the windward side of any obstacles, which leads to a telltale pattern on one side of the plants, crystals jutting out like a thousand tiny daggers. This had led to a white coating on the north side of all the plants on the hill. Rime ice is often confused with the frost we meet under clear skies in autumn, but it's different.

Rime ice is a helpful sign in natural navigation because it forms a consistent pointer over a wide area often when visibility is poor. Three ingredients make rime ice more likely: cold, wind and fog. Rime ice and fog often ride together as they are both signs of cold wet air. Rime ice points towards the direction the wind has come *from*. Cold wet winds often come from the north, but not always, so whenever we meet rime ice we tune into its trend and then it will act as a friendly compass. Rime ice takes a little practice to read intuitively, because our brain likes to think that wind pushes things away from it, but like so many of these clues, once you befriend it you will enjoy meeting it again many times each winter.

I paused for lunch and met the thorns. Once more I got in close enough to hear them scratching my jacket and now I could see another beautiful pattern. The fog had thinned and the sun's disc was breaking through. It had thawed the south side of the berries, giving them a wet radiant sheen, as if they'd been polished.

Auriga

The stars put on a more passionate show in December than in any other month, with a large number of prominent and easy-to-recognise constellations. Mighty Orion rises in the east soon after sunset. We can use all the Orion techniques we met in October and we can also use him to find two very interesting constellations. We have seen how the line that runs up the left side of the Hunter, from Saiph to Betelgeuse, takes us north. It leads us between the constellations of Gemini and Auriga, with Gemini on the left of that line and Auriga on the right. They are fascinating and beautiful constellations and have much to offer.

Auriga features in the list of forty-eight constellations that the ancient astronomer Ptolemy compiled almost nineteen hundred years ago and is a very useful constellation for finding the North Star. It consists of a large ring of five bright stars and a small triangle of three fainter ones. One of the ring stars, Capella, is impressive, the sixth brightest in the night sky and one of the three brightest visible from northern latitudes. It is hard to miss on clear December evenings.

The abnormally bright yellow-white Capella is the ring star furthest from Orion and therefore furthest north. Look near to Capella, between that star and the next clockwise in the ring of five, and you'll spot three faint stars that make a thin triangle. The triangle points roughly towards the North Star, but Auriga offers a more accurate natural navigation method and it is one of my favourites at this time of year. Look anticlockwise from Capella to the first and second stars around the ring of five. Imagine a line that goes from the second of these stars back to the first and continue this line five times that distance and you'll find the North Star.

Gemini

Anyone who hears the parable of the Good Samaritan understands the message about helping someone when it is an unpopular thing to do. How many can recall that the Samaritan gave the innkeeper two *denarii* to cover the costs of hosting the injured party as they recovered? It's an unimportant detail, but it is worth a moment of our time in December.

The *denarii* in question were Roman silver coins and we know what they looked like. On one side there was a pair of young men on horseback, the twin brothers Castor and Pollux. They resided in the night sky, as the constellation Gemini.

Almost all ancient and modern civilisations agree on one thing: there are twins in the night sky. The Persians saw Do Patkar, the two figures; in China they saw Yin and Yang, the two principles; and in India there were the twin deities, the Ashwins; the Arabians saw two peacocks, and the Egyptians a pair of plants. If anyone spends a few minutes looking at the night sky in December, they will see a pair. Once you have met the twins, you are unlikely to forget them – they stay with you.

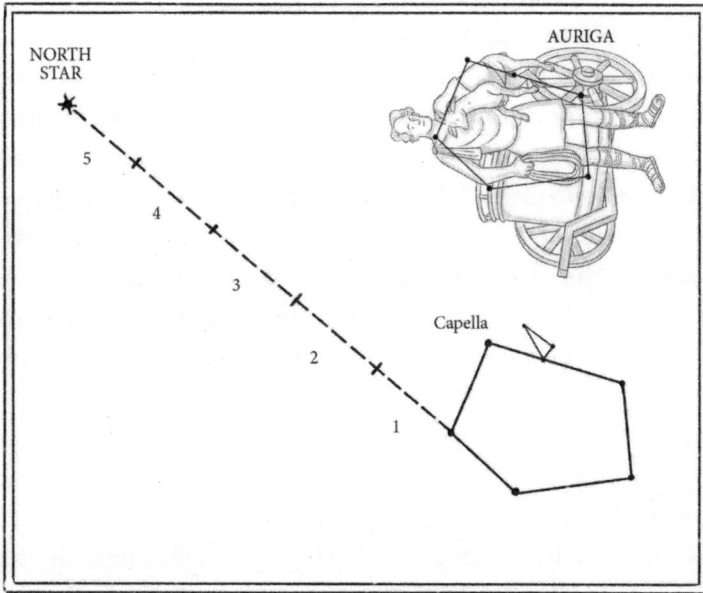

Between fifty and a hundred stars are visible to the naked eye in the constellation Gemini, but we will notice their heads first, the two brightest stars with familiar names, Castor and Pollux. They are among the brightest stars in the sky, which means in marginal conditions we can often see both when the others are hard to make out. References go back thousands of years to the way in which the twins' heads appear different, which is ironic. Castor is pure white, while Pollux is brighter and has a yellow to orange hue.

The twins can be found low in the sky between north-east and east soon after 7 p.m. in December. I like to think of them getting up at this time, because they rise horizontally, as if they're levitating out of bed while still asleep. Castor rises first, then Pollux. Once you can distinguish enough of the constellation above the horizon, you will understand why our ancestors saw twins: there is a remarkable symmetry in the whole constellation. Soon after rising, Gemini can appear like a rectangle, wider than tall, with two much brighter stars at the left-hand side.

Gemini rises in the early evening and arcs upwards, getting higher and higher until it passes through the highest southern sky through the middle of the night. By the early hours of December mornings, it is well on its way down to the western horizon, dropping below it between west and north-west as the sun starts lighting the sky again from the south-east.

If you would like another way to find Gemini, a simple method uses the Plough. Think of it as a saucepan and draw a line from where the handle joins the pan (a star called Megrez) to the bottom right star in the pan, Merak. These two stars form your Gemini pointers. All you need do is continue in the same direction for five times the length between those two stars. You'll spot the bright heads of Castor and Pollux first, then the rest of their bodies (two sides of the rectangle) continuing away from the Plough.

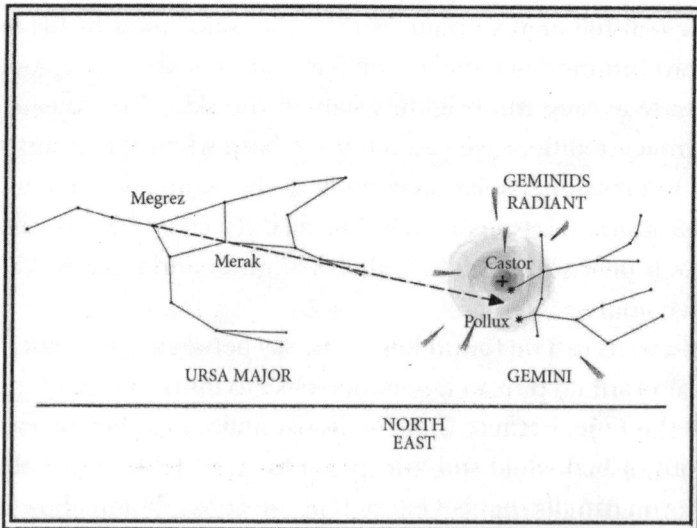

Watching Gemini rise soon after dark in December

Although we can spot Gemini over many months, early December is the time to get to know it best, because there is an excellent meteor shower in mid-December called the Geminids. The Perseids in August are probably more numerous and popular – not everyone enjoys standing outdoors in the December dark – but the Geminids can pip them for entertainment.

The shower can be seen between 4 and 17 December and normally peaks on or near the fourteenth. The radiant for this shower is near the star Castor, the first of the bright pair to rise. Look in that general area. There's no need to focus on one spot – in fact, the best way to catch shooting stars is to allow your eyes to skip to a nearby dark patch every few seconds. If you're in a group, you'll probably end up doing this naturally and improving the odds of catching them between you.

No two years are the same and trying to predict shooting stars with precision is impossible, but if we keep vigilant we will be well rewarded, with more than a hundred meteors per hour if we catch the peak of the shower. There is also a long game to be played here, as the shower is a relatively new one to astronomers. It was first observed in 1862, and is thought to be getting better over the decades.

The late sunrises of December offer a golden chance of catching shooting stars before dawn. It is a magical time. Take a moment before the sun gets up and you may be rewarded with multi-coloured meteors, lots of whites and yellows, but also blues and reds. The Geminid shooting stars are unusual because they are formed by particles of different elements from an asteroid called 3200 Phaeton. Most meteor showers form when Earth moves through the debris in the wake of comets, which are formed of lumps of rock covered with ice, but asteroids bring new ingredients to the mix and more interesting colours to the sky. (The only other impressive shooting stars to form from an asteroid are the Quadrantids, which we'll meet in January.)

Before leaving the twins, look carefully from their heads down to their feet. If the conditions are good, you will notice the background shift from deep black to grey: your eyes have wandered to the Milky Way.

Low Sun Lines

The land has a long memory. Bumps and hollows can last for centuries, sometimes more than a thousand years, if spared the brutal evisceration of the plough. There is a hill near my home with old stories in its grassy fields. The lines that run up it are not perfectly straight, but formal enough to betray human creation: the remnants of an ancient field system. The lines hide for long periods in summer but shine in December.

The smallest undulations show up best when the sun is low. It follows its lowest arc in late December, which means lines that hide for most of the year suddenly appear on sunny winter days. And we are not restricted to ancient field works: this low light transforms every landscape, because the slightest protrusion will cast a shadow when lit from the side.

This is the reason that tracking animals is easiest at the start and end of the day. The squirrel's track in the mud appears at dawn, fades to nothing under a midday summer sun and reappears at dusk. We can see some of the smallest indentations in the middle of a winter day, thanks to the lower sun.

Comparing high and low suns, we will see striking changes wherever we look and on many scales. Study the bark of two trees you pass regularly. Notice how the colours look different and textures appear similar in the middle of a summer day, but in the low sun of winter their colours now look similar but we see the gentlest crenellations appear in the bark of one and not the other, especially when the sun hits the bark from the side.

We can recreate this effect at home. Hold up an orange in a well-lit room and the first thing we notice is its colour. Move to a totally dark space and shine a torch from the side: the dimples stand out. Low light from the side mutes colour and highlights relief and texture.

The Winter Solstice and the Lag

In late December, around the twenty-first or twenty-second, Earth reaches the opposite point in its orbit of the sun from the June solstice. The North Pole points away from the sun and the South Pole towards it. At the December solstice, the sun is over the most southerly point of Earth's surface that it ever reaches: the Tropic of Capricorn, 23.5 degrees south of the equator. If you were standing on it, perhaps near the town of Alice Springs in Australia, you could watch the sun pass directly overhead at midday on the December solstice.

Wherever you are in the world at the December solstice, the sun will rise and set as far south of east and west as it ever does from your location. The further you are from the equator, the more extreme the deviation from east and west. At the equator, the effect is noticeable but not dramatic: the sun will rise 23.5 degrees south of east and set 23.5 degrees south of west. In mid-latitudes, like England, it rises and sets closer to south-east and south-west. At the Arctic Circle – 23.5 degrees south of the North Pole, there's that number again – the sun appears to rise and set at the same place: due south. In other words, the sun never climbs above the horizon. There is a whole lot of twilight to the south at midday, but the sun doesn't actually rise.

From anywhere in the northern hemisphere, the midday sun

will be at its lowest at this time of year. The winter solstice offers the longest midday shadows of the year (which is why we see more bumps in the land in December).

Christmas is snowy in our minds because it is a cute image, not because it is the time of dependable snow. (Dickens gave this image a big push when he set *A Christmas Carol* in a snowy London in 1843, when we were still in 'the little ice age', which lasted from the early fourteenth to the mid-nineteenth century, and snow was more likely. That story has probably been adapted into more movies than snowflakes will fall in London at Christmas.) We experience our lowest levels of sunlight at this time of year, but rarely the lowest temperatures because of the lag in solar effects.

The oceans and atmosphere don't respond instantly to changes in solar radiation. Anyone responsible for heating a home will know the lag effect well: we turn on the lights and see the effects instantly, but we turn on the central heating and don't have a cosy home until an hour or two later. Each season reflects the energy input of the sun a couple of months earlier. The sun turns down the thermostat in December, but we don't feel the temperature effects fully until late January or February (by which time the sun has started turning the dial back up so that we can hope for a warm day or two in April). The sun is giving us the same energy in late March and September, but the lag effect explains why March is often surprisingly brutal and September loves a late heatwave.

The winter solstice was a time of tension and release in ancient cultures. In a world without electric lighting or central heating, our ancestors were especially keen that things should at least *start* moving back in a warmer, brighter direction. The sun headed south for months as the world grew colder and colder. With only traditional beliefs based upon the habits of previous years to offer hope, there must have been a nervous fear that it might not return. What was stopping the sun continuing south, heading off altogether and leaving the world as a dark frozen wasteland?

When the sun indeed slowed and stopped, it was a cause for celebration. Shivering fur-clad proto-astronomers would announce they had noticed that the sunrise had, very slowly, stopped on its journey south. It would soon start working its way back north, promising longer, warmer days once more – mercifully! Northern cultures like to party in late December.

The Ursids

A modest meteor shower lasts from around 17 to 26 December and usually peaks shortly after the solstice, near the twenty-third. These meteors are known as the Ursids, from the Latin for 'bear', because the radiant is found near the North Star, which lies in the Little Bear constellation (Ursa Minor).

Look north near the solstice and pay the closest attention to the patch of sky between the Plough (part of Ursa Major) and the North Star. If we get clear skies at this time of year, temperatures fall sharply, so I remember it this way:

The longest nights and cold air,
Look to the north, near the Bear.

Stories Are Paths

There are only small changes in the natural world as December nears its close, but there is a revolution in our inner world and, as January looms, thoughts shift towards regeneration. The days are short, we venture out less and hunker down more: it is a season to read, watch, listen and think. It is a time for devouring stories.

Think of a story, perhaps your favourite, but any story will do. I may not know you personally, but I can say a few things with confidence about you and your chosen story. Over the past twenty-four hours, you have eaten something, drunk something, slept and navigated. Your story contains clues that could prove helpful for the last of these.

There is a lingering belief that we must clamber into ships and watch shores slip away to navigate, but once we accept that our route to the bathroom in the darkest hours of the night constitutes navigation, we are all in the same boat, so to speak.

Eat, drink, sleep and find our way: four of the things that humans do every day. And that is why these universal activities percolate through all powerful stories. Food writers have mined the old stories for insights into our historical relationship with food. Michael Pollan has described cooking as the 'essential human activity at the heart of all cultures', but he's skipped a beat. How does that food find its way to our tables? It doesn't magically appear. We have to gather it, which requires us to find our way. Navigation comes before food: it is more essential.

Who gathers the food, how and where? That is the first conversation at the heart of every culture. And it continues to this day: every household knows who provides food, who cooks, who washes the dishes and the ratios in which they do it. The slightest imbalance in these delicate scales will lead to conversations. But these conversations were all pre-empted by the chat about who would venture out to gather herbs, throw spears or pick up the Pad Thai.

'Would you mind getting a couple of onions on your way home?' This is a question that only works if we understand that the route home passes the convenience store. Onions and navigation, two ingredients in our most basic conversations.

Storytellers know they are leading us on a journey with clues and choices, and nobody understood this better than the philosophical Italian novelist Umberto Eco, who gave a series of six Harvard lectures that explored the craft of fiction. He published them as *Six Walks in the Fictional Woods*.

Stories lead us into conundrums and crises, then offer us routes out of trouble or deeper into it – the fork we face when lost in the woods. It's our job to spot the signs that hint at the best path, as we learn from the mistakes and triumphs of the characters in the story. After many years in the business, John Yorke, an award-winning British television producer and script editor, wrote a brilliant book about how stories work and why we tell them. Its title? *Into the Woods.*

Stories drop ideas, offer insights and dangle tips to improve our understanding and choices in all human endeavours. They are most abundant in the areas we share, and that is why we can learn to be better wayfinders by spotting the clues within every story.

Deep winter is the time to hone our sensitivity to the clues. It's an art that steals nothing from the stories but enriches them, adding layers to our perception and enjoyment. During the long nights and short days of occasionally unfriendly weather, we have an opportunity to continue our journeys and discoveries vicariously. It doesn't matter if we feel ourselves leaping on to broomsticks, fending off enemy hordes, or sucked into a taut psychological drama: if a story pulls us in it will also offer us clues as to how best to shape our future journeys. We grow more sensitive to the signs out there.

My visit to Ashdown Forest earlier in the year prompted me to delve into the most famous literature of the place in search of insights. A. A. Milne found charm and inspiration enough in the Forest for his *Winnie the Pooh* stories, setting them in the Hundred Acre Wood. The source of that name is no great puzzle: look at an Ordnance Survey map of the area today and you will still see the words 'Five Hundred Acre Wood' in large letters.

As sleet hit the window, gusts crept down the chimney and tugged at the flames over the logs of the fire, I joined Pooh, Piglet, Eeyore, Christopher Robin, Roo, Rabbit and company. I thought it would be an entertaining exercise to read some of the original stories, for fun but also inspiration. Would the nature of the Forest seep deeply enough into Milne's light fantasy world that I would manage to prise out a natural clue or two?

Pooh and Piglet are planning a hunt for a Woozle and timing is important. Piglet asks Pooh what time he thinks it is. 'About twelve,' Pooh replies, after looking at the high sun – an observation to warm a natural navigator on a winter's night.

There are some interesting discussions about how the shape and size of an animal's hole in the ground will reveal its likely owner. Pooh, a bear, demonstrates the infallible logic of this by getting stuck in a rabbit hole.

The intrepid pair have fun tracking animals, following foot-prints in the soil – but the number of animals they are following seems to grow. A single set of 'Woozle' tracks becomes two, then three. It's a proper puzzle until Christopher Robin climbs down from an oak tree and cracks the case: they have been walking around the same small wood until they picked up their own prints in the ground. Pooh and Piglet had been tracking them-selves. It is not impossible that this wisdom could save us from harm or, more likely, embarrassment one day.

In practical natural navigation terms, one of the gems is hidden in plain sight. Milne tells us, in the story in which Piglet meets a Heffalump, that the gang reached 'the Six Pine Trees'. The clue here is almost too obvious.

The six pines form a unique landscape feature: they stand

out as a notable, unambiguous *landmark*. If the team passed 'some trees' or 'a wood' or any other vague descriptor, it would not count as a landmark because it could be any of a thousand nearby places.

The real value of this leaps out when you walk in these landscapes. The clumps of pines scream out across the heather and grasses – they can be seen for miles. If we can find some way of pinning down their identity, some feature that makes a cluster of trees not just visible from far away but also unique, its value soars. 'Six Pines' is clearly the only clump of six pines in the area. We can never be lost if we can see something we have fixed as a landmark. If you have ever been properly lost you will know the pure, powerful joy of recognising a landmark after hours of emotions that tiptoe towards terror.

A grand, dominant isolated tree may qualify as a landmark – it may even earn a name from locals if it is a magnificent specimen that holds court over a local landscape.* But each tree is unique and we can create our own mini-landmarks if we take the time to read trees attentively. It is a good time of year to practise this as many deciduous trees are more distinctive after their leaves have fallen.

This is a practical exercise. We look for and recognise unique shapes in our landscape. Next, we name the new local landmarks: we give them a label that is fitting and memorable. And, if we choose, we can perhaps go one better and create stories from the

---

* I wrote an article for *The Sunday Times* about the tragic case of the Sycamore Gap tree that was felled, criminally, overnight on 27/28 September 2023. Its loss was felt so keenly, not only because a much-loved tree had been taken down but because someone had had the temerity to destroy a landmark and therefore change everyone's relationship with that landscape, making them feel, at a deep level, less secure.

shapes we have seen and the characters we have created. In my local woods I know three gnarly tree shapes as the Crown, the Viking Helmet and the Claw, and I get a warm fuzzy feeling each time I pass them. The brain likes recognising landmarks because this habit protected our ancestors and remains good for us.

Earlier I asked you to think of a story. Clues and signs are hidden within it that will help you shape your journeys in the new year.

The Taurus Compass

Look for the head of Taurus on a late December evening and you will meet a very rare star compass. I haven't come across it being used by anyone else today or in history. I'm sure it was used by our ancestors, but I have uncovered no record of that.

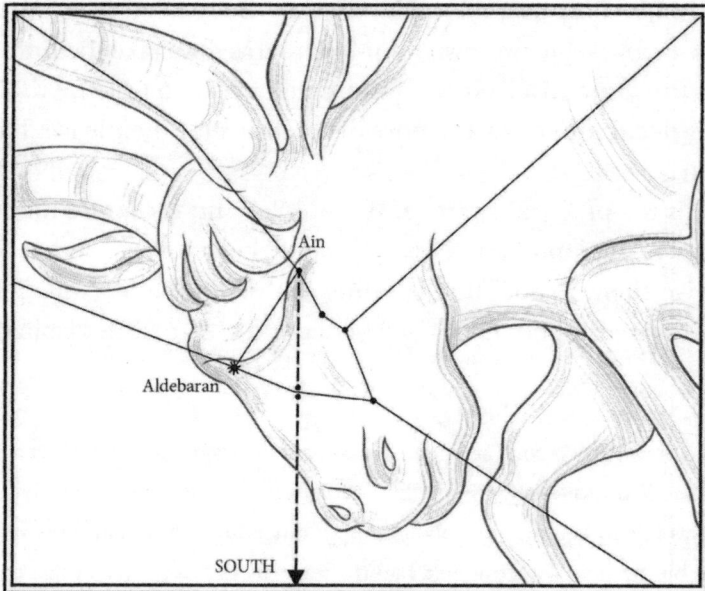

The Taurus Compass

Taurus rises in the east and rolls through the south before dropping towards the western horizon. When the star Ain is directly above those known as Hyadum III and IV, we are looking south.

Sirius at New Year

We've met Sirius already, the brightest star in the night sky. You may recall that we find it by sliding along Orion's belt.

Sirius will be at culmination, the top of its arc, at midnight on New Year's Eve. This is true every year and will be for decades, but not thousands of years. We happen to live in the right era for this happy coincidence. It also means that Sirius will be due south at midnight. I can offer no more beautiful compass or method to cap off the calendar year.

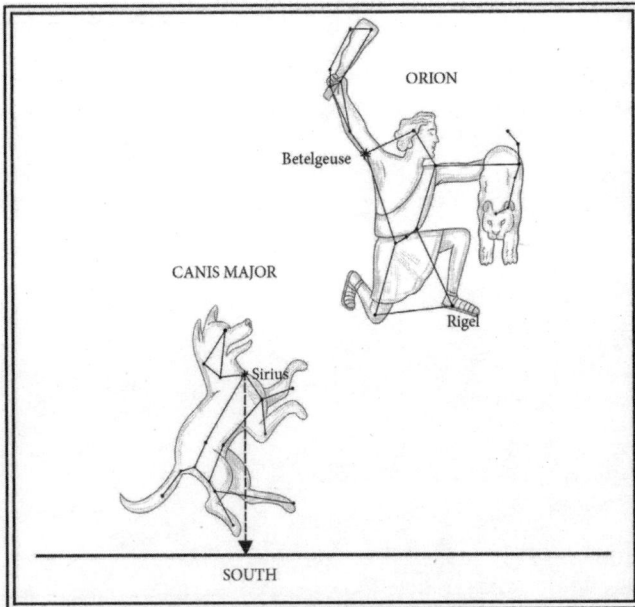

Looking south at midnight on New Year's Eve

16

January

The Quadrantids and Shamanic Radiants

—

Two Sounds

—

Marcescent Chatter

—

The Wistful Warmer

—

New Curves

—

Janus the Winter High

—

Coats and Tameness

—

Saluti, Ötzi!

The Quadrantids and Shamanic Radiants

Brave the cold of January and there are rewards. We learn to predict the behaviour of animals and meteors like a shaman.

I leaped out of the back door, warmed by a story I had read earlier in the evening about shooting stars. In Igloolik, an Inuit hamlet in the Qikiqtaaluk region of northern Canada, meteors have more than one traditional name. The Inuit elders favoured *ingnirujait*, while the young leaned more towards *ulluriat anangit*. The former means 'bearing fire or sparks'; the latter could be loosely translated as 'star shit'.

There is a traditional view in Greenland that meteors are souls on a sightseeing trip from Heaven to Hell before returning. This idea warmed me even more, as I continued my night walk up a local hill in Sussex with a cold breeze on my face and thoughts of souls in Heaven getting itchy feet: 'Heaven's all right, but shall we go for a drive and check out Hell?'

We know that two parts of the meteor showers are fairly predictable – when and where to look. But the Quadrantids have a quirk worth knowing when it comes to 'when'. They light the sky from late December to about 12 January, as Earth travels through the dust in the wake of asteroid 2003 EH1. They peak around 3–4 January. All meteor showers show this pattern of a broad window of gentle activity with a narrower peak of intensity, but the Quadrantids have a much sharper peak than other showers.

The narrow climax changed my relationship with Quadrantids and was the reason for the night walk. With the broader-peaked showers, like the Perseids, I raise my vigilance near the peak and look upwards a lot more at night, but I don't always make a special occasion of viewing them. The tighter punch of the Quadrantids makes its way into the diary and means I'll be weather-watching in the build-up.

A tawny owl called to its partner strongly a few times as I walked on, but it stopped suddenly. Perhaps portending the changes in the sky. Owls are more vocal under clear skies. Frustration swept across from the west in the form of scudding stratocumulus clouds. There were frequent breaks in the blanket, but the wide gaps were mainly to the south and the Quadrantids are a northern shower. Their radiant is in the constellation Boötes, which is easy to track down using the 'arc to Arcturus' method.

Find the Plough, think of it as a saucepan, then follow the curving handle of the pan away from its tip until you meet a star called Arcturus. It's not shy: Arcturus is the fourth brightest in the whole night sky and has a distinctive orange tint. It is the brightest star in the constellation Boötes, the Herdsman.

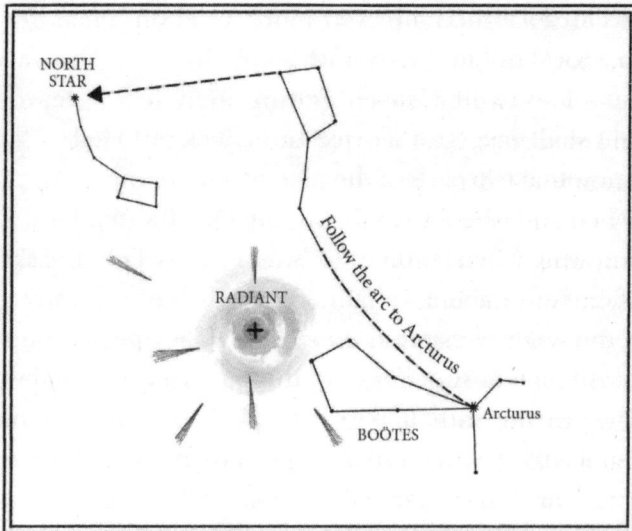

Boötes and the Quadrantids radiant

I caught a few shooting stars through larger gaps in the clouds before they sealed tight. Like the Grand Old Duke of York, I marched back down the hill. I had lost the stargazing battle, but not the war.

At home, I warmed my cold feet by the embers of the dying fire and read some pages by R. W. F. Poole. The late great country writer took a basic approach to outdoor apparel, but found this philosophy tested in his feet over the cold months. In winter, he wore a pair of thermal boots fashioned in Sweden from reindeer hide, believing that 'warm feet are the basis of righteousness'.*

I woke to find the light from the third-quarter moon cutting through a gap in a window blind. It was due south, which must mean it was close to 6 a.m. I tried with difficulty to make out the hands on my watch to confirm this, but it was a test of the watch more than the moon. If the two disagree strongly, I would trust the moon more.

On with my Norwegian jacket, and this time I carried a chair into the garden, laid my head on its backrest and gazed up at the clear sky. Any small warmth had escaped and there was a bite in the air. The Plough had swung round a good quarter since I'd last seen it, but the relationships between the stars and therefore the method are not time-sensitive: we still follow the 'arc to Arcturus' wherever the handle points.

I let my eyes skip in little steps across the northern sky and it was only a minute before the first blue scratch marked the sphere. And then another and another and another. The peak was not over yet. Between each fiery line, I found my attention wandering to the satellites that tracked across the constellations. Each year the satellites multiply, reproducing like rabbits

---

* R.W.F. Poole, *A Backwoodsman's Year*, p. 164.

and nibbling more of the dark sky. They are easy to recognise as steady pinpricks of star-level light that move across the sky. The constant speed is the giveaway: each satellite moves at its own speed – the quicker they are, the lower and closer – but their speed doesn't vary as they cross the sky. They keep a steady pace.

That pre-dawn morning I saw something modest in brightness, but rare indeed. For a couple of seconds, no more, a star near Boötes grew from nothing to a small, glowing, fiery point before disappearing again. It took me a moment to appreciate what I had seen. What can be the only deduction on seeing a single point of light, a dot that flames and fades to nothing? That a meteor is heading directly towards us. That was what I had seen: a smaller-than-a-pea missile on course to hit me between the eyes, or somewhere not far away. But I had no fear. The odds on it reaching the ground were very small and the odds on it hitting me or anyone else a lot smaller still. But not zero.

A small meteorite tore open an artery in the leg of a Franciscan friar in the seventeenth century. And one wrecked Mrs E. Hodges's Alabama roof when it crashed through the ceiling, bounced off the radio and hit her on the leg in 1954. Michelle Knapp found her Chevrolet somewhat unroadworthy after a meteorite smashed into it on 9 October 1992.

Shooting stars are considered lucky by some and more profound by others. The explorer and anthropologist Knud Rasmussen, writing about an expedition to the far north between 1921 and 1924, recorded the local belief that an Inuit woman named Uvavnuk developed strong shamanistic powers after a meteorite 'entered' her, although the exact meaning of that is not clear. Her son, Niviatsian, inherited some of her shamanic potency. I can't promise you such powers, but my night and morning with the Quadrantids allowed me to practise a technique that might convince others we hold them.

If we know the radiant of a meteor shower, we can use this to make a prediction about the direction in which we will see shooting stars move because they radiate – they head away from the radiant. It's a question of perspective: all objects move away from the radiant from the perspective of the observer. If, for example, you face towards the direction the wind is blowing the clouds *from* – let's call this 'the clouds' radiant' – you can predict the direction they will move in all other parts of the sky. Look left of the clouds' radiant and they appear to move right to left; look to the right of it and the clouds appear to move left to right. And if you look towards this radiant direction the clouds will move low to high until they're over your head; if you turn your back they will move from high to low.

We cannot predict the exact timing of the next meteor, but we can practise a little magic with unsuspecting friends, if we note where they are looking relative to the radiant. Imagine a line from the radiant through the patch of sky they are focusing on and any shooting stars in that area are likely to follow an extension of this line. Not shamanism, just good meteor science, but I'll let you decide what you tell them about your new powers.

Two Sounds

I was admiring the way a high fork in a tree had caught the falling thin branch of its neighbour, when I heard a sharp sound. A few seconds later I heard a similar staccato crack, muffled by the undergrowth between us. It came from a thin strip of woods that ran between two fields, about eighty yards to the south; the sounds had carried against the northerly breeze. Now I was listening and looking, my focus had shifted consciously. I had experienced the simple powerful awareness switch that most mammals, including humans, experience in nature in this situation. This is the law of two sounds.

The natural world has an abiotic soundtrack – leaves in the wind, rain falling, waves breaking . . . It is extremely important for prey to be able quickly to decipher the difference between an abiotic noise and an animal moving nearby. Did the twig snap because of the wind or because a predator is moving towards me?

The context is important. The sound of a twig snapping on a windy day surprises no person or animal. This is one reason why many prey animals are less inclined to venture far on windy days – it gives predators an advantage, like an audio smokescreen. However, on calmer days there are still many apparently random sounds in any natural setting. Silence exists in a vacuum, but never in a landscape. If you spend enough time outdoors you will hear every sound conceivable, including a large mature tree falling unexpectedly on a calm day, which is terrifying.

Animals can't stop what they are doing and tune into every single sound they hear. It would make life impossible – they would starve to death. Fortunately, evolution has developed an approach that allows animals to screen out most noise and focus on key messages. A twig snapping may or may not be another animal. Two sounds of twigs breaking in short succession from roughly the same direction are unlikely to be anything else. It's a game of probability: the chance of two unlikely events happening in the same zone is low enough that it is a different signal – stop what you're doing and tune in. The animals follow this approach and we can too. This is the law of two sounds.

Hunters have long known it. The art of hunting centres on a deep understanding of the patterns, habits, rules, strategies, tendencies and probabilities of animal behaviour. A single sound will put prey animals in the area on alert. A second noise changes their behaviour. They switch from vigilance to flight mode – they're off. A second sound also allows animals to pinpoint the location of the threat and shape a better escape.

Most people are more familiar with this law than they might realise, but in a different setting. If you have ever been lying in bed at night and hear a weak sound outside that doesn't fit expected patterns, it might make you curious, possibly alert. If we can explain it away, we can relax. But two similar unexplained sounds will ratchet up the adrenaline and pulse. The brain switches from hearing a noise to sensing a signal: something or someone is definitely out there. Again, context is key, and your understanding of your neighbourhood will shape your reaction.

After freezing, motionless, for half a minute and focusing on the trees through the low crepuscular light, I watched the silhouettes of one, then two, three, four and more fallow deer moving across the thin strip of woods. If they had broken only one stick underfoot, they might have passed unnoticed, but they couldn't beat the law of two sounds. Now it was time to turn the tables. I clapped once, not too loudly. The two deer I could still see through the trees froze and lifted their heads. I clapped a second time and they bolted, cantering up the hill, making a small racket underfoot.

Marcescent Chatter

A buzzard landed on a low branch only twenty feet from my head, so much closer than I normally get to them. I grew conscious of my every movement, making stillness harder – even my breathing suddenly required complex effort. I turned as slowly as I could, but it wasn't good enough: the bird launched and carved a route between the hazels. Who was I kidding? Their eyesight is eight times better than a human's. The buzzard had made me greedy and I willed the fox to pass. I sometimes see him on a dawn patrol in these parts, but never when I will it. He's too wily for that. Instead I watched a pair of squirrels jumping from branch to branch in the beeches. There are not many motives for animals to leap about with so much energy on a cold January morning. A single squirrel might have been flee-ing a threat, but the pair gave it away: they were courting. January and February are busy times for squirrels.

I closed my eyes and listened to one of my favourite winter sounds, the marcescent chatter. A woodland wind called the 'bulge' passes between the tree canopy and the ground, the zone in which we spend our time. In summer, the bulge-wind effect is quite strong as the air is forced below the leaves on the trees. But we can feel it in winter too and this is the best season to listen for it.

Many broadleaf trees, including oaks, beeches and horn-beams, hold on to dead brown leaves on their lowest branches throughout winter. Scan the lowest of broadleaf branches and any small young trees at this time of year and it won't be long before you see the light catching the stubborn brown leaves. You will come across this 'marcescence' effect in trees wherever you are and it's easy to spot in towns where you are likely to pass the occasional beech hedge with a full coat of brown leaves (one reason why beeches are popular hedge trees). When the wind brushes past the dry brown leaves they rub together and make a particular winter sound. It's like the faintest rattle, a bit scratchy, but I think of it as the 'marces-cent chatter'. It's a sound that marks the winter woods for me, but I also like trying to pick it up against the noise of a town when passing a hedge or park tree, even if it means leaning into the brown foliage.

The Wistful Warmer

The thought occurred to me, as I sat watching squirrels and listening to the leaf chatter, that I first paused in those Sussex woods two decades earlier. I've been having lots of thoughts like that recently and ascribe them to passing my half-century recently. But there is another possible explanation for these feelings in winter. They keep us warm.

An extraordinary piece of work by researchers at the University of Southampton has revealed that feelings of nostalgia can act like a hot-water bottle. Professor Tim Wildschut, co-author of the study, put it more scientifically: 'Our study has shown that nostalgia serves a homeostatic function, allowing the mental simulation of previously enjoyed states, including states of bodily comfort; in this case making us feel warmer or increasing our tolerance of cold.'

I couldn't resist getting in touch with Professor Wildschut to ask if he would try to summon up feelings of nostalgia if he was suffering from the cold and in danger of hypothermia. He was good enough to humour me: 'I would only do so if I had run out of more pragmatic solutions, like putting on extra clothing or staying indoors. Under life-threatening circumstances, like cold, hunger or thirst, nostalgia is a last resort that may help one to hold on just a little longer. "A grain in the balance", in Darwin's words.'

If you're shivering, put on more clothes, and if that fails, pull out that photo of you playing with your best friend as a child and you'll be cosy in no time. Welcome to the wistful warmer.

New Curves

A thin waning crescent moon, three days off new, struggled for height as it rolled up from the south-east. The imaginary line touching its horns pointed down to the south. There was the first glow from the sun in the south-east and, sandwiched between the sun and the moon, Venus was bright.

Recent gales had brought down storm flotsam and it lay

across the path. Thousands of dead leaves, tiny twigs and nut husks lay deep in the ruts of the forestry tracks and covered the rain channels, but the next heavy rains would clear it, like a sneeze. After heavy winter rain, look for pale sinuous lines on any slopes: this is where the rain has cut through the dark debris. There will be small mounds where the leaf litter piles up and forces the rainwater to pick a new route.

There were signs of greater mayhem ahead. A skeletal old ash tree I had known for many years, long dead from ash dieback fungus, had come down across the path. It couldn't have been there for more than a few days as I'd passed that way recently, but already the 'smile path' has formed, a curved detour in the long grass to one side of the track. There are different types of smile path, but this is one of my favourites: fallen trees and other small, determined obstacles lead to tight, well-defined smile shapes, like a joker's grin. Long stretches of deep mud or boggy ground create a broader, weaker smile, a smirk.

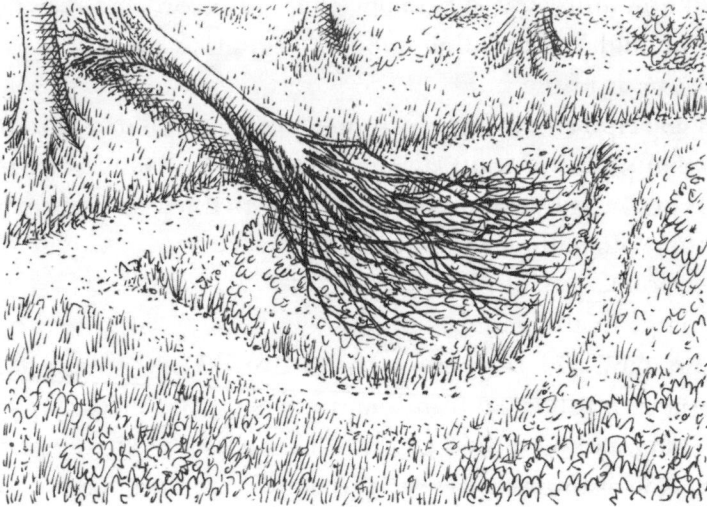

Smile path

Janus the Winter High

At the edge of the woods, a pair of mature yew trees arched over the track, meeting a few feet above my head as a dark gate. A weak winter light poured through the bare broadleaf trees beyond. I was passing a dark portal to a lighter world.

The ancient Roman god Janus was responsible for beginnings and endings, entrances and exits, and his image appeared on many gates. His name lies behind that of our month January, and he was famously two-faced, able to look forwards and backwards at the same time. One of the principal differences between amateurs and professionals lies in their perspective on events: rookies react, experts anticipate. We do well to see January as the depth of the winter season *and* the precursor to spring. A few feet from the yew trees I found fresh green leaves on a honeysuckle vine. Leaves were bursting out of a small elder tree, and there were catkins on the hazels.

A two-faced January character is easy to recognise when you know him, but he passes most people unnoticed: the 'winter high'. When the clouds clear during a winter high pressure, nothing holds in the warmth and the temperature falls precipitously, especially overnight. Winter highs are notorious for both sunshine and some of the lowest temperatures of the year and they are popular or unpopular depending on your situation. They are glorious friends on a city lunchbreak, lots of sun, blue sky and crisp frosts decorating the park. In the suburbs they burst the pipes of those away on holiday, and in remote regions care is taken to guard against hypothermia and frostbite. Visibility is impressive in cold, dry, crisp air, and high ground will offer some of the best views we will ever see. But always remember: the winter high is a Janus character and I met the other face as I ventured into the woods.

After a few days of brilliant blue skies, an oppressive grey blanket now lay heavy over the country and all colours leached from the land. There was no break in the clouds, just a dull thick sheet of grey stretching from horizon to horizon. The air was cool, but nowhere near the cold of the previous days. Gone were the wondrous sunrises and sunsets. Light levels smudged up from dawn to midday, the sun buried behind a wall of tarnished silver. No sun, no rain, no snow, little wind. A disgusting sky, rude in its monotony, but the land was still gripped by a high-pressure system. How could this be?

It was 'anticyclonic gloom'. Anticyclonic simply means 'high pressure' (cyclones are extreme lows) and the gloom bit is accurate. This ugly face appears when the winds circling clockwise around the centre of the system pass over oceans and pick up lots of moisture, enough to form clouds even in sinking air. The clouds get stuck under the falling air in the high pressure, which traps them, smothering a region in a thick blanket of grey. And the gloom was there to stay, because highs don't budge easily. Whichever face Janus shows, it is likely to stick around for days.

How can we tell when Janus is about to turn and we might see a different face or perhaps a different weather system? The direction of the wind is the key: if you sense it changing by ninety degrees or more, a significant change in the weather isn't far off. One of the most enjoyable ways to do this is to keep an eye on the way the birds are facing – if that changes significantly, the wind direction has shifted and soon the weather will too.

Coats and Tameness

I leaned against the smooth bark of a beech and looked down a firebreak in the trees. I didn't expect to see much – January is not a month of great activity – but I did know that my chances were much higher if I looked along a straight, clear line.

Barely ten seconds later, I watched a red fox trot into the firebreak and follow it away from me for half a minute, then duck back into the trees and out of sight. It was long enough to notice the rich darkness in the ruddy colour of his coat. Many animals that remain active through the winter months change their clothing for the season, including foxes, hares, weasels, stoats, wolves, caribou, reindeer, leopards, lemmings and ptarmigan. Some adapt to the scenery: Arctic foxes and mountain hares put on a whiter coat; red foxes take on a darker hue in the winter months as they don a thicker, warmer coat – they appear lightest in late summer.

The robin landed not far from my feet. It cocked its head to one side to give it a better view, then hopped closer still, appearing unusually friendly. This was a display of 'midwinter tameness', a common behaviour in animals that have to forage for a living in the harshest season. When food is abundant animals take fewer risks in their search for a meal, but when winter bites and food is scarce, the same animals cannot afford to overlook any opportunity: their appreciation of risk alters. We find we can get closer to some animals in the harsh winter weeks than in summer, especially garden birds. In truth, it is neither tameness nor friendliness, just desperation. Our ancestors had a more honest view: January was the 'wolf month' when sharp-toothed canines descended from the wooded hills to the villages.

Saluti, Ötzi!

In 1991 a pair of German tourists, Helmut and Erika Simon, stumbled across human remains on an icy ridge in the Alps, near the Austrian-Italian border.

After the police arrived, work began to estimate the date of the mountaineer's death, as this would help identify the unfortunate individual. It did not appear to be a recent accident. All mountaineers carry certain tell-tale equipment and investigators knew it would be possible to estimate the rough date of any death from the clothing and kit found on the body. Any Gore-Tex in a jacket, for example, would mean that a climber died after 1969, the year that the breathable fabric was invented. Experts in ice axes would also be able to estimate the date range of an accident, as all equipment evolves over time. A similar approach was used to establish the approximate time of death of the man in the ice. Konrad Spindler studied the axe found with the body, but he was not a policeman or forensic scientist so it was hard to be precise. He was an archaeologist and estimated the mountaineer to have died at least four thousand years ago, which changed the nature of the investigation completely.

The long-dead man earned the name Ötzi, after the Ötzal region of the Alps, and quickly became a popular and scientific sensation. The ice had mummified his body and preserved his tissues and the equipment he was carrying with him at the time of his death. Archaeologists managed to reconstruct Ötzi's lifestyle, before it was cut short by wounds that included an arrowhead deep in his left shoulder. Analysis of pollen grains and the chemical elements found in his teeth revealed the exact village where he had spent his childhood, modern-day Feldthurns, before he travelled to live in the valleys further north in about 3200 BC.

Alongside his axe of copper and yew, Ötzi had many other supplies, including arrows in a quiver and an unfinished longbow. He also carried a pair of baskets fashioned from birch bark and some simple tools. Sloes were found near the body, which might have suggested an autumn death, but the freshness of the pollen in his stomach – believed to be only two hours old at the time of death – proved that he had died in spring or early summer. The sloes must have been preserved from the previous year. There were two types of fungi in his possession, a birch polypore and a tinder fungus. The birch polypore is a common bracket fungus found on dead or dying birches and it has been used in traditional medicine for as long as we have records. Some have speculated that Ötzi may have used it to expel a parasite called whipworm. The tinder fungus is the one that always reminds me of Ötzi, especially in winter.

We know that many fungi are not only seasonal, but ephemeral, with fruiting bodies that seem to appear overnight and disappear as quickly. But perennial tough fungal bodies can be found year-round. The structure of these hardy specimens gives them properties that recommend them to fire-makers. Humans have used fungi for thousands of years as tinder, and also for transporting fire from one place to another. The idea of transporting embers may seem odd from the perspective of our era of flames at the touch of a button, but if you have ever had the pleasure of starting a fire using traditional friction methods, you will see the virtue. Carrying a glowing ember for a short journey is smarter than sweating and swearing until smoke rises over blisters. Ötzi carried several pieces of the tinder or hoof fungus; it can look uncannily like a horse's hoof. Tests revealed that he had used it for lighting fires.

I think of Ötzi when I'm walking in the cold winter highs and especially when the sun catches the dark semi-spherical domes of King Alfred's Cakes, also known as cramp balls, a fungus with the formal name *Daldinia concentrica*. I see these fungi on dead or dying ash trees – it's common to find a colony of a dozen half-golf-ball-sized black lumps on a felled stump or thick branch.

As a salute to Ötzi, there is a January ritual I like to follow. I gather some of these dark cakes and dry them for a few days. Then, when a sunny winter high has thrown a blue blanket over the land and turned down the outdoor thermostat, I light a candle using a modern lighter. I hold one of the dried fungal balls to the flame until it glows. I blow out the candle and carry the black and glowing orange fungus on a short walk in the woods, before returning to relight the candle with the fungus. *Saluti, Ötzi!*

17

Early February

Silver Floods and Sky Mirrors

—

A Tree Mystery

—

Lost Souls and Raging Water

—

Snow Mosaics

—

Winter Eyes

—

Silver Floods and Sky Mirrors

Late winter is when we learn to spot the subtle patterns in apparent chaos. Nothing is random. Every cloud, stream and snowflake has meaning.

I headed into the foothills of the Cairngorm Mountains in Scotland with Shaila Rao, the conservation manager of the Mar Lodge Estate. It covers thirty thousand hectares of high lean land and hosts the plants and animals that give this part of the world its signature wild beauty. There are sea and golden eagles and patches of the old Caledonian pinewoods stretching back, unbroken, to prehistory.

Shaila told me that the eagles aren't always obvious on first sight, but that they give themselves away by flapping infrequently. Other large birds of prey, like buzzards, might look similar, but they lack the mighty wingspan of the eagles and have to flap more regularly.

We walked away from the river that had mocked its banks and ran in countless fat ribbons across the floodplain. February is the month to look for the 'silver floods'. This is the time of wet ground, with snow melt and rain, and the sun has yet to muster the height to burn off the water. Rivers and streams swell and burst. If you find yourself with a good view, look across low ground towards the brightest sky. The light will bounce off any water that lies over the ground, painting silver sheets in the flood plains but also bright snakes in places we might never have believed the water to reach. The same view looks different at all other times of year.

Where we see silver floods, it's worth looking up. We see the silver in the water because of the light from the sky, but that light also reflects up into the sky, all the way to any low clouds. On days with sunlight and low clouds the effect can be electric: the sun reflects off the water and paints the undersides of the clouds with a more brilliant coat. It will also light any moisture in the air, giving the atmosphere brilliance.

It is worth searching for more exquisite patterns. We take our inspiration from the indigenous hunters of the far north, the Inuit, who have learned to map the ground and water by looking to the sky. From water, Inuit hunters sense distant ice sheets in the brightness of the clouds in that direction, an effect called 'ice blink'. Looking from ice and seeing darkness in clouds reveals open water in that direction, a pattern known as 'water sky' (it can look like heavy rain).

We may not navigate the same icy waters as the Inuit, but their skills offer inspiration and methodology. The key is contrast. If you are blessed with a scene that mixes extreme dark landscape areas with wide areas of water, look for the same contrasts mirrored weakly in any low clouds.

The ingredients must be right for bold patterns. We need low clouds with flat bases, dark land areas, water and some sunlight. It helps if the weather is calm – we want both water and clouds to make good mirrors. My best tip is to take a positive approach: these effects are there to be seen. Put another way, why should we not aim to see a puddle in a cloud? Failure in this endeavour is positive, we'll spot something we didn't think to look for. I regularly find rewarding patterns in low clouds above a city river.

A Tree Mystery

Looking higher up the valley, between the dominant dark pines, I could see large healthy colonies of larches. They are light-hungry trees and do best in the places that the sun reaches. They are also the only deciduous conifers in the country and leap out in many seasons, showing an untidy brown in midwinter, through bright greens in spring, darkening a touch in late summer and turning golden yellow in autumn before falling. Larch woods make fun winter walking as the light gets in and the ground builds up a soft, thick, bouncy carpet of long needles. Black grouse grazing on larch buds is a signal spring moment on the estate.

The sound of the river faded as we climbed through pines that had grown tall in the shelter of the river valley. My eyes, always tuned to asymmetry, fixed on the dark sides of the trees, where storm winds had driven rain and sleet on to the exposed south-western sides of the bark. The contrast was dramatic: the bark was black on the higher south-west side of the trees, but much paler, a faded pink-brown, on the lower valley side. The colours didn't merge or segue into each other. A distinct line divided the two. This is a clue and a compass, but a temporary one. It needs spotting and resetting after each gale. The darker, wetter bark is not guaranteed to be on the south-western side, it could be any, but once we have tuned to the side it is on after each wet-weather event, it will hold true and consistent over wide areas, until the sun or the next rains reset the trend. Wind and rain leave wet footprints on trees.

During our walk, Shaila mentioned a couple of times that the pines on the estate favoured the north side of the mountains. I made a mental note to come back to this observation as it jarred with my understanding and experience of pines. When I did, I discovered a wonderful jigsaw.

Shaila was leading a programme of regeneration, helping the trees, especially the pines, to re-establish themselves after decades of punishing over-grazing by the red deer. The main tactic was simple: the deer numbers needed controlling and, in the absence of wolves, this meant shooting them. As their numbers fell to historically proportionate levels, the trees were no longer 'nipped in the bud' and started to grow again. The pines made their return.

'We're doing almost as well as the wolves.' Shaila smiled.

But one zone proved stubbornly difficult, resisting all good efforts to help the trees. It was on the south-east side of one of the mountains. Looked at through any one of the layers, this was a puzzle. The soil, altitude, weather, climate and aspect were all suitable for the pines, but they would not thrive. Now, after hundreds of rifle cracks, the deer numbers had been brought under control, but still the trees refused to flourish. It was a mystery.

The answer lay in a sunbeam. If you have spent time outdoors in winter, you will know the joy of the moment when the sun lifts just high enough to warm. The deer know this feeling well. There were no longer too many on the estate, but those that remained were not spread evenly. They were packed into zones. The deer were congregating on the south-east side of the mountain, waiting for the mid-morning sun to warm them. The smaller numbers had gathered in tighter concentrations, thanks to the habits of the sun, which had killed off the pines on that side of the mountain. This helped explain why the pines favoured the north side of the mountains. Pines love sunlight and prefer the southern sides of hills, but so do the deer and they held the power in these mountains.

'We tried chasing them, but no point . . . They're soon back there. They like the rays in the morning.'

The trees endure hard weather in these parts, but they do it in different ways. The spruces cope with heavy snowfall by letting their drooping branches usher the snow downwards with gravity; we hear clumps and thumps as it slides off and hits the ground, especially after the temperature lifts a degree or two. The pines have more rigid, less floppy branches and hold them closer to horizontal. They lose whole branches with a violent crack. The pines also shed them after extreme cold snaps. Shaila told of the time that the thermometer went down to minus 30 degrees centigrade at night. The following day the spruces were unmoved, but branches fell from the pines all around and some had come down, trunk and all. There was no wind, just bitter cold under open skies.

Lost Souls and Raging Water

I stopped suddenly. There were bold asymmetries in the ice patterns on the dirt track. A long thin line of ice ran along the south side, but there was none on the north. The sun struggles to reach the south side – there is often more shade from growth to the south of the track – and finds it easier to warm the north.

Towards the end of our time walking, I listened to stories of those who had got lost in those mountains. They would pitch up at Shaila's home or one of the other nearby buildings in a rattled, anxious state. They had reached safety, but were confused; a debrief would reveal their past hours. They had made a popular mistake, one I have made in the past.

After growing disoriented and then lost on high ground, they had followed a water course downhill, reasoning this must lead them towards their start point. The problem was that they had crossed the ridgeline, stepped over the watershed, without realising it. It's an easy mistake to make in old mountains because the highest ground is gentle and rounded, worn by millions of years of erosion, unlike the jagged peaks of young summits. The weary walkers had followed the water down into a totally different valley, all the way to the edge of civilisation. They struggled to believe how far they were from where they felt they must be. Still, they were safe. As the old navigator's joke goes, water will lead you home, if not to yours, then at least to somebody else's.

We paused by a mighty bridge and the water roared loud and angry beneath it, slamming into the dark rocks below. The stone arch of the bridge reached a good thirty feet above the rocks of the valley, but the river was in spate and threw itself up at the bottom of the bridge in angry white spurts. This is the time of year, as the meltwaters flood the valleys, to look closely at bridges. It really helps to practise seeing the character of any watercourse in February and tying this to the nature of the bridges – high arches hint at tempestuous water. In six months, the waters will have dropped and we'll find it hard to believe that the meek river could ever lose its temper or trouble us. If we learn to sense the meaning of the bridges in late winter, the water finds it harder to trick us into thinking it's harmless at other times. Throughout the year, when we're near watercourses we don't know well, it's worth remembering, if we don't want a nasty surprise:

High bridges and heavy rain,
Think twice, then think again.

For the same reason, this is the season for admiring waterfalls – the cataract that underwhelms in September will quicken the blood in February. I thanked Shaila and continued on my way, keen to explore and hopeful that I wouldn't need to knock on strangers' doors.

Snow Mosaics

There was a small mountain near the ski resort of Glenshee that I picked to study snow. It looked, from its base, like the perfect candidate: a short walk would take me to a zone above the tree-line where I would find hundreds of patches of snow, but also many darker stretches of heather and grass. I would have the opportunity to study the meaning in the mosaic of remnant white patches.

I crossed a small stream and walked uphill, sticking to the grass and threading my way between clumps of heather. The wind channelled between the summits, heaving and sighing over the mountains, tugging at the water in the stream.

In one direction the land was white; opposite, it was dark. South-facing snow thaws more quickly than north-facing at the same altitude. Here's the twist: we see south-facing slopes when we look north and vice versa. That means we see more snow when looking south, which is perfectly logical but a little coun-terintuitive as we associate the south with light and warmth. 'Look south for snow.'

We will see the same effect painted beautifully on the moun-tains below the wings of any aircraft.

At the edge of my eye, the snow moved. Our peripheral vision is bad at detail but good at sensing motion and flagging it to our brain. My eyes had been low, picking a route between sodden mud and heather, but the motion at the corner of my eye was enough to pull my head up. The snow moved again. I focused as best I could on the restless patch as my brain sifted through dozens of scenarios to try to understand what was happening. We all get this feeling regularly. It's a sign the brain is aware of something in our environment that needs attention but not why. It does this quickly and automatically as it's one of its evolutionary priorities. There are a hundred things we can ignore easily, but if there is anomalous fast motion in your field of vision your brain will nudge you to work out what it is. Try to ignore a plastic bag flying past you on the wind. Impossible.

The snow moved once more and this time a lump left the main patch and bounded up the hill away from me. For a fraction of a ridiculous second, I thought it might be a white dog, but then I recognised a mountain hare in its splendid white winter coat. I experience the same joy each time I see these magical creatures, and I'm always pleasantly shocked at how big they are. The hare moved quickly and without apparent effort up the steep slope – hares flee uphill – and disappeared behind the heather on a ridge. I changed my heading towards the snow it had crossed, hoping to find its tracks. I did, but they were weak, thanks to the snow having formed a firm crust during the recent cold snap. The dark droppings were easier to make out: small black pellets on a white canvas.

The cold southerly wind was on my back for the first hour and I was grateful that I was turning into it regularly to investigate things – it kept me wise to the wind's duplicity. In the mountains it is too easy to think of identical distances being equal. They are not. A mile with your wind on your back is not the same as a mile with it on your face. The walk back would be across a harsher world.

The greatest challenge was taking notes and photos. An ungloved hand would protest after only seconds in the mean wind so I relied on two layers. Some tasks meant taking a mitten off and relying on the thin glove underneath, which allowed a few minutes before the fingers smarted. Work in these conditions is trying, the days are short and the work so much slower than scribbling and snapping away under endless hours of June sunshine. But the joys are unique and I've never seen a white hare under a high sun.

We need not dwell on every gale-bent hummock or clump of snow I met that day. Instead, let me share my growing collection of snow-reading tools. Each one allows us to see another layer and together they make a meaningful picture.

First, we have the wrestle between altitude, temperature and gravity. The higher we go, the colder it is and the more likely snow will remain for long periods. However, snow, like water, will head downwards until something stops it. That is why it is common to find thin, hard, icy patches high on a slope, and deeper, softer, slushier snow further down.

The wind shapes the places snow collects, which influences where it lingers – deep snow lasts longest. There is normally at least one 'beast' each winter, when a weather system carries a very cold air mass from frozen continental land. In 2018, a high-pressure system over Scandinavia led to clockwise winds that ushered freezing polar air over the UK. The thermometer plunged, schools closed and the media had a lot of fun talking about 'the Beast from the East'. The late artist and author Robert Gibbings put it well: 'Reason, will power and the warmest clothes are powerless against an east wind.'

Vertical strips of snow will line one side of the trees after every snowstorm. Once we have tuned into which side that is, we can use it as a dependable compass over many miles. This is one of my favourite winter compasses. Each winter I venture into woodland I don't know well. First, I walk for about ten minutes towards the snow strips on trees, then turn ninety degrees and walk with the strips visible to my right for ten minutes. I turn again and walk towards the bare side of the trees, then turn a final time and walk for ten minutes with the strips on my left. The four sides of the square lead me very close to where I am trying to get to – back to my start point – but, as with all natural navigation exercises, there are always small errors and understanding these yields valuable insights. For instance, walking ten minutes uphill creates a shorter side than ten minutes downhill. Or it can be subtler, the wind bending as it works its way around a proud rock, changing the snow-strip patterns downwind of it.

The same snow-laden wind leads to bulges on the windward side and tails on the downwind side of any obstacles in the snow's path, like tree stumps. If you are getting into a car after a night of heavy snow, notice how it has built up more on one side than the other. Then look at the patterns on the ground nearby. Finally, zoom in and study the patterns around tiny obstacles on the car, like an aerial or wing mirror. Then forgive yourself for being late for something less important than reading snow stories.

On a larger scale, this wind leads to more snow accumulating on the sides of any hills or mountains. And it creates fascinating, sometimes dangerous, sculptures over ridges, including cornices, the overhanging ledges of snow that tempt some poor souls to walk out over a treacherous bridge made of water and air. One cornice expert suggests that we should never be close enough to a snowy edge that we can look down over it – if we can see over the edge, there is the terrifying possibility that we are standing over a few feet of snow and a thousand feet of air.

The two grand painters, sun and wind, lead to north–south and east–west asymmetries and the effects can overlap. More snow arrived from the east; more snow thawed on the southern side . . . The north-east side of the mountain has the deepest snow.

When the snow stops falling, the wind continues to act. It picks up any loose snow and carries it until it falls out of the flow, which leads to snow accumulating in any wind shadows. It fills in any hollows in the landscape. Many of the patches I could see on the mountainside highlighted small dips in the land, places the wind struggles to reach and the snow comes to rest. The wind carries dry snow, which is more common during very cold snaps, over any bumps or higher parts, then drops it and lets it gather in the dips. This paints any depressions in the land white, like a fingerprinting powder. After a light snow shower, paths and animal trails appear as white lines across a dark hill.

When the temperature rises above freezing, the wind carries this thawing air across the land and leaves its mark. The warmer air melts snow quickly, but the hollows and other wind shadows hold on to their snow for longer, compounding the lasting effect of the deep snow there. A cold nor'-easter can bring in heavy snow and cover that side of the mountain, but a week later, a mild sou'-wester might thaw any snow that has survived on that side. The north-east and south-west sides of the mountain look quite different.

Let's return to the sun's influence. The southern sun thaws the south-facing slopes first, but it also warms the land unevenly because dark surfaces absorb more heat than light ones – parked black cars lose snow faster than white cars. This means that a landscape of mixed vegetation is likely to have more snow on the lighter colours. On the hills around me I saw little snow on the dark heather, a lot more on the pale grasses between. Two effects were in play, the sun warming the dark heather more quickly *and* the heather standing taller than the grasses, allowing the wind to scour it clear of snow.

Snow patches appear random only if we let them. In truth they create an intricate portrait of the elements' waltz with the landscape.

Winter Eyes

Very sadly we lost our old family dog, a beloved miniature Schnauzer, Dreyfus, as I was writing this chapter.* It was peaceful, but sad, my wife and I resting our hands on him as he slipped away on a rug on the floor of the vet's surgery.

We'd been through a lot together, Dreyfus and I, mostly play, a little work, and he appears in a few of my books. He taught me plenty about animal body language and I will never forget how he would signal the presence of other animals in subtle changes in poise and gait. Or the late December day many years ago that we returned from a local trip and he greeted us with his head held low, revealing that we had left the bedroom door open. Our efforts to lighten Santa's workload had been compromised.

Dreyfus saved one of his best lessons for his last days. During his final week he struggled to walk and some days we could barely tempt him into the garden, let alone the woods. On one of his last ever proper walks, the sun had long set and I lost sight of him for a moment in the darkness. For many years this would have been of no concern, but in his vulnerable state I started to worry. The light from my torch caught his eyes and a pair of turquoise circles shone back at me. It is a colour I had seen so many times but I'd never considered how different it was from the colour I saw in our other dog, our Jack Russell, Dotty.

Many animals have a layer at the back of their eyes called the *tapetum lucidum*. It is a reflective layer of cells that maximises any low natural light available and is especially common and noticeable in nocturnal creatures. The colours we see vary with the animal species; yellow, orange, green and blue are common.

---

* Dreyfus was named after the chief inspector in the *Pink Panther* movies, for reasons that escape all of us today.

Size, number and height above ground offer our first clues. A pair of penny-sized eyes a foot off the ground could be those of a dog, a fox or many other animals, but once we add colour, the range narrows. Green is very common in dogs, when seen head on, but foxes are often white. There are clues in alignment too – a pair of close eyes fixed on us is likely to be a predator; hunters need eyes near the front of the head as binocular vision offers better clarity and distance-gauging. Horses have large eyes, but like many prey animals, their eyes are positioned on either side of the head, offering an incredible 350-degree view, but that means we often see only one bright eye at a time.

If there is no reflective layer at the back of the eye, the light can still bounce out but we see red, as this is the colour of the back of the eyeball. In other words, the colour red in torchlight, or flash photography, is a sign of no *tapetum* – and therefore poor night vision.

The reflective layer has helped nocturnal creatures survive for millions of years, but more recently it has proved a vulnerability. Hunters use a bright light to seek out animals at night. If I hear a diesel engine off-road after dark, it is often paired with a searchlight sweeping the hills from a 4x4. This hunting technique, known as 'lamping' or 'spotlighting', is popular with legal hunters and poachers and is effective for two reasons. First, the animals that had been using the cloak of darkness to hide suddenly appear as a strikingly bright pair of eyes. Second, these animals have not evolved to associate bright light with danger so it doesn't trigger their flight responses. Instead of fleeing the danger, they stand stock still, mesmerised by the light, until the gun fires. The effect is visible from distance and those hunting with a dog have to train it not to take advantage too early: they are taught not to 'bolt the beam'.

The last time I noticed the colour of Dreyfus's eyes at night, I could see the sickness in them. I'm not going to pretend that

I could see anything precise and I certainly couldn't have diagnosed anything, but they were not the eyes of a healthy young dog. Many animals' eyes change over their life, most dramatically in the first three months and near the end. A white reflection from the eyes when we expect to see a different colour is known as 'leukocoria' and can be a symptom of disease in many animals, including humans.

Dogs with blue eyes during the day are less likely to have a *tapetum lucidum* and therefore probably don't have strong night vision; this is especially true in smaller dogs. In other words, dogs with blue eyes by day or red eyes at night will need more light. Pigs and many rodents, including squirrels, also lack the reflective layer and make poor night scouts.

Interestingly, blue eyes in humans mean something quite different. It is a sign of lower levels of melanin, which increases sensitivity to light and the owner's discomfort if a torch goes on suddenly. Blue-eyed people squint more at sunsets.

A Sting in the Tail

February is a poor month for shooting stars. Those living in more southern latitudes might glimpse the Alpha Centaurids, a weak shower that peaks in early February. Peaking is not the right word for these meteors, they fizzle shyly and barely register. A good one to miss.

We have seen that Scorpius is famously a summer constellation and we won't spot him in the evening at any time in winter, because he is lost in the sun's glare (the sun is in front of Scorpius in early December). But there is a little Scorpion surprise: we can catch him before sunrise in February.

As we know, the stars rise four minutes earlier each day than the sun, and by late winter Scorpius has moved far enough ahead of the sun that we can spot him before dawn. If you are an early riser, look south before sunrise and you'll spot him low in the sky. Using the same method we learned in July, Scorpius points perfectly south in the pre-dawn of late February, which I find a pleasant twist in the tail of the month.

Buds

The trees may look bare and certainly there are few leaves. Only the real outriders, like elder, have leaves. But February is the month to savour the buds on the trees. After months of dormancy, they are changing by the week, morphing in size, shape, colour and texture.

Tree buds are genius little bundles. They contain not just the genetic plan of how to emerge as a shoot, burst into leaf or blossom as a flower, but the energy needed to get started too. Remember that balmy, lazy August weekend last year, when you sat for hours with friends around cool drinks, chatting lots and doing little? The trees were harvesting some of the same sunlight and packing it into the buds. Keeping an eye on them is an excellent way to stay ahead of the obvious. The swelling of the buds gives us several weeks' lead time on the moments that most consider spring in trees, when the green leaves unfurl. The easiest way to do this is to glance at the buds you pass daily. Nothing very much will happen for several days and then quite a lot.

Now it is time to retreat, because there is a beautiful effect, which we can see from a distance. If you watch carefully, you'll notice that woodlands change colour as the buds swell, before a single leaf has emerged. Buds come in many colours – browns, greens, reds, yellows and the black of ash – but they are a different hue from the branches. As the buds swell, they add a tint to the woods and the trees change colour when seen from a distance. The effect is most dramatic when we look down and through hundreds of bare branches from a small height. Look down on trees from a neighbouring slope and watch them take on a pink colour. It is a cheering pre-vernal sign.

Sunrise and Sunset Disagree

A week may slide by in January without us noticing the change in shortening nights, but once February arrives, we definitely start to sense it. The days grow longer and the thermometer wobbles upwards.

We may notice sunsets getting later before we feel sunrises coming earlier, which doesn't seem logical. You're not imagining it. The angle of Earth's axis and the elliptical path of Earth around the sun affect the rate that sunrise and sunset times change with the seasons.

Sunset times change faster than sunrise times in late winter, as we emerge from the winter solstice. In mid-latitudes, we may find the day is about an hour and ten minutes longer at the start of February than it was at the start of January, but it is not shared evenly. Sunrise will be about twenty-five minutes earlier, but sunset is perhaps forty-five minutes later.

In the weeks before the winter solstice we see the opposite: sunrise moves later more quickly than sunset draws earlier.

We Go Again

Trouble may still lie ahead, but there is now a lifting of spirits, a rising belief that winter may have done its worst. The change is welcomed by most without hesitation, but farmers take deep breaths. Preparations must be made, soon the change will be too rapid to ask what needs doing – spring is a time for action, not getting ready for it.

Once more, Nature is counting with both hands. On one, it

senses the shorter nights and limbers up, ready to uncoil. On the other it tots up the warm hours and, finding few, bides its time. Somewhere between the start and end of the month, there will be a mild spell and now the hands shake and agree that there is enough light *and* warmth. Wheels start turning.

In a moist fertile spot, lit and warmed by the rays from a sun that no longer hides in a pathetic low arc, there will be a hundred winged insects or more in a pillar of frenzied flight. The wings catch the sunlight and signal change. We don't need to know the insects' names – call them gnats if politeness demands it – for the dance is what matters. The insects may see it as part of courtship, males seeking females, but for me it's a different celebration, one that marks the coming together of light, warmer air, warmer ground and moisture. Remember, the smaller the creature, the more sensitive and responsive to any changes in the environment it will be, which makes insects our vanguard of change. The fluttering column of wings puts us on watch. It is a twitching of the needle that sits at the edge of winter and spring. Land that was frozen a fortnight earlier is now gloop and gulls swoop inland to pull worms skywards.

The sunlit insects were a signal, telling me I must try hard not to step on a frog. When February warmth arrives, the amphibians emerge from hibernation and charge from all corners towards the fresh water. They are fussy about temperature. The day can lengthen all it wants, but frogs, toads and newts are immune to its overtures unless the thermometer also climbs.

Toads are a little warier than frogs, and wait for a more determined uptick in temperature. The frogs normally beat the newts into the water too, which is a good plan, because the newts will gobble frogspawn and tadpoles. There used to be an unwritten rule that the newts would give the frogs a head-start, a couple of weeks maybe, before they slipped in and went on the rampage. Recently they have been closing the gap.

February can be an eerie time for a night walk. The new drumming of the woodpeckers during the day gives way to owl calls, which add an edge to the mood among the dark-cloaked trees. A startled deer darts invisibly from its bracken bed, cracking stems and disappearing with the softest thunder under its hoofs. The pulse drops for a moment, but then the fox mating calls cut through the wood, sending volts up the spine and turning the blood in my neck to ice. I take a torch on all evening walks at this time – and suffer its night-vision vandalism – not because I'm scared of vixen sounds, honestly, but because otherwise I will, on return, slip on one frog and land on another pair, improving the mood and well-being of none of us. There are rumours that licking the skin of certain toads can lead to hallucinogenic trips, but the paths near the pond wriggle, wobble and hop without the need for toad-skin narcotics.

The pond is never quiet or still now and the hours around dusk are riotous. Ripples spread from the shallows and the males attract females with their croak and cling to them in an embrace called the 'amplexus'. The eggs are fertilised outside the female, which wriggles in the clutches of specially adapted fingers on the male's front feet.

If you head into the woods, you will meet some bird clues on your way in. Before reaching the edge, look for the 'sentinel' bird. Scan prominent perches that stick out from high on the trees at the edge of the woods. A vigilant bird may spot you and signal to the others, vocally or by flying away noisily, that you are on the way. The birds are serious about territory in February and unforgiving of trespass. In other months they may let us sit on a park bench or a tree stump and enjoy a quiet pause, but now they protest. The smaller birds vocalise their unhappiness, breaking the peace with staccato alarm calls as they flit up and down the branches. They are fidgety and noisy with displeasure.

The sheep on the hill appear to have drunk coffee for the first time, there is a laughable energy and lack of purpose in their movements. I have watched them countless times traipse in orderly files towards some temptation, but this is different. They are charging across their field, hopping as if their tails are on fire, stopping suddenly, pausing for a moment, then charging off in some other direction. I soon spot their mad leader. The clichés about sheep hold much truth; they are followers so when a dominant individual gets energetic and excitable the others join in.

Those sheep remind me of an interesting story about these disciples. Many years ago, a shepherd in the southern Levant was struggling to get his flock to cross a lively stream. The animals lined up on one side of the fast-running water, stared at him and refused to budge. The shepherd didn't remonstrate or reason with the animals, he used his wisdom to act in a way they couldn't resist. He knew one of the dominant ewes, grabbed her lamb and leaped across the torrent. The mother followed and so, in short order, did the others.

The insects, the amphibians, the birds, the sheep, the buds on the trees, the Scorpion in the sky . . . They all whisper the same message. We go again.

Your Season

We have now immersed ourselves in the science and the experience of looking for nature's signs through the seasons.

Our personal experience begins with solitary observations. We learned, for example, that July is a good time to look for stories in grasses and Scorpius in the night sky. We enjoy meeting these two signs as individual characters and then we start, slowly, to appreciate that they are not isolated but part of the same tapestry. As the sun lowers in the north-west, we pick up the scent of wildflowers as we feel a gust that bends the tall grasses in a new direction. Soon we spot the scorpion climbing near a tall cloud in the distance. Then we remember that gusts and towering clouds are a sign of unstable air, a warning of storms, which are more common as summer matures. The scents, the bending of the grasses, the shape of the cloud, the unique constellation all reflect that one moment back to us. The patterns paint this time of year, not the word 'July'.

Pick two things outdoors, any two things, and there will be a connection, a seasonal bridge between them. As I write this, it is mid-morning in late February and a good writing day, the skies are sombre and rain beats against the cabin windows. I can hear the last of the birds' morning chorus. They are late, but that is not surprising: the dawn rhythms of animals creep later on overcast days. The sounds and timings of the rain and the birds were connected and both belonged to that February moment.

Today is the season for you to craft your own moment.

18

Appendix: The Moon and the Seasons

Over the following pages I will share some rare moon knowledge that leads to new seasonal skills and great satisfaction, but there will be challenging times along the way. The path to lunar wisdom is beset by thorns.

The moon follows its own cycle and its rhythms don't align with the Earth–sun annual relationship. This means we can't predict the moon's behaviour using only months in the way we can with the sun. We can estimate with great confidence where the sun will rise on any date in a hundred years' time, but we can't predict where the moon will rise in a week's time, until we learn a new method. We can only predict the moon's behaviour when we learn to pair its phase – its shape – with the month.

Full Moons

A full moon appears full because it is opposite the sun, with Earth between. When we look at a full moon, we see a bright round disc (an unusually bright one – a helpful way of gauging whether you are looking at a full moon is that it should look both round and extraordinarily bright; a full moon acts as a mirror and reflects the sun's light straight back to our eyes).

The full moon's position leads to behaviours that are logical and opposite to those of the sun at this time of year. The sun is highest in the sky on the summer solstice; a full moon is lowest in the sky at this time of year.

As we saw in June, if there is a full moon at the time of the summer solstice, it will move in a cycle opposite to the sun, with opposing timings and directions.* As the sun sets in the north-west, the full moon will rise in the south-east. As the sun rises in the north-east, the full moon will be setting in the south-west. You may have spotted that the full moon is following a short arc, south-east to south-west, which may sound familiar. It's the same short arc that the sun follows in December – full moons mimic the arc of the sun in six months' time.

A full moon at the time of the summer solstice will be low in the sky and pass through south at midnight. By midnight, I mean the middle of the night, when the full moon is at its highest.†

The full moon is opposite the sun at all other times of the year, too, and this introduces a helpful method. We can think of the full moon doing roughly what the sun does in six months' time – because that is the opposite time of year in the Earth – sun cycle. Try this for yourself: how should we expect a full moon to behave in late December?

---

* For simplicity, all timings and directions in this chapter are approximate.

† In natural navigation, midday and midnight describe astronomical moments, for example, when celestial objects reach their highest point in the sky, not what it says on your watch. This may be close to midday or midnight on your watch, but your watch is never as accurate as the sun, moon or stars. If you plant a stick and then mark the end of shadows cast by the moon, you will find they get shorter as the moon rises and longer as it sets. They are shortest when the moon is highest, when it is due south – the shortest shadow cast by the moon will point perfectly north. The moon casts weaker shadows than the sun, so this works best on bright surfaces: snow and sand are good, but I have done it on a grass lawn many times too. It makes for a late night, but a memorable one.

In late December the sun is rising south-east and setting south-west and follows a short, low arc. The December full moon will rise north-east, set north-west and follow a long high arc – which is what the sun will do in six months' time.

A full moon will behave as the sun does in six months' time at any time of year. A full moon near the equinoxes, late March and September, will rise and set near to east and west and pass through south at a medium height in the middle of the night. (Because an equinox is always six months from an equinox, the opposite behaviour is actually the same behaviour for the moon.)

How will a full moon behave in August? We now have two ways to tackle this.

The sun will rise east north-east and set west north-west in August, the full moon will rise and set on the opposite side of east and west, rising close to east south-east and setting west south-west.

Or . . . six months from August is February. In February, the sun will rise between south-east and east, east south-east, and set between south-west and west, west south-west.

New and Half Moons

OK, we've corralled the full moon and can predict its behaviour at any time of year, but we're often dealing with something less neat. Fortunately, we can keep things straightforward by remembering the fundamental meaning of the moon's phase: the shape of the moon tells us where it is relative to the sun.

The closer to a circle the moon is, the fuller it is and therefore the closer to being opposite the sun it must be. The smaller the moon's crescent (the nearer to new) the closer to the sun it is in its cycle. A new moon is close to the sun, which is why we don't see it, and its habits match those of the sun. A new moon

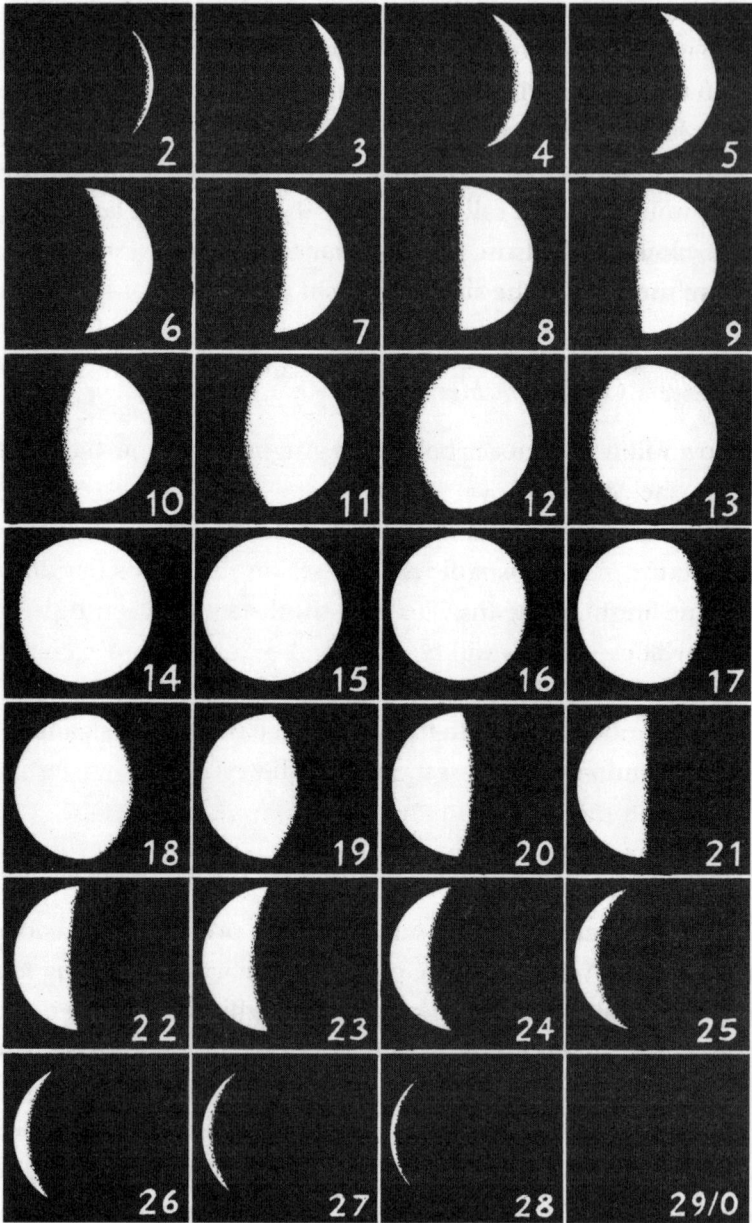

Each day the moon's shape changes and
reveals where it is relative to the sun

rises and sets in roughly the same part of the sky as the sun and also passes across the southern sky in the middle of the day, like the sun. This is academic as we can't see it because it is hidden by the blinding glare of the sun, but it is still helpful, because it reminds us that a new moon is very near the sun. Which means a very young moon, say a two-day-old thin crescent, must be quite close to the sun. We should expect thin crescents to behave similarly to the sun at all times of year.

Volunteers Only from Here . . .

We are ready to consider the times when we see half of the moon, the phases known formally as 'first-quarter' and 'third-quarter' moons (confusingly referring to the quarters of the lunar cycle, not the shape we see). If we see that half of the moon is bright, it means we are halfway between new and full moons. These moons will behave in a middling way relative to the sun, neither aligned with it nor opposite it.

At the June solstice, for example, half-moons rise and set near east and west and pass through south at a medium height – higher than the full moon and lower than the new moon. The same is true at the December solstice.

If we see that the right half of the moon is bright, this is a 'first-quarter' moon; if we see the left half is bright this is a 'third-quarter' moon. Both moons are a quarter of the cycle away from the sun and behave roughly as the sun will do three months away from the time we see it, but . . . we need to know which way to go, because three months ahead is very different from three months back.

I have a trick for remembering how to work out whether to go forwards or backwards in time.

A *first*-quarter moon *wins the race*. It sounds *faster*, so we go *forwards* by three months.

Imagine you see the right half of the moon is bright in late March. Where will this moon set?

OK, the right half is bright, which makes it a first-quarter moon. First sounds fast, so we go forwards three months. The moon will behave roughly as the sun does in three months' time, that is, in June. We know the sun rises and sets well north of east and west at this time, so we can expect a first-quarter moon to rise well north of east, rise very high in the southern sky and set well north of west in March.

How about if we see the left half is bright in March?

This is a third-quarter moon. We go back three months to December. We can expect this moon to rise well south of east, pass low through south and then set south of west.

That is enough to play with until you're very comfortable with these ideas. When it comes to natural navigation with the moon, I recommend taking small bites and chewing. Read a bit, think a bit, look a bit, rest and repeat. The moon is one of my favourite natural navigation signs, but it's easy to take on too much and suffer indigestion.

Once you are well practised at predicting the moon's behaviour when it is a full or half-moon, you may feel ready to take on the more challenging phases between, which requires a little interpolation. I won't go through every possible permutation, because all I need to do is explain the simple logic that every phase of the moon must be between two of the phases we have already met. A moon that is halfway between a third quarter and full will behave halfway between the moon at those two phases.

Let's imagine that we see a four-day-old moon in late December. This will look roughly halfway between new (nothing) and first quarter (right half bright). We can expect it to behave halfway between the sun's behaviour in December and March (forward three months). So, we can expect it to rise roughly halfway between south-east (December sun) and east (March sun), that is, east south-east, then climb a little higher than a winter sun in the south and set between south-west (December) and west (March), so west south-west.

I salute you for even reading this Appendix and empathise if your head hurts. But it's only a series of stepping stones, none of them unreachable. Take another step when you're ready and always feel free to take a step back. The moon is the wildest celestial beast in the natural navigation zoo, but it proves to be a fascinating companion when we tame it.

Acknowledgements

There were constant reminders during the writing of this book that the solitary profession of writing is no such thing. An unusual one came when the name of my UK publisher changed and I woke to find that the sun still rose in the east and everyone I work with on my books still had the same names and personalities (technically, I moved from the imprint Sceptre to Hodder Press and the sun only rises due east on the equinoxes).

The Hidden Seasons is the title of a chapter in my previous book, *How to Read a Tree.* There is a sense that this book rose like a tendril from the humus of thoughts and discoveries during the writing of that earlier book. Writing that one chapter opened up so many intriguing questions and possibilities that could not be explored within its pages.

Wherever the idea came from, no book of mine is written on a whim; quite the opposite, they come after a long internal campaign to not write them (if you don't start a book, it can't take over your life, exhaust you or leave you howling at the moon). And all my books come after a parallel, equally long, but much more satisfying and productive series of discussions with the very professional people who made this book possible.

From the first mooting of the idea to the ongoing collaborative effort, I would like to thank my literary agent, Sophie Hicks, and my UK and North America publishers, Rupert Lancaster and Nicholas Cizek. The support you have shown me and constant contact between us mocks the image of the lone writer. Thank you, Sarah Williams and Morag O' Brien, for the very important work you do, it helps make this strange career possible.

I would like to thank the brilliant teams at Hodder & Stoughton and The Experiment, not least Matthew Lore, Rebecca Mundy, Jennifer Hergenroeder, Olivia French, Ella Young, Alice Morley, George Biggs and Dominic Gribben.

Thank you, Hazel Orme and Lucy Buxton, for your excellent help with the text, and Neil Gower for your continuing patience and skill in beautifully illustrating things that are hard to describe, using only my words and laughable sketches. Thank you, Joanna Boyle, for your enthusiasm in tackling astronomical challenges.

Thank you to everyone whose name appears in the book, but also to those who helped in other ways, including Juliet Anderson, Sandra Bell, Shaila Rao, Kevin Hobbs, Ross Cameron, Rosemary Fricker and the team at the Cambridge University Botanic Garden, Steve Thackeray, Miles Irving, Tom Fortune, Emma Cunis, James Chiavarini, David Jaclin, Rod Kent, Ruby Taylor, Pascal Wyse, Chris Watson, the Sussex Wildlife Trust, Mya Bambrick, Peter Thomas, Tim Blackburn and Jeremy Mynott.

Thank you to everyone who has come to a talk, joined a walk, been on a course or read any of my earlier books, you helped make this one possible.

Thank you to my friends. I'm so grateful to have friends who are kind when things are tough, but season the good times generously with rudeness and derogation.

I would like to thank my whole wonderful family. You're all in here even when you're not.

Select Bibliography and Sources

Books

Allen, Richard Hinckley, *Star Names*, Dover Publications, 1963

Berman, Bob, *Secrets of the Night Sky*, Harper Perennial, 1996

Blackburn, Tim, *The Jewel Box*, Weidenfeld & Nicolson, 2023

Clarke, Philip, *Where the Ancestors Walked*, Allen & Unwin, 2003

Friend, Mari, *Small Wonder*, Blandford, 1991

Gibbings, Robert, *Coming Down the Wye*, J.M. Dent & Sons, 1947

Gibbings, Robert, *Lovely Is the Lee*, J.M. Dent & Sons, 1947

Gurney, Peter, *Shepherd Lore*, Wiltshire Rural Life Society, 1985

Hillman, William, *Photoperiodism in Plants and Animals*, Carolina Biological Supply Company, 1979

Hutton, Ronald, *The Stations of the Sun*, OUP, 1996

Leigh, Cordelia, *Nature's Playground*, Collins, circa 1940

Levi-Strauss, Claude, *Myth and Meaning*, Routledge, 2001

Lumsden, P.J. and Millar, A.J., *Biological Rhythms and Photoperiodism in Plants*, Bios, 1998

Macdonald, John, *The Arctic Sky*, Nunavut Research Institute, 2000

Milne, A.A., *Winnie the Pooh*, HarperCollins, 2016

Moore, Patrick, *Naked Eye Astronomy*, Lutterworth Press, 1976

Mynott, Jeremy, *Birds in the Ancient World*, OUP, 2019

Parker, Eleanor, *Winters in the World*, Reaktion Books, 2022

Poole, R.W.F., *A Backwoodsman's Year*, Pan Books, 1990

Ruggles, Clive, *Ancient Astronomy*, ABC Clio, 2005

Spindler, Konrad, *The Man in the Ice*, Weidenfeld & Nicolson, 1994

Staal, Julius D.W., *The New Patterns in the Sky*, The McDonald & Woodward Publishing Company, 1988

Sutton, Charles Nassau, *Historical Notes of Withyham*, Alpha Editions, 2019

Thomas, Stephen, *The Last Navigator*, Hutchinson, 1987

Thompson, Christina, *The Sea People*, William Collins, 2019

Vince-Prue, Daphne, *Photoperiodism in Plants*, McGraw-Hill, 1975

Wyman, Harold, *The Great Game*, Fieldfare, 1993

Articles

Andrew, C., Heegaard, E., Høiland, K., Senn-Irlet, B., Kuyper, T.W., Krisai-Greilhuber, I., Kirk, P.M., Heilmann-Clausen, J., Gange, A.C., Egli, S., Bässler, C., Büntgen, U., Boddy, L. and Kauserud, H., 'Explaining European Fungal Fruiting Phenology with Climate Variability', *Ecology*, Vol. 99, No. 6, 2018, pp. 1306–1315

Augspurger, C.K. and Bartlett, E.A., 'Differences in Leaf Phenology between Juvenile and Adult Trees in a Temperate Deciduous Forest', *Tree Physiology*, Vol. 23, No. 8, 2003, pp. 517–525

Augspurger, C.K., Cheeseman, J. and Salk, C., 'Light Gains and Physiological Capacity of Understorey Woody Plants during Phenological Avoidance of Canopy Shade', *Functional Ecology*, Vol. 19, No. 4, 2005, pp. 537–546

Bertin, R., Searcy, K., Hickler, M. and Motzkin, G., 'Climate Change and Flowering Phenology in Franklin County, Massachusetts', *The Journal of the Torrey Botanical Society*, Vol. 144, No. 2, 2017, pp. 153–169

Bonacina, L., Fasano, F., Mezzanotte, V. and Fornaroli, R., 'Effects of Water Temperature on Freshwater Macroinvertebrates: A Systematic Review', *Biol Rev Camb Philos Soc.*, Vol. 98, No. 1, 2022, pp. 191–221

Corbet, P.S., 'Orientation and reproductive condition of migrating dragonflies (Anisoptera)', *Odonatologica*, Vol. 13, No. 1, 1984, pp. 81–88

Dale, A., Galic, D., Leuty, T., Filotas, M. and Currie, E., 'Hazelnuts in Ontario — Biology and Potential Varieties', Ontario Ministry of Agriculture, Food and Rural Affairs, 2012

Deng, C., Ma, X., Xie, M. and Bai, H., 'Effect of Altitude and Topography on Vegetation Phenological Changes in the Niubeiliang Nature Reserve of Qinling Mountains, China', *Forests*, Vol. 13, No. 8, 2022

Diamond, S.E., Frame, A.M., Martin, R.A. and Buckley, L.B., 'Species' Traits Predict Phenological Responses to Climate Change in Butterflies', *Ecology*, Vol. 92, No. 5, 2011, pp. 1005–1012

Dumitraşcu, M., Marin, A., Preda, E., Ţibîrnac, M. and Vădineanu, A., 'Trampling Effects on Plant Species Morphology', *Rom. J. Biol, Plant Biol*, Vol. 55, No. 2, 2010, pp. 89–96

Fitter, A.H. and Fitter, R.S., 'Rapid Changes in Flowering Time in British Plants', *Science*, Vol. 296, No. 5573, 2002, pp. 1689–1691

Gordo, O., 'Why are Bird Migration Dates Shifting? A Review of Weather and Climate Effects on Avian Migratory Phenology', *Climate Research*, Vol. 35, No. ½, 2007, pp. 37–58

Harju, L. and Huldén, S-G., 'Birch Sap as a Tool for Biogeochemical Prospecting', *Journal of Geochemical Exploration*, Vol. 37, No. 3, 1990, pp. 351–365

Horbach, S., Rauschkolb, R. and Römermann, C., 'Flowering and Leaf Phenology are More Variable and Stronger Associated to Functional Traits in Herbaceous Compared to Tree Species', *Flora*, Vol. 300, 2023

Jackson, M.T., 'Effects of Microclimate on Spring Flowering Phenology', *Ecology*, Vol. 47, No. 3, 1966, pp. 407–415

Jyske, T., Järvenpää, E., Kunnas, S., Sarjala, T., Raitanen, J-E., Mäki, M., Pastell, H., Korpinen, R., Kaseva, J. and Tupasela, T., 'Sprouts and Needles of Norway Spruce (*Picea abies* (L.) Karst.) as Nordic Specialty—Consumer Acceptance, Stability of Nutrients, and Bioactivities during Storage', *Molecules*, Vol. 25, No. 18, 2020, 4187

Kauserud, H., Heegaard, E., Semenov, M.A., Boddy, L., Halvorsen, R., Stige, L.C., Sparks, T.H., Gange, A.C. and Stenseth, N.C., 'Climate Change and Spring-Fruiting Fungi', *Proc. R. Soc. B.*, Vol. 277, No. 1685, 2010, pp. 1169–1177

Kauserud, H., Stige, L.C., Vik, J.O., Okland, R.H., Høiland, K. and Stenseth, N.C., 'Mushroom Fruiting and Climate Change', *Proceedings of the National Academy of Sciences of the United States of America*, Vol. 105, No. 10, 2008, pp. 3811–3814

Khan, Z.H., Islam, M.R. and Tarefder, R.A., 'Determining Asphalt Surface Temperature Using Weather Parameters', *Journal of Traffic and Transportation Engineering (English Edition)*, Vol. 6, No. 6, 2019, pp. 577–588

Klopatek, J.M., 'Phenology and Microclimate', *Field Station Bulletin*, Vol. 5, No. 1, 1972, pp. 10–16

Lechowicz, M., 'Why Do Temperate Deciduous Trees Leaf Out at Different Times? Adaptation and Ecology of Forest Communities', *American Naturalist*, Vol. 124, No. 6, 1984, pp. 821–842

Leopold, A. and Eynon, A.E., 'Avian Daybreak and Evening Song in Relation to Time and Light Intensity', *Condor*, Vol. 63, No. 4, 1961, Article 1

Linde, K., Kriston, L., Rücker, G., Jamil, S., Schumann, I., Meissner, K., Sigterman, K. and Schneider, A., 'Efficacy and Acceptability of Pharmacological Treatments for Depressive Disorders in Primary Care: Systematic Review and Network Meta-Analysis', *Ann Fam Med*, Vol. 13, No. 1, 2015, pp. 69–79

Martínez Usó, M.J., Marco Castillo, F.J. and López Ortí, J.A., 'The Lyrids Meteor Shower: A Historical Perspective', *Planetary and Space Science*, Vol. 238, 2023

Nizinski, J.J. and Saugier, B., 'A Model of Leaf Budding and Development for a Mature Quercus Forest', *Journal of Applied Ecology*, Vol. 25, No. 2, 1988, pp. 643–652

Olsson, C., (2014), 'Tree Phenology Modelling in the Boreal and Temperate Climate Zones: Timing of Spring and Autumn Events', [Doctoral Thesis (compilation), Dept of Physical Geography and Ecosystem Science], Department of Physical Geography and Ecosystem Science, Lund University

Palacios, C. and Abecia, J.A., 'Lunar Cycle and the Frequency of Births in Sheep', *Biological Rhythm Research*, Vol. 42, No. 4, 2011, pp. 283–286

Primack, R.B., Laube, J., Gallinat, A.S. and Menzel, A., 'From observations to experiments in phenology research: investigating climate change impacts on trees and shrubs using dormant twigs', *Annals of Botany*, Vol. 116, No. 6, 2015, pp. 889–897

Rappenglück, M., 'The Pleiades in the «Salle des Taureaux», grotte de Lascaux. Does a rock picture in the cave of Lascaux show the open star cluster of the Pleiades at the Magdalénien era (ca 15.300 BC)?', in Jaschekm C. and Atrio Bárendela, F. (eds.), *Actas del IV Congreso de la SEAC "Astronomia en la Cultura"* (Proceedings of the IVth SEAC Meeting "Astronomy in Culture"), Universidad de Salamanca, Salamanca, 1997, pp. 217–225

Richardson, A. and O'Keefe, J., 'Phenological Differences Between Understory and Overstory', *Phenology of Ecosystem Processes*, 2009, Springer New York, pp. 87–117

Roche, C., Thill, D. and Shafii, B., 'Reproductive Phenology in Yellow Starthistle (Centaurea solstitialis)', *Weed Science*, Vol. 45, No. 6, 1997, pp. 763–770

Seghieri, J., Floret, Ch. and Pontanier R., 'Plant Phenology in Relation to Water Availability: Herbaceous and Woody Species in the Savannas of Northern Cameroon', *Journal of Tropical Ecology*, Vol. 11, No. 2, 1995, pp. 237–254

Staples, E., 'Indian Ocean Navigation in Islamic Sources 850–1560 CE', *History Compass*, Vol. 16, No. 9, 2018

The dawn chorus: I am grateful to the excellent work done by Diego Gil and Diego Llusia in their review of the scientific literature and equally grateful to the many scientists cited within that review, including, but not limited to: H.A. Allen, F.H. Allen, M.I. Avery, J.R. Krebs, K.S. Berg, R.T. Brumfield, V. Apanius, J.S. Bolsinger, V.M. Cassone, D.F. Westneat, W-M Chen, W. Cresswell, D.M. Dominoni, R.A. Fuller, D. Gil, D. Haskell, B. Kempenaers, M.T. Murphy, T.H. Parker and H. Tillin, C.E. Staicer, R.J. Thomas and J.E. York.

Visser, M.E. and Both, C., 'Shifts in Phenology Due to Global Climate Change: The Need for a Yardstick', *Proc. R. Soc. B.*, Vol. 272, No. 1581, 2005, pp. 2561–2569

Wake, R., Misugi, T., Shimada, K. and Yoshiyama, M., 'The Effect of the Gravitation of the Moon on Frequency of Births', *Environmental Health Insights*, Vol. 23, No. 4, 2010, pp. 65–69

Zhou, X., Wildschut, T., Sedikides, C., Chen, X., and Vingerhoets, A.J.J.M., 'Heartwarming Memories: Nostalgia Maintains Physiological Comfort', *Emotion*, Vol. 12, No. 4, 2012, pp. 678–684

Websites

earthsky.org/astronomy-essentials/halloween-derived-from-ancient-celtic-cross-quarter-day/

www.scientificamerican.com/podcast/episode/death-by-lightning-is-common-for-tropical-trees/ [27/11/23]

en.wikipedia.org/wiki/The_Paris_Concilium

www.botanic.cam.ac.uk/the-garden/gardens-plantings/snow-drops/ [10/01/24]

www.bergundsteigen.com/wp-content/uploads/2021/08/60-62-Auf-der-sicheren-Seite.pdf [10/02/24]

www.discoverwildlife.com/animal-facts/amphibians/under-stand-frog-breeding-behaviour [10/02/24]

web.archive.org/web/20150103171458/http://www.rogerco.pwp.blueyonder.co.uk/jenyns/jenyns4.htm [26/02/24]

blogs.scientificamerican.com/news-blog/darwin-200-years-later-evolution-by-2009-02-02/ [26/02/24]

www.the-scientist.com/do-epigenetic-changes-influence-evolu-tion-70591#:~:text=Besides%20RNAs%2C%20epige-netic%20ofactors%20such,the%20fitness%20of%20future%20generations [02/04/24]

www.timesofisrael.com/erupting-with-flowers-before-spring-almond-tree-a-bounty-of-jewish-symbolism/ [03/05/24]

www.scottishfield.co.uk/scotland-travel/theres-more-to-the-cuckoo-than-its-famous-call/ [26/06/24]

www.researchgate.net/profile/David-King-45/publication/344027150_WIND_CATCHERS_OF_MEDIEVAL_CAIRO_PART_ONE_SEPT_2020_This_work_is_in_two_parts_This_is_Part_1_containing_an_overview_of_the_historical_sources/links/5f4e7ee4a6fdcc9879bff22b/WIND-CATCHERS-OF-MEDIEVAL-CAIRO-PART-ONE-SEPT-2020-This-work-is-in-two-parts-This-is-Part-1-containing-an-over-view-of-the-historical-sources.pdf [13/08/24]

gathervictoria.com/2017/03/10/the-herstory-of-food-gone-missing/ [29/12/23]

www.washingtonpost.com/weather/2021/03/29/japan-kyoto-cherry-blossoms-record/ [06/05/24]

www.alaskanbeer.com/2021/06/12/tip-of-the-spruceberg-the-one-of-kind-story-behind-our-sitka-spruce-tips/ [15/04/24]

www.theguardian.com/lifeandstyle/2022/feb/05/secret-to-bringing-droopy-houseplants-back-to-life-led-light

www.commonground.org.uk/what-we-do/ [16/11/23]

www.sciencedaily.com/releases/2020/11/201130101309.htm [18/11/23]

www.dorsetcouncil.gov.uk/-/wildlife-of-dorset-heaths [28/11/23]

www.poetryfoundation.org/poems/45362/locksley-hall [07/12/23]

ui.adsabs.harvard.edu/abs/1997ascu.conf..217R/abstract [07/12/23]

www.rmg.co.uk/stories/topics/what-are-pleiades [07/12/23]

www.bbc.co.uk/news/science-environment-67658650 [15/12/23]

www.si.edu/spotlight/buginfo/bugnos [08/04/24]

www.bumblebee.org/bodyTempReg.htm [09/04/24]

www.scientificamerican.com/article/why-do-bees-buzz/ [10/04/24]

www.thejc.com/judaism/jewish-words/shkediyah-rndbp206 [03/05/24]

allpoetry.com/The-Shepherds-Calendar--July [31/07/24]

en.wikipedia.org/wiki/Dog_days#CITEREFEvelyn-White1914 [12/08/24]

duas.com/dua/314/dua-for-the-rain-to-stop [16/08/24]

www.telegraph.co.uk/news/2024/08/18/why-the-skies-are-turning-red-over-britain/

www.woodlandtrust.org.uk/blog/2019/04/dawn-chorus/ [16/10/24]

https://www.youtube.com/watch?v=9bOlLKjDxzs [04/11/24]

For more information on the sources used in writing *The Hidden Seasons*, please see www.naturalnavigator.com.

Index

Page numbers in *italics* refer to illustrations